praise for FIFTEEN DAYS

"Blatchford has a remarkable ability to convey the intensity of the emotions experienced by soldiers and their families. Do not expect to remain dry-eyed after reading this book." —*Calgary Herald*

"[R]equired reading . . . as a reminder that Flanders Field is a glorified final result while Kandahar is a gory ongoing reality." —*National Post*

"Few are better armed with the necessary mix of rebar steel, journalistic talent and heart-on-the-sleeve emotion in order to document their journeys than [Christie Blatchford]." —*Edmonton Sun*

"A vivid and heroic portrayal of death in Afghanistan. . . . *Fifteen Days* is a good start to understanding the Canadian men and women who are fighting [there]." —*The Chronicle-Herald* (Halifax)

"*Fifteen Days* . . . goes deep, and it goes personal. Blatchford gives [soldiers] more than just faces, she gives them life. And, for those who died wearing Canada's uniform, she gives them a life that no newspaper has the length and space to describe, and no television documentary can convey in an hour's time slot." —*London Free Press*

"By far the most deeply personal and startlingly honest account of Canadian soldiers since they first stepped foot in Afghanistan. . . . By earning their confidence and respect, Christie Blatchford has delivered a candid and often painful account of their most difficult days. She is a master at capturing the truth of a moment, the humour and the heartbreak. The book is so vivid that I could feel the unbearable weight of the fallen."

—Lisa LaFlamme,
National Affairs Correspondent, CTV National News

CHRISTIE BLATCHFORD

FIFTEEN DAYS

STORIES OF BRAVERY, FRIENDSHIP, LIFE AND DEATH
FROM INSIDE THE NEW CANADIAN ARMY

 Anchor Canada

COPYRIGHT © 2008 HOUNDHEAD ENTERPRISES INC.

ANCHOR CANADA EDITION 2008

LIBRARY AND ARCHIVES CANADA CATALOGUING IN PUBLICATION

Blatchford, Christie
Fifteen days : stories of bravery, friendship, life and death from inside the new Canadian Army / Christie Blatchford.

Includes index.
ISBN 978-0-385-66467-7

1. Canada. Canadian Armed Forces. Princess Patricia's Canadian Light Infantry. 2. Afghan War, 2001– —Personal narratives, Canadian. 3. Canada—Armed Forces—Military life. 4. Soldiers—Canada. 5. Afghan War, 2001– 6. Soldiers—Canada—Biography. I. Title.

UA600.B548 2008   958.104'7   C2008-902005-7

COVER IMAGE: AR2006-A020-0017A, Sangin, Afghanistan, Photo courtesy of the Canadian Forces Image Gallery, National Defence. Reproduced with permission of the Minister of Public Works and Government Services, 2008. Corporal Robin Mugridge

JACKET DESIGN: CS RICHARDSON

PRINTED AND BOUND IN THE USA

Published in Canada by
Anchor Canada, a division of
Random House of Canada Limited

Visit Random House of Canada Limited's website: www.randomhouse.ca

BVG   10   9   8   7   6

Yes, makin' mock o' uniforms that guard you while you sleep
Is cheaper than them uniforms, an' they're starvation cheap.

—RUDYARD KIPLING, "TOMMY"

Contents

—

Author's Note

—

WHEN IT CAME to writing this book, my initial approach was pure newspaper reporter: You start at the beginning, period.

Even decades ago, writing about National Hockey League games for *The Globe and Mail* on deadline, I couldn't manage to file what's called "running copy." Basically, this is the middle of the story, and the game. The idea is that you get this done early, then write the top of the piece once you have the final score. More able colleagues can do it in their sleep, but I always had to start with the first paragraph and go to the second and so on. I couldn't write word one until the game was over.

I brought this rigid blockhead mentality to the book. The beginning, I figured, must be the introduction, because that's what comes first. In January 2007, I was just back from spending the Christmas holidays in Kandahar. Exhausted, as you always are when returning from Afghanistan, I wasted about three weeks on the stupid introduction. I'd write a couple thousand words, go to bed feeling satisfied, and wake up appalled: Everything I'd written was about me, and why I was writing this book I had no clue how to write.

Every morning, I destroyed what I'd written the night before.

Finally, I threw myself upon the mercy of the small group of women with whom I run a few times a week. We met, as usual, in Judy Wolfe's kitchen, and there, desperation in my voice, I told them my problem: I had no fucking idea how to write the fucking thing, no plan, just a lot of stories destined to move only me to tears, since I was apparently incapable of putting them to paper. I begged them to skip the run, and they agreed immediately.

As selfless as that was, I should mention it was so bitterly cold that one of our number, Karen Falconer, also known as the Weather Pussy for the obsessive way she monitors all storm fronts that come within five hundred kilometres of Toronto, had already cancelled and was missing in action.

These women are a clever bunch with diverse skills, none of which I have. Wolfe is a strategic planner by trade; Mary McIntyre is marketing director for a leading architectural practice, plus a talented jewellery designer who attends the Ontario College of Art and Design part time; Margaret McNee is a lawyer; and Janis Caruana, a legal assistant, raised with her husband, Abe, five daughters in a house that had only one full bathroom when the kids were little.

(As a measure of the state I was in, McIntyre resisted the temptation to crow about the exchange she and I had had a few months earlier. Out running one day, she asked if I had a structure for the book yet. "What structure?" I'd snorted. "Mary, I'm a *writer*. It'll come.")

Within an hour, they had me a plan: I was to buy a big roll of paper and write down the people and elements I wanted in each chapter. I had to have a physical map of what the book would be.

I bought the supplies that same morning and followed my marching orders, starting with one of the stories—of a battle on August 3, 2006, in which four Canadians were killed—I'd told my friends. Putting down on paper what I wanted to include in this one chapter gave me the template for the others.

My three trips to Afghanistan were spread out over ten months of 2006; the war itself is seasonal, so there are quiet periods and busy ones. I didn't think that telling the story in a purely chronological way would work. And there wasn't a theme, really, except that I wanted to reveal the soldiers as I had found them.

While mapping out the story of August 3, I wondered whether I could tell the story through a number of significant days, days that as the boss of the book I could pick. As it turns out, I already had them all in my head: August 5, when Ray Arndt was killed; July 9, when I was caught in a battle and walked in the blood of a young reservist named Tony Boneca; April 22, when Lieutenant Bill Turner, a letter carrier I'd met on one of my visits, was blown up in a massive bombing; March 4, when Tim Wilson's organs were harvested and he died; May 17, when Nichola Goddard, whom I knew only as a soothing voice on the radio, was killed.

Pretty soon, I had fifteen big sheets of brown paper taped to the walls of my little home office. I wrote down the days as they came to me, and then I wrote the chapters in the very same order. I had not only my structure, buggered up as it is, but also the title of my book.

Much later, I realized that I'd mixed some of the stories that were hardest to write, where the connections were deep and personal, with some that were just a little easier. Some of the dates really are significant, certainly in terms of who was lost and sometimes because of what was learned, but all of these days matter to me because they speak to the character of the Canadian soldier.

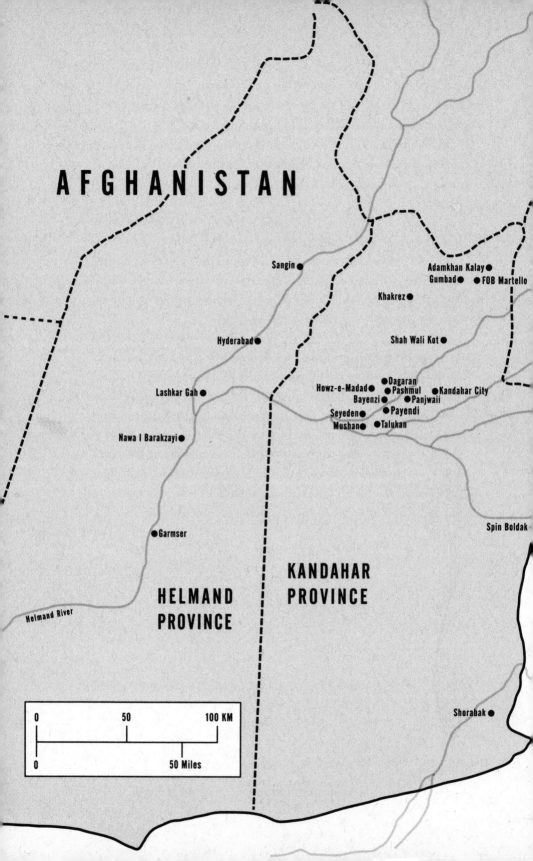

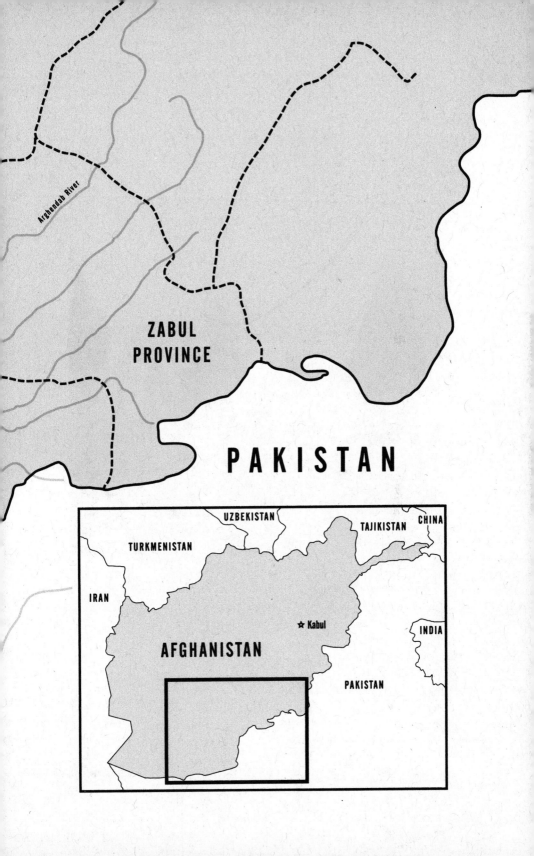

Arghendab River

ZABUL
PROVINCE

PAKISTAN

UZBEKISTAN   TAJIKISTAN   CHINA

TURKMENISTAN

IRAN

☆ Kabul   INDIA

AFGHANISTAN

PAKISTAN

Ramp ceremony for Pte. Kevin Dallaire, Sgt. Vaughan Ingram, Cpl. Bryce Keller, and Cpl. Christopher Reid

3 August 2006

—

"Blackest day of my life. Four perfect men lost, seven others injured. . . .
The day will be marked by acts of heroism—some witnessed, some
described to me. I will have to tell the story someday, when I can do so
without choking up."

—FROM IAN HOPE
TO CHRISTIE BLATCHFORD
SATURDAY 8/5/2006 1:40 P.M.

By July 2006, Task Force Orion was a killing machine.

Named for the conspicuous constellation of stars known as the Hunter, Orion was the Canadian battle group made up of the soldiers of the 1st Battalion, Princess Patricia's Canadian Light Infantry in Edmonton; a company from the 2nd Battalion and a battery of gunners from 1st Royal Canadian Horse Artillery, both based in Shilo, Manitoba; and combat engineers.

Even into the early spring, the soldiers of Roto 1, as the seven-month tour in Kandahar Province was called, had confronted many tests that tax a soldier's resolve and ingenuity. But they had yet to face full-fledged combat.

The troops were being blown up regularly, killed and maimed by Improvised Explosive Devices (IEDs) planted by an enemy who went unseen and largely uncaught.

They met endless groups of village elders, and older Afghan men who appointed themselves elders, in countless *shuras*, or consultations. Most of these were peaceful, if occasionally galling, because the soldiers suspected, and in a few cases damn well knew, that some of the same men laying bombs by night or with certain knowledge of who was doing so would sit cross-legged with them by day, swilling glass after glass of chai tea and nodding agreeably.

The Canadians patrolled on foot and in armoured vehicles and spent long stretches exploring territory, climbing stony hills, searching caves, and living rough far away from the huge base at Kandahar

Air Field (KAF) or the little strong points they periodically called home.

"We were basically introducing ourselves—we're not the Soviets, we're not the Americans," Chief Warrant Officer Randy Northrup, the Patricias' Regimental Sergeant Major (RSM), says of their long, slow start. "We were pissing in our corners. Our mantra was, Go do something, in case he just don't know who his daddy is."

I spent four or five days in March 2006 out with Alpha Company's 3 Platoon, and the only nerve-racking moment came as we were climbing to 6200 feet and a boulder gave way under Captain Sean Ivanko, who was checking out a far-flung cave. He dropped several heart-stopping feet before nimbly grabbing on to another chunk of rock.

Things were so quiet in those days, even pastoral where we were, that I remember wondering to myself, in that remarkably condescending and vainglorious manner journalists the world over have perfected, if the Patricias weren't playing soldier and maybe laying it on a little thick for my benefit.

In any case, for all that they dared, tried to tantalize, and practically begged the enemy to reveal himself, in those early months he did not.

Lieutenant-Colonel Ian Hope, the Patricias' commanding officer, remembers that they'd receive intelligence that the Taliban were in a particular area. "Where are they?" "Everywhere." "What villages?" "All of them." "When?" "Every day." "What about the mountains?" "In the mountains too."

The Taliban almost certainly were there, probably much of the time, but this was their turf, and they alone would decide when the battle was on. "They weren't ready to fight," Hope says. "They weren't ready to fight until sometime in April."

Because the Patricias were then operating on their own as a Canadian battalion, the considerable fighting they did in late spring and early summer of 2006 received scant attention.

But fight they did, spending weeks in contact—which means in contact with the enemy—and meeting the Taliban in the first of what would add up to more than fifty significant and fierce engagements.

Jon Hamilton, the then twenty-nine-year-old captain of the reconnaissance or recce platoon, first fired his weapon on February 4 in his initial week on the ground in Afghanistan during the operational handover from American troops. At that time, the event was so startling he was quizzed about it.

"I remember actually sitting down with the colonel and the operations officer and they were going, like, 'Okay, what the hell's going on here, Jon?' I was like, 'I fired my weapon in support of coalition troops. I don't understand what the problem is here.'"

Hamilton believes he was the first Canadian soldier on the tour to fire a shot, and suspects that as soon as word of it got back home, which in our age means almost instantaneously, military bureaucrats in Ottawa had their knickers in a knot. "Now," he says, "that seems so stupid . . . so insignificant compared to what lay ahead."

By the end of July, Hamilton, his two dozen men, and the rest of the battalion were battle-hardened and so inured to the roar of combat that they were lighting up smokes and cracking jokes with rounds raining down on them.

"This is the kind of stuff you get used to," Hamilton says. "And it's not complacency or laziness. It's just the shit that happens in battle, it's the human mind protecting itself from going insane or something. It's the way soldiers are."

For recce, July 4 was the turning point.

Hamilton's platoon was doing a route reconnaissance near the spot where he'd first fired his weapon months earlier, about 160 kilometres north of Kandahar city and sufficiently far north of Forward Operating Base (FOB) Martello that they were out of the comfort zone, and range, of their enormous artillery guns. They had the usual Afghan complement—the always present "Afghan face" of every mission, though Hope says in retrospect that the only Afghan face they saw consistently on their operations was that of the Taliban. With recce in this instance were some Afghan National Police (ANP), the least-loved element of the Afghan National Security Forces (ANSF).

En route, the small convoy found a village road blocked off with rocks at both ends. Hamilton stopped to question the village elder and was told the Taliban had been there during the night.

"Why would they block off the road?" he asked himself. "Is there somebody high up here? They know we're gonna stop, they need to slow us, and that gives them time to bugger off. That's kind of what we were led to believe."

Guard up, moving single file, their little group of G-Wagons— recce travelled the whole tour in these versatile Jeep-like boxes, the least protected of Canada's otherwise armed-to-the-teeth fleet—was just cresting a small rise when Sergeant Jeff Schnurr, the 3 section commander, looked off to the right.

The army has a formal procedure for the sighting of enemy, just as it has a formal procedure, or form, for every eventuality and every thing. That's both why it works and why it can make smart men crazy. This particular procedure is called a fire control order, and it's supposed to be done the same way every time—something like, "Contact, reference hill 600 metres left."

But what Schnurr barked to his light machine gunner Corporal Jimmy Funk was, "Jim, they're on the right! Fuck 'em up!"

"The old expression, Catch somebody with their pants down," Hamilton says, "well, literally, that's what we did. These guys were obviously armed, they had the chest rigs on [brassiere-like systems of straps and pouches for carrying ammunition], and they were having their lunch by the river. And they were undressed—you know, shoes off and everything."

Hamilton, Schnurr, Sergeants Willy MacDonald and Mars Janek, and about three others moved in on foot, while the rest of the platoon remained with the G-Wagons, gunners spinning around the turrets as the Taliban began to return fire.

"These guys didn't have a chance," Hamilton says. "We just wiped them out. And I can remember seeing half a dozen of 'em and looking through a scope and shooting and watching guys drop. I thought, Jesus, this is a turkey shoot, these guys are done. There's got to be at least six bodies down there. I look over at Willy, and we just kind of looked at each other and I just gave the order to cease fire. Because we had clearly won the firefight."

The Taliban is respected, however reluctantly, for retrieving their dead and wounded as scrupulously as the Canadians do; their practice is to maintain harassing fire just long enough to pick up their fallen comrades. And that's what they did, buying themselves time until they could run out through a wadi, one of the dried-up riverbeds that are far more common than actual rivers in the south.

It wasn't long before Hamilton and MacDonald were down by the stream. They found clothes everywhere, the remains of the men's lunch, shoes, five or six AK-47s and a Rocket-Propelled Grenade (RPG), but only one dead body, a young man of seventeen or eighteen at most, his chest rig full of bullet holes.

Hamilton was infuriated. He'd seen men falling with his own eyes through his scope, and so had MacDonald. Besides, "I know the difference between troops making shit up and not, and I know my guys just aren't like that. And I know myself, I watched this guy drop, where the hell is he? I told Willy, 'We only found one, where the fuck are they?' And he [said], 'I dunno, man.'"

Then they spotted a blood trail, and what Hamilton had learned in an advanced reconnaissance course taught at Gagetown, New Brunswick, was suddenly useful. When he took the course, he remembers, he'd thought, "What the hell, this is World War II stuff, tracking Germans through the hills. What a waste of time. I knew so much then."

So they followed the trail, about 300 metres from the actual contact itself. "We picked it up, we lost it, we picked it up, we lost it, and sure enough, we come up to a bush and there's a guy lying underneath and an ANP guy is pointing at him."

The injured man was older than the dead teen, maybe twenty-five, and he was bleeding from a round that had entered his buttocks and exited through the front of his leg.

Hamilton's head filled with memories of lost friends and colleagues—particularly Captain John Croucher, seriously wounded in a May 25 IED strike—and, with adrenalin from the firefight still flooding through him, he was enraged.

"Willy had to calm me because I was pissed," he says. Looking at the wounded man, "I said, 'Why the fuck should I pass you up?' And I was telling him this through my interpreter, and I said, 'If I was under the bush there, bleeding, and you came across me, what would you do to me?'

"And he said, 'Oh, I'd take you back to my compound and heal you up,' and I said, 'That's bullshit.'

"And I know it, because about two days earlier, out in Helmand Province [the British AO, or Area of Operation], they caught two Brits and they basically beheaded one of them and dragged the other behind the truck, so I know what they do to people they catch.

"And I said, 'That's bullshit. Because I'm better than you, because *we're* better than you, I will heal you up and patch you up and take you back.'"

Hamilton had with him a medic, who did tend to the man's wounds—good thing, too, because it took about three hours before a Black Hawk landed to take the Talib to the base hospital at KAF.

While they were waiting for the chopper, the platoon rounded up the captured weapons, but had to retrieve them from the ANP because they had found the injured man first and "had already scrounged everything off the guy, so it was just a complete waste of any possible intelligence that was on him. But those pricks had already rifled through him. I managed to claw back the weapons from them, and I gave them the RPG and then was told we're not allowed to give them RPGs and it was a fight to get it back. You almost have to punch them out to get stuff back from them."

That was Hamilton's first real firefight as a commander, and it was an all-round success.

"I don't pretend to be Rommel or anything like that," he says. "It's just the conditions were right: We managed to surprise them, I had the terrain advantage with that high ridge there, and for once—probably the only time—we probably outnumbered them. And had superior firepower, all those things that as a commander, in the perfect war, in a perfect battle, you want to have checked off in your box."

And, thanks to Schnurr's giddy announcement, recce came up with what Hope later called "the best fire control order I have ever heard. We preach 'effects-based planning' so as to determine the clear definition of what exact effect it is that we want to produce upon the enemy," he said in an email. "Clearly, throughout the tour, I wanted to 'fuck 'em up' more often than not, but I am too educated to articulate with such clarity an exact meaning."

From July 4 onward, Hamilton says, "anyone who even messed with us, and they picked on us because we looked smaller and weak, we just hammered the crap out of them with everything we had."

It was during this period that recce conducted what Hamilton describes as "recon by force—drive till somebody shoots at you." The platoon was nicknamed the Bullet Magnets by Major Kirk Gallinger, with whose Alpha Company it most often worked.

The lessons came as fast as the RPGs for the sophisticated young Hamilton, who was raised in the small rural town of Norwood, Ontario, and environs but who spent two years in his wife Carolina's home country, Venezuela. There he picked up a bit of Spanish and took bets on sports for a bookie, before coming home and landing a job in the export-import field (he brought meat from Mexico to Brampton) he had studied at college.

"And I hated it," he says. "Detested it."

He applied to the military but didn't hear a word for eight months—typical for the Canadian army circa the turn of the century, which usually acted as though applicants ought to be grateful if they were even given a look and whose top speed tended toward the glacial. "I thought it was dead and gone—'No, we don't want him'— and then I got this call out of the blue."

He was twenty-three, and he was in.

Hamilton's grandfathers had both been in the military. One, Major-General G.G. Brown, was a former colonel of the regiment who fought in the Second World War. Brown lived in Calgary, but the family had a small cottage on an island in Quebec where they all gathered in the summers. "He loved to spend time with his grandkids. He'd appoint one sergeant-major for the day, make sure the chores got done. I had no idea what a sergeant-major was at that age, but then he'd tell us enough, stories about him being wounded."

But it was his grandfather Hamilton, a volunteer with the Toronto Irish, who really intrigued him. "Like he couldn't even say 'World War 2' without getting choked up, and it always stuck with me. What made him tick like that? What made him like that?"

Hamilton heard about his paternal grandfather's experiences largely through others, learned that he had seen action in Sicily, then all the way up the Italian boot until finally reaching Holland. "Holland was where it really got to him," Hamilton says. "I remember him telling me, 'We went in and saw the children there, they had nothing to eat,' and that was it, just knowing the kind of compassionate man he was with children, and everyone else."

For the longest time, he believed that Grandpa Hamilton "might have been upset that he had to kill somebody else, and that's why he was crying. But now I know it's not the case. Losing your mates beside you, that's what chokes . . . not that we're born murderers, but it's something we have to do, and we . . . it's something that had to be done."

On July 13, in a village called Hyderabad in central Helmand Province—known as the Green, both because it is lush with poppies and because exorbitant proceeds from those plants make it what Willy MacDonald calls the moneybelt of the Taliban— Hamilton had his first up-close brush with the spectre that had so haunted his grandfather.

The soldiers had travelled at night, through a huge dust storm that allowed them to make excellent time. They were to take a quiet peek at a compound where it was believed a Taliban commander— called an MVT, or Medium-Value Target, in army-speak—was holed up and opium and IED-making cells were being housed.

The original plan was for Hamilton and a complement of eleven soldiers to go in dismounted with some Afghans, but there were the usual minor screw-ups and delays—vehicles getting stuck and the like—and Hamilton was beginning to think the mission had been called off just as Gallinger handed him a satellite phone. It was Hope, and the CO told him to get going: They wanted recce in, and out again, before first light.

Hamilton drew up a quick plan—as formal as battle procedure often got in Afghanistan—and finally began to move.

They went through the village—Hamilton remembers that the first call to Muslim prayer was floating gracefully on the air—and arrived at a little mud bridge, the only way across to the compound, located on the west side of a canal that linked to the Helmand River.

As one element of the platoon secured the near side of the bridge, Mars Janek and his two men moved single file across it to secure the far side. On Janek's thumbs-up, the rest of the platoon began going across. It was still dark, MacDonald says, "but with colours changing as dawn quickly approached."

The 155-millimetre guns of the 1st Royal Canadian Horse Artillery's A Battery fired an illumination plan off in the distance to distract enemy eyes from the small recce group. Just as half of the platoon was across the bridge, three people were spotted running through a field to the west.

The men on the bridge stopped, adopted fire positions, and waited, while MacDonald jogged past them to the far side—the only sounds he heard made by his men chambering rounds in their rifles—where Hamilton was in an irrigation ditch.

At the same time, Janek moved with his two men to the cut-off position north of the compound.

"That," says MacDonald, "is when the world around us exploded."

A hail of gunfire—from AK-47s—and RPGs came from an estimated twenty-five to forty enemy spread in a horseshoe shape covering the west, south, and northwest.

"We had to position ourselves to counter that," Hamilton says.

He had Jeff Schnurr up on a hill, and another small group on the other flank keeping up the fire.

But Janek's detachment had been ambushed from the compound wall and was now cut off, thirty metres from the rest of the platoon.

"I couldn't fucking find them," Hamilton says.

With MacDonald directing fire from Schnurr and machine gunner Jimmy Funk, Janek's crew made its way back to the relative safety of the irrigation ditch. Only, Mars Janek was missing. MacDonald and Hamilton were trying frantically to locate him, visually and on the radio, when someone yelled, "Mars is hit!"

Janek had been shot in the back, the round stopping in the plate of his body armour, and had the wind knocked out of him. When he could catch his breath, with the platoon still taking fire, he fell into another ditch.

"I think he's fucking dying or something," Hamilton says.

He didn't know that the medic, Private Jason Lamont, had "made a decision," as MacDonald puts it, a decision for which the young man, now a corporal, would be awarded a Medal of Military Valour.

"Without direction or concern for his own well-being," MacDonald says, "Lamont got up and sprinted through approximately thirty metres of open terrain, under a heavy and concentrated enemy fire, in an attempt to get Janek."

Hamilton, who knew only that Janek wasn't answering his calls, says, "The medic was just a wee, wee guy, ninety pounds soaking wet, you know that type? And he had run over. Mars is about six fucking four, about 270 pounds, he's a huge Slovak. And obviously [Lamont] went over to see if he was all right, and he was all right, and [Lamont] had come back.

"I didn't see that.

"Next thing I see is Mars still lying there and I said, 'I'm fucking going to get Mars,' so I ran over. I thought he was really hurt, and as I was running over, I thought, 'How the hell am I going to pick this big son of a bitch up?' I fucking grab him and I pulled him out of the ditch and start to help him across and he said, 'Fuck, Hammy, I'm all right.'

"And I just, I tell you, I'm better with it now," Hamilton says, "but the first time I had to tell this story I burst into tears because I just love the guy so much, and I just couldn't stand him not being here."

About twenty to thirty minutes later, A Company's 2 Platoon rolled up in their Light Armoured Vehicles (LAVs), and with the compound burning and the enemy beginning to flee, recce temporarily withdrew to safety under the welcome boom-boom-boom of the LAVs' 25-millimetre cannons.

When the platoon returned not long after to exploit the scene and assess the battle damage, they found five confirmed dead and another five to ten suspected dead; weapons and ammunition; raw opium paste so concentrated, Hamilton says, "that if you touch it it'll absorb into your skin and really fuck you up" and with a street value of about $15 million (U.S.); high-value intelligence items that can't be identified; and anti-Canadian jihadist propaganda.

"I got my interpreter to translate the first part of it," Hamilton says, "so I could relay back to command what we had found, and it said that all Afghans should basically rise up and jihad against the invaders, especially the United States, Britain, and Canada. It carried on with some ranting and crap.

"But in a weird way, I felt proud to be a Canadian.

"Ever read those history textbooks on D-Day? And it's all American and British troops? And I'm Canadian, dammit, and we were there, and so I guess it was finally nice to be recognized by the enemy. . . . We're big enough to be recognized by guys who hate us, powerful enough to be recognized by those who hate Western society."

And that was July.

The Afghan sun was relentless. I was there for most of the month, and even when I got up at 6 a.m. and opened the tent flap, the whiteness outside was so blinding I more often than not emerged in a stumble, as surely as if I were drunk.

The day I landed in Kandahar the temperature hit 60 degrees Celsius (the big thermometer outside the media tents at KAF hit that number, then stopped working). Even on the mountaintops, where it was coolest, A Company's 3 Platoon once measured the temperature at 45 degrees Celsius.

July saw the troops drinking at minimum six litres of bottled water a day, more often between twelve and eighteen.

July was all combat.

These were not the isolated skirmishes of peace-stabilization missions, such as Canadians had performed in Bosnia, nor the one-off fight like the valiant men of the 2nd Battalion of the Patricias waged at the Medak Pocket in Croatia in 1993.

This was new—or rather ancient—because it was war.

July was a daily diet of long battles that went on for hours and stretched the battle group thin over six hundred kilometres in seven separate districts over some of the most treacherous terrain in Afghanistan.

I had last seen the soldiers in early April.

When I caught up with them just three months later, I barely recognized them. They were exhausted and skinny (many sweated off twenty pounds in the heat, some as much as forty), and even if there were only a troubled few with the thousand-yard stare (and usually then just for a short time), most of them obviously had been through the wringer. But while the long period of IED-wrought helplessness, the enemy as ghost, had had them looking a little hunted, now they more resembled hunters.

They were a killing machine. "We were," says Ian Hope. "I kept telling officers, 'You need to encourage and push a moral sense of force. Morally, you have to feel superior.'"

Just when they might have imagined they had experienced every horror and every triumph, felt every emotion and whipsawed from adrenalin rush to terrible grief and guilt at being alive and back again, it turned out they hadn't.

—

SERGEANTS PAT TOWER and Vaughan Ingram from Charlie Company were cranky.

Ordered to the Forward Operating Base at Spin Boldak—Spin was supposed to have been Charlie's AO but in practice almost never was—their 9 Platoon had sat out virtually all of July's fearsome fighting.

God knows, the troops deserved a respite.

They'd had a busy and wearing three months, much of it living on hard rations and in the dirt of a small Afghan National Army (ANA) camp called the 530 compound just off Highway 1, which runs west from Kandahar through the volatile Panjwaii district.

The 530 didn't even have a tent.

"It looked like the Alamo or something," Tower says, "just this big mud-walled compound. Had the grossest frigging Johnny-on-the-spot in Afghanistan."

From the 530, they conducted dismounted patrols, shot and were shot at, and had the usual close calls, the closest on May 29, when Corporal Tim Nowlan asked Ingram for a cigarette.

In position as one of two rear air sentries—who travel standing up in the LAV, rifles at the ready, heads and upper bodies exposed—Ingram ducked down into the carrier to grab his smokes just before an RPG came roaring into the space he'd occupied.

"If he'd been standing up, it would have cut him right in half," Tower says. Ingram, a handsome Newfoundlander from the hamlet of Burgeo, dined out on that story for a while, telling the troops how smoking had saved his life.

As it was, two other RPGs hit Ingram's LAV in that ambush, and he and four others were injured seriously enough that they were choppered to KAF for repairs.

Ingram was still picking shards of metal out of his skin days after returning to the field, and in a picture Tower has from that time, the big man with the telltale shrapnel face looks more like a spotty teen than the thirty-five-year-old hard charger he was. As Ingram told Hope, he was but "temporarily ugly."

Tower's own LAV was hit in the same ambush, one RPG blowing up underneath the vehicle, flattening the tires and dropping the suspension, the second exploding against its side.

I winced when I heard that, because I had been in Tower's first LAV, back in early April, for a punishing twenty-four hours as we made our way to FOB Robinson, then a primitive patch of near-desert about 100 kilometres west of Kandahar in the badlands of Helmand Province.

Possessed of a dry wit and easy confidence, Tower is one of those guys so baldly competent in virtually everything he does that even a dopey reporter recognizes it immediately; I felt safe beside him.

At that time, Charlie Company's mission was to secure the little FOB where just a week earlier one of their own, twenty-two-year-old Private Rob Costall, and U.S. Army Medic John T. Stone were killed in a vicious three-sided Taliban attack that sprung from the surrounding compounds and small hills.

If the loss of Costall and Stone wasn't warning enough, the potential perils of the mission were clearly spelled out for the soldiers in detailed briefings. But the troops were eager for their first real action, not only of the tour but also, for many, of their entire careers.

As Tower said then, "I've been waiting for this all my life."

As it turned out, it was quite a storied crew and a memorable trip, for all the usual mixed-up reasons.

In addition to Tower, who in 2006 was awarded the Star of Military Valour, in the LAV with me were Corporal Paul Rachynski, Private Joe Rustenburg, and Master Corporal Tony Perry, all of whom received Mentions in Dispatches. And throughout that endless trip—interrupted by a traffic accident that seriously injured two young privates, Dawson Bayliss and Daniel Mahlo; vehicles that got lost or broke down; and alarming reports of suicide bombers driving through the congested streets of Kandahar, trying to find a clear route to our convoy—there was on the radio the constant, soothing voice of a young woman named Nichola Goddard, a Forward Observation Officer (FOO) who then had only forty-five days to live.

However, the fight the troops had expected at FOB Robinson

never materialized, and it wasn't until May that 9 Platoon really got into the shit.

On June 15, back in Canada, I got an email from Tower, describing the platoon's third visit in recent weeks to Panjwaii. "Every time there has been some action," he wrote, "but nothing like this last time."

On the first visit, Captain Goddard was killed; on the second visit, the platoon was ambushed; on this third visit, there was a company-sized contact.

With a section on leave and Warrant Officer Shaun Peterson still back at KAF going through detox for a bad bite to the ankle from a five-foot viper, the platoon was under-strength and down to twenty-one men. They were sweeping dismounted through the village of Seyeden, on high alert because "we'd go into these compounds, and there'd be the laundry out, and the people were just there—and they're gone."

The area is a rat's maze of high mud walls tight to both sides of all roads and any driveable wadis, the branches of grapevines so close they brush and scratch against the tops of the LAVs.

"We had to start heading north," Tower says, "so I see where there's a corner to head north into this town, I go around this corner, and there's this guy at the end of it."

The man started backing up, "so I know there's something a little fishy," Tower says.

"And he's about fifty metres away and the thing is, you always go, 'Does he have a weapon? Does he have a weapon?' That's the big thing. If he's got a weapon, you can engage. So I'm looking and looking: Does this guy have a weapon? Has he got a gun?

"That's all I'm thinking: Does this guy have a gun?

"He just [pulls one] out of nowhere—because it was in his mandress, I could see it—and he just starts blasting at me with an AK."

The man's first rounds zipped along the side of the wall and sent up clouds of dust, and "he's blasting through the dust at me and I'm blasting through the dust at him, and I'm near the end of my magazine, I know I'm almost out of ammo. I go, 'This isn't working,' because I can hear rounds just going all around me."

With his section right behind him now firing, Tower ducked back around the corner and he and the platoon commander tossed a couple of grenades and then sprinted up the alleyway.

The alley opened up into a big grape field, and from a tree line on the far side of it, Tower says, they took fire again. His platoon, spread out in an extended line returning fire, was soon joined by another section of men and the engineers attached to the company that day. Together, the soldiers formed a fire base so that 8 Platoon could come up the flank.

"As they were moving into position to do their flanking," Tower says, "that's when two of their privates were wounded."

They were Kory Ozerkevich, now a corporal, who took a round to the armpit, and Brent Ginther, who was so seriously shot up in both legs that he was, Charlie Company commander Bill Fletcher says, "within five minutes of bleeding out" when evacuated by chopper.

With all that and more behind them, 9 Platoon surely had earned a rest by July, and the FOB at Spin offered that.

It has a kitchen, for one thing, so the troops didn't have to eat the loathsome, preservative-laced rations, some of which come with those silica packs that most often accompany non-comestibles. It has small brick buildings, and compared to sleeping in the dirt at the side of a LAV, that is downright cushy.

But to Tower and Ingram, the relative luxury sat like punishment or exile; they were sidelined.

"I know how I felt," Tower says. "I was pissed off, especially when you heard everything going on in Panjwaii and Helmand and you're listening to the radio and you hear about guys getting killed and wounded, you just want to be there. So I was pissed off. I think most of the guys wanted to be there. I know, talking to Ingram, I know him and I, we'd sit around and bitch about it to each other."

Things seemed to be winding down, in any case. The end of the tour was now in sight, the first of the Patricias had already left for the long trip back to Canada and others were getting "posted" (being posted out of the regiment to new assignments).

Then, late one night, Tower learned they were going back to KAF and then on into Panjwaii yet again. There, with Hamilton's recce platoon, 9 Platoon would be attached to Hope (the CO is always called Niner on the radio) and his tactical detachment of engineer and artillery assets (called Niner's Tac) with whom he always moved.

They were to be in the area of the notorious White School.

There are actually two White Schools, though they are often referred to as a single unholy entity. Both were built in 2004 with funds from the U.S. Commander's Emergency Reconstruction Program (CERP). The southern school is in the village of Bayenzi, the northern one near Dagaran.

The school in Bayenzi had been a festering sore for the Patricias for months, and would remain so for their successors, the 1st Battalion, the Royal Canadian Regiment.

As far back as May 17, Hope remembers, the villagers complained to the local ANP that the Taliban had slept in the school overnight and turned children away in the morning. The Patricias duly rode to the rescue hours later and cleared the school, but when the traditional summer harvest break came and the students were off, the Taliban returned.

Again and again, the Canadians went back to give them the boot—a total of six times, Hope figures. And almost every time, it was a dangerous trip along Highway 1, which in the Panjwaii region is called Ambush Alley, with a hard fight at the end.

Now, they had multiple reports of another Taliban group holed up in the area, with fighters sleeping in the school again, a Taliban checkpoint established on the Arghendab River, and the Taliban's white flag flying over the bazaar.

In addition, the ANP commander had received a call from the fellow who owned the marijuana field on the north side of the wadi. The man wasn't phoning to report the forty Taliban hiding in his field, but rather to complain that they were crushing his hash.

The initial plan was to move past the White School—Nick Grimshaw's Bravo Company coming down from the north and

Niner's Tac with 9 and recce platoons moving through the south—and seize the Bayenzi market. But as Hope says, "Missions evolve."

"I tell you," Grimshaw says, "certainly in my company, the guys were very, we were not looking forward to going there whatsoever. It was gonna be our fifth time going in. We knew what we were going up against.

"We knew the roads were impassable with LAVs because the bridges had been blown, we knew there were IEDs in the road, and we knew the Taliban were going to fight, going to stay and fight."

The majority of Grimshaw's men—from the 2nd Battalion—were slated to land at home base in Shilo, Manitoba, in just two weeks. "So there was that mindset: 'Man, we're so close to the end here, what's going on.' But we had a job to do and we got on with it."

Hamilton was simply happy the CO wanted him along. "He had a lot of faith in my men there and I know that," he says. "I was honoured. Anything he wanted done, I'd do it for him. Wasn't an issue."

At Patrol Base Wilson (PBW)—the grimy base named after Master Corporal Tim Wilson, killed in a vehicle accident in early March, that sits just off Highway 1—Hamilton and Peterson, 9 Platoon's acting commander, got quick orders from Hope and then sat down to figure out "how we were gonna do this exactly."

The convoy left PBW in the wee hours of August 3, drove in total blackout across Highway 1 toward the Panjwaii district centre, and headed northwest toward the wadi, 9 Platoon in the lead, then recce and Niner's Tac.

Just after 4 a.m., Tower's platoon spotted men armed with RPGs and AK-47s on a mud wall to the west, and engaged for about fifteen minutes, taking "out all those enemy."

At 4:13 a.m., about 150 metres from a bridge, the third LAV in the line struck a remote-controlled IED.

Grimshaw, north and on the other side of the Arghendab River, could see the flash in the sky and knew it was a bomb of significant size. "We could see the LAVs firing, and I was thinking, 'Here we go.'"

It was the platoon commander's LAV—hard-luck Peterson, who'd been bitten by the snake and blown up a couple of times. He was concussed—hell, he was still concussed from an earlier IED strike—and badly shaken up, but he wasn't the most badly injured; the LAV driver, Corporal Chris Reid, was mortally wounded.

The medics worked frantically on Reid. "They did CPR for forty-five minutes until the bird came," Randy Northrup remembers. "Sweating buckets, all for naught."

As they waited for the helicopter, Hamilton and Ingram, by default now the 9 Platoon commander, went forward to secure the scene, all standard procedure whenever there's a blast.

What they discovered stunned them: well-prepared firing points for IEDs, defensive positions around the bridge, an RPG with ammunition, spider (initiation) devices for bombs, and by his count, three more IEDs, some already half-buried in the soft ground.

Pat Tower also saw water bottles in the trees, blood trails, and "prayer mats all laid out."

In the final tally, Hope said in a "lessons learned" presentation he delivered in Edmonton, there were five IEDs placed along a hundred-metre stretch of road leading out of the wadi and up to a bridge over a small canal.

With so many bombs about, they called in the Explosives Ordnance Disposal (EOD) team, composed of combat engineers and navy officers, to come on foot to have a look, and they brought their LAV to blow up what they found.

"They got about ten feet," Hamilton says, "and BOOM! Another IED goes off. I was dismounted, walking back toward the bridge when the thing went off, and I just remember walking—BOOM! It kind of knocked me over a bit, and there was just this terrible, just toxic cloud of grey smoke and mist, and just disgusting chemical smoke-type thing.

"It knocked the transmission right out of the fucking thing [the LAV]," Hamilton says, but the engineers inside walked away with only three injured—bumps and bruises mostly, no one seriously hurt. Indeed, the men inside were so composed they told the troops, desperate to come forward to help them, to stay back because there were cook-offs, or smaller blasts, still exploding.

Hamilton brought Hope, who was only 150 metres away, up to have a look.

The school was tantalizingly close, maybe four hundred metres, but the mission had changed from a clearance of suspected Taliban positions to a large recovery operation.

As Hope tells anyone who will listen, "Everything in Afghanistan submits to incredible frictions. All plans change with the breakdown of one vehicle, the wounding of one soldier."

Despite army doctrine to the contrary, it was Hope's practice to stop everything in order to extract his casualties. "One may criticize the inevitable loss of momentum this brought," he says. "To this I respond that the destruction of no number of Taliban was so important as the safe evacuation of one Canadian—or ANSF."

Similarly, he knew, no number of dead Taliban was equal to the propaganda value the enemy would claim if a LAV was abandoned on the battlefield, so he always recovered vehicles too.

While all this was going on, Grimshaw's Bravo Company was involved in a significant fight near the north school.

It was barely 9 a.m.

"We'd never seen this intensity," Hope remembers. "At first light, we saw their defensive positions: they'd put holes in all the walls, the irrigation system was a trench system, they were wired up for multiple IEDs, rockets lined up."

By about noon, as they were waiting for the signal from the EOD boys to begin extracting the dead vehicles, Hope got intelligence that their silent night move had worked, and that a Taliban commander had been caught flat-footed and was now trapped in the south school to the west.

With one man dead, four injured, and two vehicles already down and disabled, the CO decided it was too risky to send the LAVs any further, and that the only option was to press on dismounted.

Hope remembers asking Hamilton and Ingram, "Can you guys

take that school?" Ingram, with that long, slow smile sliding across his face, replied, "Hell, yes."

Hamilton and Ingram had never worked together before, just knew one another a little.

Shortly before the battalion headed overseas, Hamilton had instructed a resistance-to-interrogation course. At one point, he needed help with what he calls, with uncharacteristic delicacy, "some very active demonstrations. . . . I had [Ingram] act as a guard, actually, and he just got right into it, eh?" He called Ingram Iggy, as most everyone did, as people call him Hammy.

Now they planned as best they could. They divvied themselves up, with Hamilton leading a group, which included the trusty Willy MacDonald, to the White School up along a canal, and Ingram taking the other, which included Pat Tower, up a ditch that ran parallel.

"Two separate axes of advance on either side of the road," Hamilton says. "At least give them two things to shoot at, instead of one."

They split up their ANP—instead of the promised one hundred, twenty-six men had shown up—and then waited for the Apache attack helicopters to arrive.

The sections stepped off, as they call it, "and sure enough, from in behind us, the shooting starts, and it's with Vaughan Ingram there, and the shooting is going in behind us," Hamilton says.

It was, as they realized later, only harassing fire. "Looking back on it, they [the Taliban] were buying themselves time, just to set us up," Hamilton says.

Meanwhile, he and Ingram couldn't get their coms working.

"For some reason I can't talk to him," Hamilton says. "Everybody thinks it's nice and easy, that you can talk clear to people, [tell them] what's going on, but you can't. People forget about the radios, and they don't always work, and you don't always have the full idea of what's going on."

So he made his way back, found Ingram in the ditch, and jumped in.

"Private [Andy] Social is to the left of Vaughan there, and I'm beside Vaughan, and we're talking, lighting up a smoke, and Social gets a round in his plate and he fucking gets in the ditch . . . and we go, 'You all right?' And he goes, 'Yeah, fuck, I'm fine.' He just got it in the plate, but he's shook up."

With the firing still going on, Social got the dry heaves, and Hamilton and Ingram started to ride him just a bit. "You know what," Hamilton said, "it's just, be thankful you're alive, you're all right. You got everything. Now we can fucking make fun of you, it's the old soldier's way."

The plan was always for the Patricias to push the attached ANP into the school, the old "Afghan face" dictum, with the Canadians supposedly "acting in support" of them. The ANP actually made it into the school, but the moment they started to move for the bazaar and take fire—it was sporadic, what Hamilton compares to being "in the woods and there's someone duck hunting beside you"—they pulled back.

"All I see is a fucking sea of blue of these guys coming back, running away from the school," he remembers, "and I go, 'What the fuck?'" Hamilton was furious. "Part of the plan was to get the ANP in front of us as we approached the school, because it's their fucking country, and every mission we're supposed to have an Afghan face on it, and I thought, 'You know what, it's about time they started fucking coming good on this, let's get them up there. Fucking, you know what, I hate to say cannon fodder, but you know what, it's time for them to take the fucking lead. We'll push up behind and make sure they do it right.'"

He got on the radio to Hope: "I said, 'Sir, this is the situation. There's small-arms fire coming from the vicinity of the school, the ANP have run back, and they're hiding in the ditch right now.'

"And he goes, 'Jon, you're going to have to hold their hand and take them in there. You have to lead the way in there.'

"And I said, 'Roger that, sir.'"

Deep down inside, Hamilton says, he knew all along he'd have to do that anyway.

By now, Ingram had discovered that the canal didn't go all the way to the school, and that he and his men would have to join Hamilton and go up via the ditch on the north side of the road.

It was late morning now, and the withering sun—temperatures were between 57 and 60 degrees Celsius—was taking its toll. Both platoon signallers, who carry the radios, batteries, and heavy coms gear on their backs, in addition to the usual seventy pounds of ammo, body armour, and weapons, had collapsed with heat stroke.

"It's not heat stroke where you just say, 'I'm too hot, I don't feel like fighting,'" Hamilton says. Men were staggering with it, fucked up, not making sense. Matt Tibbetts was one of the signallers. He kept apologizing, telling Hamilton, "Sir, I'm sorry."

"You don't be sorry, you're humping that fucking radio," Hamilton told him.

The heat stroke casualties were dropped at cut-off points, to be rounded up when things were quieter.

There were now fourteen soldiers, Canadians all, who formed the assault element and were positioned tight to a mud wall running along the south side of the road.

Using the wall for cover, under continuous small-arms and RPG fire, they began making their way to the school, one small section moving as another kept up suppressing fire. With this fire-and-movement technique, the men gained about two hundred metres of ground and hit the wall's end.

The school was very close, about 150 metres away, but across open, flat terrain.

Corporals Bryce Keller and Mark Bedard, the pair manning the General Purpose Machine Gun, or C6, had covered the first group of men as they made the dash to the school, but they were beginning to fail in the punishing heat. They didn't know whether they had enough left to make the run to the school themselves.

MacDonald asked whether they could, given a few minutes to rest and drink. As Hamilton says, through the sheer force of his leadership, MacDonald can pull the last and best from his men.

The second group, unaware that the machine gunners weren't with them, made their run, and as they moved, Kevin Dallaire was hit in the chest with a round.

"The soldiers scrambled to get him to cover and dress his wounds," MacDonald says, but in the ensuing confusion, he and the machine gun team lost verbal and visual contact with them. "It was decision time."

He told Keller and Bedard they could stay and cover him or make the run with him. "I told the two soldiers that the run would be under enemy fire, with no suppression from the assault element. The troops knew what had to be done." MacDonald grabbed the spare C6 ammo and barrel to lighten Bedard's load, "and we prayed and began to run."

Bullets whined off the ground around them, buzzing in their ears. RPGs roared by their heads.

As soon as they got inside the school—they were actually in small outbuildings, two bathrooms, male and female, separated by about eight feet and a wall a little higher than chest height—MacDonald says Ingram grabbed Keller and placed him in a firing position to "suppress the enemy fire which was now almost overwhelming."

MacDonald looked around. "I realized things were really bad . . . the situation was dire." Inside the school, they had Dallaire, wounded but still alive, and another five or six fresh heat stroke casualties.

Hamilton was in one of the bathrooms, MacDonald in the other. Some soldiers were still laying down suppressing fire, some were throwing back water, some were catching the faint breeze that wafted in the alley between the little buildings.

MacDonald was trying to call in artillery support; he's a trained Forward Air Controller, or FAC. After about thirty minutes, he was finally shut down at the brigade level "because of the risk of collateral infrastructure damage," he says.

"Colonel Hope became very angry at that. On the radio," Hamilton says.

Hope's end of this fiery exchange with General Dave Fraser was heard by more than a few sets of ears. The CO was "screaming for bullets" (the artillery's big ones). Gallagher, the guns commander who as always was with Hope, was also screaming for bullets, says someone who heard them on the air.

But the North Atlantic Treaty Organization (NATO) had just taken over the reins from the Americans in Afghanistan, and the rules for artillery had changed overnight from so-called "danger close" distance of 250 metres from buildings to the "peacetime safe distances" of 750 metres.

Fraser turned down his CO cold—the first and only time the Patricias were denied fire support by the higher-ups—and if Fraser was correct in abiding by the rules of the game as NATO wanted to play it, many were furious that, as one of them put it, "After seven months of this shit, he didn't trust his people on the ground."

Hamilton, meanwhile, did some calculating, figuring it would take four men to get Dallaire back to safety. With the heat stroke casualties, he realized he simply didn't have the numbers to get the soldiers out on their own.

He got on the radio and told Hope, by now at a casualty evacuation point no more than five hundred metres away, that he had people going down from the heat.

The discussion of whether to bring in the artillery was still going on, Hamilton remembers, because "I was talking on the radio, next thing I recall is a big boom and my ears were just ringing."

A lone RPG had hit the wall of the eastern bathroom, devastating the area, the shock wave knocking down the soldiers in the western toilet. "The soldiers in the eastern building were not as lucky," MacDonald says. "Corporal Keller, Private Dallaire, and Sergeant Ingram were all killed." Four others were wounded, including Hamilton.

"It was that kind of same dark black-grey cloud there was with the IED there," he says, "and kind of the smell of cordite, and I felt something hit my foot and I said, 'What the hell is that?' It took me about a split second to know I'd been hit. I didn't know what the fuck it was, and this all seemed to take forever but I know it was fairly quick. I remember thinking, 'Well, when the dust clears I'm probably not going to see my foot there.'"

The smoke cleared.

"I looked down at the desert boot I had on—I usually wear my personal-bought $300 handmade mountain boots, and I'm kind of glad I didn't that day—but there was blood coming through my right foot obviously, and I saw the boot was still there, so the foot had to be there to some extent, and I said, 'Fuck, I gotta get on the radio.'"

What Ian Hope and Randy Northrup heard, back at the casualty collection point, was, "If you don't get LAVs in here now, we're all gonna die. If you don't get LAVs in here now, we're all gonna die."

Hamilton remembers saying it, but in his memory—probably because it is inconceivable to him that he would have failed to use his favourite expletive—it was: "Get those fucking LAVs up here now!"

Then he called for MacDonald, just across the channel between the two buildings: "I said, 'Fucking Willy, get the fuck over here!' I leaned on him, again, when I needed to and again he came through for me."

Disoriented from the shock wave, and with enemy fire—machine guns and RPGs—still raining down, MacDonald made a break for it.

"As I came around the corner," he says, "I was assaulted by what I saw. Three soldiers appeared dead, and several more were writhing in agony from their multiple injuries. Those that were not hit by enemy fire were either hysterical or unable to do anything but stare at me in disbelief and shock. The only person in control was Hammy."

MacDonald apologized, of course, for not getting there sooner. Hamilton looked him in the eyes and said, "Don't worry about it, Will. I knew you'd come for me."

MacDonald then did what he describes in the very mildest of terms as dressing Hamilton's wound, putting a tourniquet just below his knee to stop the bleeding.

Hamilton will have none of that: "Not only was he there as a fucking physical support, he was there as an emotional support—you know, telling me I was a good leader and I did a good job, you know? He was just always there for me. I just, as a commander, I couldn't have asked for a better right-hand man."

Next, Pat Tower burst into the bathroom. He had been working his way up to the school, with his guys, when Hamilton's cry for help came over the radio. All he'd had to hear was that there were casualties: He grabbed Master Corporal Cole, who was suffering terribly from the heat but refused to be left behind, and the medic, Corporal Nic Lewis. They did "a runner"—sprinting, under heavy fire, across those 150 metres of open ground. They weren't even sure where anyone was; they just ran in the general direction of the school.

Cole later found a bullet hole in his magazine pouch. As Tower says in his casual manner, "I tell you, there was a lot of shooting going on at us as we were doing this runner."

They went, first, to the western building. Corporal Jason Hoekstra had picked up the C6 ("Shoot until you fucking die," MacDonald told him), because Keller was dead. Private Andrew Gorman was in the doorway of the other building, "and Gorman," Tower says, "he's not really part of our platoon, he's a storeman normally, but he's still a Patricia. So Gorman's in the doorway, and I tell Gorman, 'Give me a bit of covering fire,' as I'm going to come over to the other side. So he starts shooting, and I come around and as I come up I can see that he's wounded, like his hand, like he's shooting but he's wounded, blood coming off him. Right on, good job, Gorman."

MacDonald remembers seeing Tower and his band of two arrive. "I said, 'Thank God you're here, Pat. How many guys do you have?'" MacDonald thought, hoped, prayed, that Tower had come in a LAV.

Tower looked at MacDonald. "And I go, 'Where's Vaughan?' and he goes, 'Vaughan's dead.'"

Arriving right behind Tower was Master Corporal Tony Perry in his LAV, and right behind him was Master Corporal Kiwi Parsons in his.

Just as Tower had moved at the first word of casualties, the two crew commanders had heard Hamilton's terrible transmission and that was all it took.

"Jon called for help," Ian Hope says, "and I had a few seconds of real hard decision making, weighing the probability of another LAV killed by an IED."

Major Mason Stalker, the battalion's operations officer based at KAF, had managed to push three fresh platoons into the area to help out, and Hope asked Perry to relay a message to Ben Richard of Alpha's 2 Platoon, to mount up and go to the school.

But instead, as the CO watched, Perry and Parsons pulled their LAVs ahead of Richard's. "Seeing where they were," Hope says, "it made perfect sense and they were doing the right thing." He had to fight back the almost overpowering urge to mount up and go himself.

"They didn't even wait for the order," Hamilton says of Perry and Parsons. "They knew that the road was full of IEDs, said, 'Fuck it, our boys are in trouble. We're going.'"

The LAVs each fired four hundred rounds on the way.

Hamilton saw Dallaire and Keller. "It was obvious that they were gone. I just remember looking at Vaughan there, and he just kinda looked up at me, and I thought, 'Fuck, he's all right,' and then he just slumped his head over to the side."

Hamilton was on the radio, calling for help, but MacDonald remembers the moment in detail. "Vaughan was dying and he knew he was dying, but he had a field dressing in his hand and he was trying to do first aid on one of the boys. I think it was Bryce Keller, but it might have been Dallaire. Vaughan looked up at us and said, 'I think I'm slipping, boys,' and then he just died. His head dropped and he was gone."

It took the three LAVs to get everyone out of the White School. The wounded, MacDonald at Hamilton's side, went in one, the dead in another. The ANP were already in their trucks.

"Hiding," says Hamilton. "If I could have shot them, I probably would have shot the ANP, I think."

They arrived at the casualty collection point, where the CO and RSM were in a piece of modular tent off the back of one of the Bison armoured vehicles that are always used as ambulances. Hope's VHF (Very High Frequency) coms were down, the satellite link was iffy, and rounds were still clipping through the top of the tent. He was in a sweat-soaked T-shirt at the very back, surrounded by his bleeding and moaning men, trying to work three radios to control the fight, have the unexploded IEDs cleared so the two disabled LAVs could be recovered, and get the mass casualty evacuation under way.

"I was unsure whether or not my messages were transmitting," he says, "because I wasn't receiving anything, so I wasn't sure anyone could hear our requests for support."

Back at KAF in his command post, Lieutenant-Colonel John Conrad was monitoring Hope's progress on the radio net. "I heard fear and stress in Ian's voice as he ordered both medevac and equipment recovery off the battlefield. It was as rattled as I have ever heard Ian become, understandably so. I learned later from him that he could hear nothing on his end of the radio, so in the middle of that difficult fight he had no idea if any of his calls for assistance were being heard or acknowledged by any of us. They were."

As the logistics boss, Conrad and his troops had pulled off miracles before—particularly when the battle group was sent deep into Helmand Province to take back two district centres and the National Support Element (NSE) had to keep the soldiers supplied over 350 kilometres for the better part of a month.

Conrad sent out a convoy of Bisons, wreckers, and lowbed trailers to bring back the two damaged LAVs under the command of Lieutenant Doug Thorlakson. The recovery column had to lay up beside the Panjwaii district centre until the soldiers were able to drag the dead LAVs back to a safe point, where Thorlakson's crew could load them up.

"It was a crowded area by the district centre," Conrad says, "with a decent-sized market replete with civilians."

Thorlakson was standing watch in his Bison with a C6 machine gun when a vehicle, driving erratically, appeared.

"He used hand signals to get it to pull over, and for a moment it did," Conrad says. "I expect this was for the driver to say a final prayer, or screw up his courage, because he immediately pulled out into the centre of the road and began accelerating toward the parked recovery convoy."

Thorlakson "walked his stream of machine gun fire up the road and into the windshield of the car," Conrad says. It detonated instantly, pieces of shrapnel flying.

Except for minor injuries, the Canadians escaped unscathed, though one piece of shrapnel just missed Thorlakson's carotid artery and lodged in his neck. Unfortunately, in the crowded area, twenty Afghans, including some children, were killed. It is small consolation to realize that many of them—or others—likely would have been killed if the bomber had swerved into the convoy as planned.

But Thorlakson, Conrad says, "had fulfilled the apotheosis of duty—given the precious gift of life back to his men, some of whom would most certainly have been lost. He also saved nearly all of our holdings of fighting vehicle recovery equipment."

Conrad and his deputy commanding officer (DCO) met the men at the base hospital when they returned. "The soldiers were badly shaken," he says, "and there were many tears of remembrance, tears of relief, and tears for what very well could have been additional tragedy on an already black enough day. I was so proud of Doug. Taking out a suicide bomber, particularly a vehicle-borne bomber, is next to impossible."

But when he went to see General Fraser that night, Conrad was astonished at his reaction. "I was so proud of Doug," he says, "but the boss immediately went on the offensive: 'Did he use the ROE properly? What was Doug doing out there?' He was very concerned with the number of Afghans killed in the blast. Look, no one wants to see an Afghan get hurt, but . . . it was a very odd meeting."

Fraser doesn't dispute Conrad's description, but is unapologetic.

"I take nothing at face value at the beginning," he says, "and I will ask lots of questions which may appear offensive to ensure that we have all the facts.

"At the time, ROE [Rules of Engagement] escalations were on the rise and we needed to determine what was causing it, ensure that the local people still had confidence in our abilities to prosecute the mission."

He says the incident, and his and Conrad's starkly different reactions to it illustrate the differences in their jobs. For Fraser, the shooting was but one of a myriad of pieces in his big-picture view of the mission; for Conrad at that moment, it was everything.

"War," Fraser says flatly of himself, "has a very bad effect of hardening you . . . it has made me more cold and calculating to get things done and not wait."

Later, Fraser signed Conrad's recommendation for Doug Thorlakson's Mention in Dispatches for his conduct during what Conrad calls the day's second battle of Pashmul. Yet there has been not a single public mention of the only known case where a suicide bomber was taken out before he could kill Canadian soldiers. The soldiers who were hurt that day blithely joke that their injuries were non-existent because it was "the attack that never happened."

Hope and the RSM, frantically working at the casualty point, knew nothing of this drama; all they heard was the loudest boom from the largest explosion they had ever seen. Then, the most welcome noise in all the world: an American B-1 bomber roared in low, illegally low at maybe five hundred feet, followed by two U.S. fighter jets at seventy-five feet.

"The pilots had heard our distress [signals] and decided to add a psychological boost," Hope says. It is one of the reasons why, in the PowerPoint notes he uses when he speaks about August 3, one of the key lessons learned is, "You can always trust the U.S. Air Force to help you out."

The Taliban fire stopped.

Tower, now the acting 9 Platoon commander, gathered the remnants of his men together.

RSM Northrup watched in awe. "They were morally hurting, physically just hanging on. [Tower] did the Knute Rockne thing. He goes, 'All right, I need you fucking guys to stand up. You, you're the section commander; you, you're the second-in-command. Shut the fuck up, this is what I want. I want everything inventoried. I need a movable force, I want ammo, weapons, dismounts. Gentlemen, it's time. It's your turn. Get on with it.'"

Within fifteen minutes, Northrup says, the shattered soldiers reported back to Tower through Kiwi Parsons, and Tower reported back to Northrup: "I've got these vehicles running, fully crewed, distributed ammo, where do you want us?"

"He was stellar," Northrup says. "You think you only see that kind of shit in the movies until you actually live it. It was inspiring."

Hope, seeing Tower ready to fight, with the fresh platoons at his side, was aching to send the men back in to finish the job. He fought his emotions, his desire for retribution. With no ANA to leave behind to solidify whatever gains they might make, any victory would be fleeting and too costly.

In the bright haze two Kandahar mornings later, the ramp ceremony for the fallen four was held. Fresh out of hospital, Jon Hamilton was there in his wheelchair. Willy MacDonald and Pat Tower were among the twenty-four pallbearers.

In video I saw afterwards, Tower was at the rear of Vaughan Ingram's casket, thinner than I've ever seen him. His glasses kept slipping down his nose. He looked vulnerable, as you would when bidding farewell to your best friend.

In a picture that appeared on the cover of *Maclean's* magazine, MacDonald, at the front of the casket, was clearly visible. The picture broke the hearts of his family and friends, he says.

Just as the photographer took the shot, Willy MacDonald had spotted Hammy in his wheelchair. "He began to cry," MacDonald says, "and I was biting my lip and trying not to cry myself."

As the caskets passed, Hamilton rose to his feet: "There was no fucking way I was sitting down for that."

Platoon mates MCpl. Ray Arndt and Cpl. Ash Van Leeuwen

5 August 2006

—

"When he walked, if I walked on a certain side and was holding his hand,
I could tell there was a limp. I noticed it much more if we were dancing,
because he always compensated for it. But he danced."

—DARCIA ARNDT, ON HER LATE HUSBAND
MASTER CORPORAL RAY ARNDT

By the end of July 2006, Darcia Arndt had just barely been able to stop keeping the phone right by the bed at night.

In little more than a week, her newly muscled husband—when he came home on leave in May, she took one look at his six-pack and squealed with delight, "Who are you? What have you done with my husband?"—would be leaving Kandahar.

She remembers thinking, "He's gonna be out of there in nine days. He's almost done, right? I don't need the security of having the phone right there." For the previous six-plus months of his tour in southern Afghanistan, she had.

Ray Arndt was an Eddie, a member of The Loyal Edmonton Regiment, Alberta's oldest infantry reserve regiment and the only infantry militia regiment remaining in the province's capital.

Though many of Canada's twenty-five thousand reservists serve as part-time soldiers and never leave home, a growing number are signing up for overseas tours, with others opting to work full-time on contracts. And reservists are increasingly playing a key role in overseas missions, making up as much as 20 percent of troops on the later rotations in Bosnia, for instance.

In fact, for the tour of the 1st Battalion, Princess Patricia's Canadian Light Infantry, two proud Alberta reserve regiments—the Eddies and the Calgary Highlanders—provided almost all the soldiers for the force protection platoon that had the dangerous job of escorting the resupply convoys which travelled to and from the hottest spots in the volatile south. Ray was one of them.

Tellingly, because soldiering was such a large part of the man he was, the first time Darcia Kope, then all of twenty-three, laid eyes on him, he was in uniform. They met at a regimental dinner at the Jefferson Armoury, Darcia on a date arranged through mutual friends, as the guest of Gordie Legarie, then an Eddie and now a member of the regular air force.

"We walked into the junior ranks mess, and everybody got a drink and was chatting and smoking, and I saw Ray standing there and I thought, 'Ohhhhh, I'd like to get to know him.'"

Later, Ray admitted that from his side of the room, he had thought, "How did Gordie ever get *that?*"

There was and is nothing wrong with Gordie, and rather a lot that is admirable: When Ray was killed, his body returned to Canadian Forces Base (CFB) Trenton for the repatriation ceremony, Legarie drove from CFB Borden, about a hundred kilometres north of Toronto, to see Darcia.

As she emerged from the long black car ferrying Ray's family and friends, the first person she saw was the kind young man who had been her date that night in 2003. "He sat by my side the entire time in that VIP room," she remembers. "He did not leave my side. He held my hand, took me outside for smoke breaks."

For Darcia and Ray, there had been an immediate and powerful sense that they had found one another at precisely the right moment. "He'd just gotten out of a long relationship and was still very hurt by that, and I just was like, I'm ready to find the one I want to settle down with, I'm not gonna go date any random guy. I want to find the one . . . and he was kind of tired of the go-nowhere relationship."

Their first proper date was on Remembrance Day that year, another signal that Ray was no "weekend soldier," as reservists are sometimes called, and that if Darcia and he were to last, she would have to be part of this world of his. It was all new to her.

Darcia was raised in Tofield, a small town about ninety minutes east of Edmonton, and later on an acreage after her mother married the man Darcia calls Dad. There is no history of military service in her family other than an aunt who was a Sea Cadet. Before meeting Ray, Darcia had no connections to soldiers but for her girlfriend's husband and a few of their friends.

The Eddies are a particularly tight group. As Ray's friend and platoon mate in Kandahar, Ash Van Leeuwen, says, "That's the thing about our unit. Because you've got that relationship, you get to learn everyone's background—this is this guy's girlfriend, and she's gonna stick around a while. Ranks kind of float away after-hours, sergeants mingle with privates. . . . It's a real regimental family."

Darcia also learned pretty quickly that Ray wanted to get in at least one overseas tour, so desperately that he'd already tried a couple of times, coming painfully close to making it to Bosnia in 2002, the year before they met.

And if a single human feature can be said to capture the glorious lunacy of the army—any army, probably, but particularly the Canadian army—it would be Ray Arndt's left foot.

"It was a birth defect," Darcia says, "and they'd had to do numerous surgeries. I believe the foot was turned all the way around. It was a club foot." After each operation, Ray the boy had had to learn to walk again. He had done so, but the end result was a right foot that was a size 9 and a left foot that was a size 6. He couldn't wear normal shoes, only fitted running shoes from specialty stores and, his favourite because of the way they hug the foot, cowboy boots.

The foot didn't pose a problem until he became an Eddie and the depths of his magnificent stubbornness were well and truly plumbed. The army had a policy of one pair of boots per man; rules were rules, and they weren't about to bend them.

"Something so simple," says Van Leeuwen. "Right-sized boots. He had to fight to get in. This was his spirit. It wasn't like, 'They won't give me the right-sized boots.' He fought that, he fought to get in. I forget for how many years, but it probably happened that for most of his military career, he had the wrong-sized boots on."

The reserves were then still emerging from decades of perceived irrelevance. In 1965, the government slashed the militia by twenty-two thousand men and closed dozens of units across the country, a devastating blow it took thirty years for Ottawa to even acknowledge.

Well into the new century, Canadian reservists on exercise were regularly denied ammunition, with enough of them crying, "Bang! Bang!" when they "fired" a shot that the term "militia bullets" was coined.

The ammunition shortage for reserve units persisted into January 2004. I wrote a column at that time for *The Globe and Mail*, quoting the commanding officers of two militia units, the Argylls and Sutherland Highlanders in Hamilton, Ontario, and the Seaforth Highlanders in Vancouver, who described in detail how the militia was starving for ammunition except for those units that had been selected for Afghanistan and were in training.

So, in the scheme of things, denying one lanky reservist with a buggered-up foot was small potatoes. If it cost Ray a spot on a tour to Bosnia—his left foot, sloshing about on training marches in a boot three sizes too big, blistered so terribly he couldn't walk properly and wrecked a knee—there were plenty of others eager to go. There always are. As Van Leeuwen says, "In the reg force, if you don't want to go, you can find a way out of it. Reservists? We're all screaming to go."

"What's funny," Darcia says, "is that a lot of the guys didn't know about his foot" until Ray joined the 49th Battalion Pipes and Drums Band, made up entirely of Eddies. "So they're all wearing kilts and those socks up to the knee that fold over, and it was very noticeable. He had this little skinny itty-bitty leg and this regular leg. They started calling him Chicken Leg. But nobody really knew about it, unless they were really close to him. It wasn't something he talked about."

Even before the regiment got word, around Christmas of 2004, that the Eddies could be going to Kandahar, Darcia was used to not seeing much of her new beau. Shortly after they met, he moved to Wabasca in northern Alberta, driving for an oil rig supply company. He'd come down to visit on occasional weekends, but most of their early relationship was conducted over the phone.

Soon, she knew, he was going to try for Afghanistan. "I had a vague idea that January, February," she says. "We had discussed it. . . . I knew how much he wanted it, I knew how badly he wanted it. I knew I could never say, 'No you can't go.' If he didn't go because of me, he'd end up resenting me for it. And I didn't want that, so we talked about it for a long time, and I said, 'Just go do it, get it over and done with, you'll come home and we'll start our lives.' Just do it. He wrote his name down on that piece of paper, and training started."

Workup or buildup training for the Kandahar mission meant nine months away in Wainwright, the former Second World War intern-ment camp (for German prisoners of war) turned full-fledged base turned training centre about two hundred kilometres outside of Edmonton. With more than six hundred kilometres suitable for live-fire practice, Wainwright has long been the army's main training base in western Canada and is destined to become the primary national one.

Before training began, Ray was "finally fitted with real boots, two pairs, one size 6 and one size 9," Darcia says. He had finally raised enough of a stink, or perhaps it was because, with the Afghanistan mission fast approaching, the army needed him as much as he needed it. It was short of instructors, and all that summer Ray and his friend Grant Trudel, then an Eddie who joined the regular force in 2006 (taking the usual one-rank demotion that comes with such a transfer) and is now a Patricia with the 3rd Battalion, ran training for the platoon.

In the middle of all this, Ray and Darcia bought a townhouse, moved in together—Van Leeuwen remembers being "voluntold" he'd be helping—and picked November 19 as their wedding date.

Intense training started in September, with the Eddies away for nine weeks at a stretch. Darcia remembers that Ray managed to sneak home on Thanksgiving for four hours. She had been three hours away at her mum and stepdad's, but drove down to see him. "He had fresh cut flowers," she says, "for Happy Thanksgiving, and he looked cute, but he stunk. He grew this nasty moustache when he was gone and I said, 'You stink and you need to shave.' So I spent Thanksgiving Monday sitting on the bathroom counter because he spent forty-five minutes in the shower, and then while he gave himself a haircut and shaved, we chatted about what he'd been doing for the last six weeks. Then he went right back."

Darcia was worried about whether Ray would even make it back for the wedding. "I'm this freaking-out, nervous, spazzy bride; we were uncertain if he was even going to be home. Then, right at the end of October, he got home."

They were married in a Lebanese hall ten minutes from their townhouse and had two hundred people for dinner.

Before she knew it, February 2006 had rolled around, and Darcia was driving with Ray to the sprawling base in Edmonton.

"He said, 'I have to stop and see Grant first, he's working at the duty desk,'" Darcia remembers.

"'What could you possibly have to see Grant for this early in the frigging morning? Couldn't you have done this three days ago?' His family was late; they're running late, we're running late. We missed roll call, that's how late we were.

"He said, 'I have to give Grant this CD,' and I just thought it was something he had borrowed and he just wanted to make sure his buddy got his stuff back, right? And I was so mad about it: 'You wait till the last minute.'"

On the disc were two documents, one a letter to Darcia, the other Ray's wishes for his funeral service.

Van Leeuwen arrived in Afghanistan on February 11, but remembers the platoon's pit stop en route at a coalition-friendly base in the Middle East called Camp Mirage. "We saw the desert sun rising for the first time," he says. "It was totally, 'We're actually here, this is real!' This fireball came out of the sky, it wasn't even fully over the horizon and we were dripping, there were stains on the concrete barricade from sweat falling off our heads."

Then it was on to Kandahar. "We land on this great big base," Van Leeuwen says, "and it's cool first thing in the morning. We arrived at the end of their winter."

The first three nights at KAF, he says, their tent was flooded from the rain. "I remember reading that Afghanistan had had thirty years of drought, so what the hell was going on? We were wet, someone lied to me. This wasn't on the poster."

But whereas back in Wainwright no one knew quite what this platoon of reservists—a good many of them still students at college or university—was going to be doing in Afghanistan, Van Leeuwen found to his relief, "We finally had a job to do. . . . They didn't care if we were reservists, they just knew we were gonna provide security for transport."

The first crew that went out, he says, "had their first contact on the way back, two RPGs scream across the hood of their G-Wagon, bounce off the hood. One of the guys from the Bison got a mag and a half off. They drove right to the tent lines [when they got back to KAF], shouting, 'We got contact!' Just that sheer excitement of 'We just cheated death and no one got hurt and this was the real deal.' We [reservists] always deploy, but we finally had our hands on something really tangible, you know? It wasn't one of those things: 'Reserves can't do it today.' This was our job, and it wasn't going to get done if we didn't do it."

That first contact happened in early March. "It was just a buzz, like static, that moon dust just hovering above the ground from the vibrations. We stayed outside, all thirty of us here were just buzzing." Van Leeuwen remembers a soldier taking one drag of his smoke and it was gone, he was so wired.

The next morning, though, the platoon was kicked out of bed to do its first ramp ceremony, likely the one for Corporal Paul Davis, killed in a vehicle accident on March 2, with Master Corporal Tim Wilson, injured in the same crash, dying two days later at the U.S. military hospital in Landstuhl, Germany. The platoon's celebration deflated. "It was totally like, no delusions," Van Leeuwen says. "We're playing for keeps now." He remembers being on the pistol range later that day when a fellow Eddie told him, "We'll probably be sending guys from this platoon home in boxes."

The day Van Leeuwen turned twenty-six, he was doing live fire at Tarnak Farm, the very place where, on April 18, 2002, four Canadians, Patricias from the 3rd Battalion, had been killed in a friendly fire incident when an American pilot mistakenly bombed them during their live-fire exercise.

He remembers those first runs into Kandahar city, how he looked at everyone and everything suspiciously, when it was all fresh and new and the instructions came fast and furious. "'Don't move your body, look with your eyes.' 'Watch the whole environment, watch how the traffic's moving, watch the people, watch for white Corollas.' I'm watching white Corollas. They said maybe it's a taxi, I'm watching taxis.

"But by the end of it, I knew where all the alleyways were, knew, okay, I come around this bend, I got an open space ten metres wide, a hundred metres long with alleyways inside of that, so cover that. I know there's a break in the centre of the road here, here, and here. So I know to hold the rifle, put down the C6."

Van Leeuwen laughs at the memory that when he first arrived, "I had escape-and-evade money on me, extra rations. At the end of it, it was kind of like walking into a 7-Eleven in a bad neighbourhood."

When the combat team began moving into the mountains and out to the far-flung FOBs, so of necessity did the big trucks of the National Support Element—bringing the soldiers everything from fuel to bullets—and so did the platoon of reservists who escorted the convoys.

At first, they had just enough people to do the job. Then soldiers began going on leave, and there were the Hurting Jacks, the men who would go to an FOB on a supply run and stay there, dogging dangerous runs. "Had a guy who spent a month and a half at an FOB," Van Leeuwen says, "came back with a great big beard. We were depleting, going out [beyond the wire] every day, at least once a day. I remember Kandahar was a big deal, then we're going to the mountains, Helmand, Spin Boldak. We had to supply them, bring troops. One day we'd be bringing troops, medical supplies and rations, ammunition; the next day [we'd go] to Kandahar" to pick up soldiers going on leave. They recovered disabled vehicles. They did everything, went everywhere.

From his vantage point in the turret with the C6, Van Leeuwen watched Ambush Alley—Highway 1 from the Panjwaii district to Kandahar city—stretch out like a child during a growth spurt. "It started off being, like, two kilometres and it grew to be fourteen kilometres long," he says, "and you puckered, you didn't sweat, and you didn't breathe." And then they'd arrive intact, and he'd be giddy with the loveliness before him.

He remembers one particularly harrowing day, when Kandahar was abuzz with a visit from Afghan President Hamid Karzai. Van Leeuwen says Karzai wanted to visit his grandmother's house and a hospital, so the city was crawling with security agents and the sky was thick with hovering Black Hawks. The platoon had to recover four vehicles, return to KAF, and then go back out through Ambush Alley.

"And it was just beautiful where we were," he says. "They just did the harvest, so you just had this stubble, stubble fields, and it was all golden."

Naturally—and it did seem natural then—on the way back to base, the platoon was attacked for the second time that day, a reminder that Afghanistan is the black widow of nations, dangerous even when alluring.

Back in Edmonton, Darcia talked to Ray every day on MSN chat and every Sunday on the phone, the days of warriors being incommunicado for weeks and months long over. But she knew little of the dangerous work he was doing. Or rather, she knew, but she didn't know, as Ray told, but didn't tell. Charlie Company commander Bill Fletcher once described this dance, in which he and his wife also regularly engaged, as: "I lie, and she pretends to believe me."

"Ray didn't tell me a whole lot," Darcia says. "He didn't give me a whole lot of information. He'd tell me about PT [physical training], he'd tell me, 'We gotta go out,' but he wouldn't give me a lot of detail about what 'going out' meant.

"He kind of sprung it on me one day, about going on a convoy, and I was like, 'What?!' He said, 'You knew that was going to happen,' and I said, 'Yeah, but I thought maybe you'd tell me before you started,' and he said, 'I can't.'"

Darcia was angry, and worried. She phoned Grant Trudel, whose transfer to the regular force came in before the Afghanistan mission so he didn't go overseas, and learned to her chagrin that couples usually work out a secret code, so that soldiers who are leaving the base can alert their wives without breaking operational security.

Ray's attitude was, "Well you know now, get over it, don't worry about it." After that, he'd just say, "I won't be able to talk to you tomorrow," and she'd know. "So I knew it was happening," Darcia says, "and I knew when it was, but I didn't know where."

She watched television news compulsively. "I was glued to the TV," she says. "He would always tell me, 'Quit watching the news,' because I'd see something and then right away, when he came on MSN, I'd be like dah-dah-dah, telling him what I'd heard. He'd kind of get mad at me, tell me to stop watching, I was freaking out for no reason. And I'd hear stuff and I'd tell him and he'd say, 'That happened five days ago,' or 'I haven't a clue what you're talking about.'

"Grant got a few calls," she says, "because I was climbing the walls, freaking out with all this stuff going on, and he'd come over and talk to me about it, calm me down."

For all that Ray was always calm and rational, Darcia's constant worrying began to take a toll on their young marriage. "It was causing a lot of communication barriers between us," she says, "and there wasn't a lot he could do to calm me down, talk me through everything. He wasn't always able to do that when he was on the other side of the world."

Finally, Ray told her in a serious way to stop watching the news. "'Why do you need to see that?' he asked. And I said, 'Well, I wanna know if anything happens to you.' And he said, 'You'll know before it hits the news. You will know. Just quit watching.' And I think I quit watching at the beginning of April."

Trudel certainly knew what Ray was doing. "I knew he was going out. I knew he had a couple of close calls," he says. But he says that all the soldiers knew what was in store for them. "I knew from the get-go, as part of the workup training, knew that was part of the mission. I knew as soon as I volunteered my name, we were going to be in a lot of shooting. We geared our training toward that ahead of time, because we knew."

Darcia leaned on Trudel, and on another wife whose husband had been deployed. "We communicated on a daily basis," she says. Sometimes, by comparing the few details the two husbands disclosed, "we would kind of meet in the middle with what we knew and figure it out." She also discovered marriedtothecanadianforces.com, which gave her "a different sort of connection. It kind of made you feel you're not alone in the world, that there are other wives, and men too, married to people serving overseas. And it was just nice to know that other people had the same fears as you."

Ray came home on leave in May. Darcia picked him up at the airport, and though he was obviously jet-lagged, he "looked fantastic! From the minute he got there, he started doing a lot of PT. He was always a very lean guy, very slim. There was hardly an inch of fat on him. But I wouldn't say he was really muscly." His neck had grown two inches, he had some muscle definition, and he was tanned and gorgeous.

Darcia kept working for much of their first week together, and then they left for Playa del Carmen, Mexico, on a belated honeymoon. "I was just excited to go anywhere," Darcia says, "because I had never been anywhere, I had never been on an airplane, it was just really exciting to go on an airplane. It seemed so surreal the whole time there, like, 'I can't believe we're here!'"

Two days after they returned, she threw a big barbecue for Ray, and then three days after that she was in the car again, driving him to the airport. It was both harder and easier than the first time, when he deployed. The scene at the base, the first time, was difficult because "there's a whole bunch of other people standing around and crying, people you don't know, people you know, family . . . everybody bawling. That was really tough; for two days after, I was depressed." The second time, they went to the international airport (soldiers travelling on leave usually fly commercial), and while there were about ten others on Ray's leave block, "there weren't that many of them, not a whole lot of standing around and sobbing and stuff."

Yet this had its own peculiar pain. "As he's getting ready to go through the gate, pushing the cart, and he's holding my hand and then your hands sort of slowly pull apart, I started to cry and he gave me this look. . . . It was easier, because there weren't all those people, and harder, because I had him back for those three weeks and I have to let him go again."

Other than a new jumpiness—"When I stepped on bubble wrap and it went pop-pop and I just about got a punch to the head"—and a hard time driving on the first few outings, Ray had seemed fine on his visit home. "[It's] normal," Trudel says. "[You're] constantly scanning, constantly feeling for the rifle."

But after Ray returned to Afghanistan, Darcia found their conversations getting longer, as often at Ray's instigation as at hers. "He started emailing me at work, saying, 'I won't be able to talk to you tonight.' That started happening much more frequently." Some nights, they were on MSN for two hours.

"I know he did it intentionally," Darcia says. "I know there were days when he didn't have to get up early and he got up early anyway [the Edmonton–Kandahar time difference is eleven and a half hours]. I think he was maybe trying to make up for it a little bit? That's the way he was. Mind you, I'd go a little crazy after talking to him.

"He always tried to protect me, whether it was here or whether he was there, and I think the extra-long conversations had a lot to do with that, making it feel like everything was okay. But he also knew what a constant worrier I was. I worry about everything. I still worry about everything, from the smallest itty-bitty things to the biggest things. That's just my nature."

She remembers the day she said, "I guess I better let you go," and he said, "No, I can talk to you a little bit longer."

They talked about the things she was doing at the house—she had the windows replaced, bought new blinds and curtains—and about Bugs, their sweet fat rabbit, "and, of course, about how much you miss each other, that's a given. It was more one-sided, though," Darcia says. "On my part, and I think that makes people vulnerable. He'd sometimes give off these macho tough-guy vibes."

Trudel says that by acknowledging how much he misses someone, a soldier can open himself up to making mistakes. "When you're over there, you're in protection mode. All your normal brain functions are shut right off. It's all survival, and how am I going to do this, do that, whatever? If you take your mind off that, off normal survival mode, if you start talking about home life, it opens up a weak spot in your own head. . . . The survival mechanism for us over there, you just go into shell mode. You become really withdrawn."

Darcia could feel the difference, would phone Trudel almost in tears. "There were numerous emails I sent to Ray," she says, "totally venting, saying I cannot deal with this disconnection, this emotional and mental breakdown that we're having, you know? He would actually email me back, madder than a friggin' hornet, you know, 'So what do you want me to do?' I called Grant lots of times. He'd come over and help me sort myself out. I realize that's the way it has to be," she says. "In your head, you know, but in your heart, ouch, that hurts."

As the tour drew down to weeks, Ray was so excited about coming home. "Top three," says Darcia, with that burbling, lilting laugh of hers: "A cold beer; sit on the couch with a beer in one hand and the remote in the other—he never did that when he *was* home—and I can't tell you the third one. And I think the beer did come first."

He was ready, she says. "He said to me a number of times, close to the end, 'I can't wait to get home and finally start our lives and have babies with you,' and stuff like that."

She had plans for the August long weekend. She'd jumped into the military part of their life in a big way, was on the regimental dragon boat team. Practices were scheduled, but she was going to skip Friday's and go to her girlfriend's place. She and Ray planned to talk on Friday night, but then on Thursday night he emailed her and said he wouldn't be able to, so they moved it to Sunday.

"So then, Friday the 4th I went to work and something was just nagging at me to go online—I never go online at work—but just go online," she says. "So I logged in and he wasn't online, but I figured he'd be getting ready for bed and probably checking his email, so I sent him a quick email and said I'm online."

Five or ten minutes later, Ray came online, and "I talked to him for about forty-five minutes, and both of us were so happy that we got to talk and everything . . . we'd missed a couple of days already, so it was nice to be able to just touch base and get a grasp on what we were doing."

The next morning, Darcia woke up to a ringing phone, now not right by the bed as it had been for most of Ray's tour. "I remember being really mad. Who was phoning me at stupid eight o'clock in the morning?" she says. "And I went running for the phone, and I answered it, and the voice said he needed to come to the door.

"I knew that something was wrong—and this is going to sound really funny, but I remembered to put on pants—and I just remember running down the stairs, just going, 'Please let him be hurt, please let him be hurt.' And I answered the door and as soon as I saw their expressions, I knew. I knew right away. I don't remember if they said, 'Your husband,' or 'Your husband Master Corporal Arndt,' but whatever it was, 'had been killed in Afghanistan in a motor vehicle accident.'

"And I think I kind of stood there and kind of looked at them with this dumb expression on my face, and I remember saying, 'No, you're wrong.'"

Then she lay down on the couch in the living room of the little townhouse where she and Ray were going to really begin their life together, and she sobbed. There were three or four men present: a padre and the Eddies' regimental sergeant major and deputy commanding officer were most certainly there. They let her cry until she stopped, and then they asked if there was anyone they could call. She asked the padre to call Ray's sister, because she knew it was more than she could bear.

She herself phoned Trudel, who couldn't quite understand what she was saying, but caught enough to know that he should get the CD with the in-the-event-of-my-death letter and funeral instructions. She called her mom, waking her, and couldn't make her understand either, so handed the phone to the padre. And then she called Aileen, her girlfriend, and said, "'The bad men we don't want to come are here.' Those were my exact words to her. She knew exactly [what I meant]."

For the next two weeks, Darcia was never alone unless she wanted to be. She was swept up in the arms of the remarkable military institution known as the regimental family. Whenever a unit is deployed overseas, a small shadowy group of officers, non-commissioned officers (NCOs), and soldiers remain in Canada and pray never to get any work. Some of them belong to "the rear party," the section that remains behind to keep the families of the troops informed and prepared. They may arrange Family Days and picnics or send out newsletters or set up websites with news of the troops, but their most wrenching task is to notify the relatives of soldiers who are killed or injured.

Having delivered the worst news possible, knowing that the sight of them thereafter will only cause pain, the men of the rear party effectively vanish from a family's view, reappearing only for the returning repatriation ceremonies in Trenton and for funerals and memorials across the country, with which civilian Canada has now become familiar. But others take over. Just as dead soldiers have escort officers—Ray's was Lieutenant Rob Glidden, his platoon commander—who are with them from the moment their bodies leave Kandahar, so do their relatives have assisting officers, or AOs. These are the men who tend to the grieving and worried and ferry them from coroner's morgue to funeral home or from the U.S. hospital in Germany, where the most serious of Canadian wounded are treated, to Fisher House, the homey residence nearby where families stay for peanuts a night.

AOs carry luggage from airport to hotel to car and back again; manage passports and tickets; offer a drink, cigarette, shoulder, tissue; dispense comfort and advice; feed the mourners, clear the dishes, pass the food, distract and play with children too young to comprehend. They are at once counsellor, butler, secretary, chauffeur, nursemaid, and political adviser.

For Darcia, this man was Lieutenant Mark Johnson, an Eddie, of course. Thirty-eight and a new father, Johnson was up early that Saturday morning, playing with baby Rowan, then about two months old, when he got a phone call telling him that Ray had been killed in theatre and asking if he would act as the assisting officer.

"I was in Darcia's living room by noon," Johnson says. The experience was the "most important thing I've ever put my uniform on for," though sometimes achingly sad. "You can't really be around grief without wearing it a bit yourself."

"Mark was pretty much glued to my hip from the day of the accident for two weeks straight," Darcia says.

He shepherded her through the blur of those first days. He managed the houseful of people she had and arranged the flights and hotel in Toronto for thirteen of Ray's family and friends who went to Trenton for the repatriation ceremony.

"We ended up driving out to Trenton on Tuesday, August 8," Darcia says. "I was a basket case. They pretty much had to force me to get into the car. It was all hitting home. If I didn't do it [go to Trenton], it wasn't real. So I pretty much sat in silence the entire way."

Except for seeing Gordie Legarie, her date on the night she first met Ray, Darcia says she removed herself from what was happening. "Even when the bagpipes played and the casket came out of the plane it was still like I wasn't there."

It was only when she walked up to the hearse that it hit home. "Yeah, this is frigging happening. When we all got back into the car, all I wanted to do was go to sleep. I was tired, I was crying, I just wanted to go to sleep."

Johnson kindly but firmly took charge. "He said, 'No, you need to watch us drive off the base and you need to watch the hearse drive in front of us, you need to watch us drive through Trenton. It's very important that you do that.' And I remember being really mad at him, for making me do that. All I wanted to do was sleep. I was upset and exhausted and I'm not really here, and I don't want to see that car with the flag inside driving in front of me."

But Darcia did what Johnson asked. She forced herself to look out the window. Outside the fence around the base, along the road, were knots of people standing silently, as there would be knots of people on overpasses along the 401 highway to Toronto.

I've been to Trenton for a repatriation ceremony. Those people were there then. They are always there, clutching Canadian flags, weeping, standing very straight. They line up outside the fence, they can see and hear almost nothing of the sombre service on the tarmac, they wait uncomplainingly for hours in rain and cold. I met a man there who had come to every repatriation ceremony and then one day nearly came for his own son's—his boy, a soldier serving with the 1st Battalion, the Royal Canadian Regiment, had just been injured and was in Germany, soon to come home.

"There were civilians saluting—saluting the police, the military police, saluting us—as we drove by. It was like, wow, what respect," Darcia remembers. "I realize why now, and I'm not mad at him [Johnson] anymore."

Back in Edmonton, there was another grim whirl of activity: picking out Ray's casket, another ceremony when Ray's body returned, arranging the funeral in Edson—Ray was a product of the Yellowhead Highway, born in Hinton, raised in Peers, and schooled in Edson—and at last the viewing.

"I really wanted to view Ray," Darcia says, "so they arranged that. I'd asked them in Toronto, how does he look? Robbie Glidden took me into the office, before I went in. He told me he needed to reassure me he'd been with Ray the entire time. Any time they'd needed to do something with Ray, he was there, whether it was to move him from box to casket, or dress him, or do his makeup or whatever, he was there, and I thought that was funny at the time. I thought it was funny he would tell me that, was so adamant about having to explain that to me.

"And I asked him again, 'How does he look?' He said, 'I'm going to tell you, he looks fine. He looks okay. He's got a lot of makeup on, but he looks okay.' And it still sounded really weird and now I know why, now I know why he told me that.

"It's because it wasn't Ray at all. And I think he needed to reassure me that he was there and that someone didn't fuck up. Because it was so not the man you see in his picture, not at all. It was not that face. Because of the extent of the injury, and the makeup, there was just too much damage for them to repair.

"Ray's face was quite long; this face was round. So you know, I said, 'That's not Ray. That's not him.' And I remember standing there for ten or fifteen minutes, just looking at him to try to find one thing that was Ray. His eyes weren't even the same way, seriously.

"But the one thing I did [recognize] was his hands. And I remember saying that to the guys, because they wouldn't let me go in by myself of course. I remember saying to the guys, 'It's not him, but those are his hands.' I would recognize his hands anywhere."

She felt three things, she says. She was relieved that Ray didn't look worse, she was disappointed he didn't look more like the man she loved, but mostly, "I was comforted to know that I would remember his hands. That was always a source of great comfort to me. I mean, on our wedding day, standing in front of the pastor, he was squeezing my hands and the pastor mentioned us squeezing our hands, a lot of people had seen the squeezing motion of the hands and even made comments about that.

"That's our thing. That's what we do."

—

Ash Van Leeuwen has written a story about August 5, 2006, which he calls "My Last Afghan Sunrise."

He and the rest of the force protection platoon were up before dawn for the ramp ceremony for the four Patricias from Charlie Company—Chris Reid, Vaughan Ingram, Bryce Keller, and Kevin Dallaire—killed two days earlier.

"I had just finished a stint with this group," Van Leeuwen says, "and I could recall their faces." It was a lot to take in, he says. "We were almost home, we had won so many battles, done so much good. Shouldn't our reward be to go home to our loved ones?"

By then, the platoon of Eddies and Highlanders had done a total of 173 runs outside the wire, but even so, Van Leeuwen says, there were always last-minute hiccups. "This was the time when you'd find the usual suspects, leaning up against our beasts of machines, smoking and joking, talking tall about some half-assed adventure."

As usual, Van Leeuwen was beside Ray Arndt, with whom he was always paired. They were on their way to Spin Boldak, by the Pakistan border, on a route along Highway 4, one of the best roads in the country, and at the time one of the safest—though that changed. They'd driven this route before, and as Van Leeuwen says, "We knew every bump, outcrop of rock, and bad guy hidey-hole. It was as straightforward as it gets."

"The mountains are far, far back, and you can see for miles," says John Conrad, the lieutenant-colonel who commanded the National Support Element of which the force protection platoon was a part. "The first forty-three kilometres were like the Trans-Canada Highway, but then the last thirty-five-odd are just really, really bad, all busted up. But I liked it because it was not IED country. Of course, you're looking at the main supply route of the Taliban, but they don't want to fight there. They want to get up Highway 4 to get where their action is, Panjwaii or Shah-Wali-Kot. So, for my soldiers, I didn't feel any stress—or less stress—when they were going that route."

Van Leeuwen, as he always did, looked in his small black Bible for a suitable prayer and picked one: "Prayer to Guardian Angel," which he thought fitting for the four lost men who were on their way home. "Angel of God, my holy guardian, appointed by God for my protection, I beseech thee: Enlighten me this day and protect me from all evil; help me to do good and show me the road to salvation."

For the first time, he was the rear gunner (usually he manned the C6 machine gun as lead gunner). Adam Keen was driving; Jared Gagnon was lead gunner and the guy who would go dismounted if there was trouble; Ray Arndt was the crew commander. It was to be a standard run to Spin—Rancho Relaxo, Van Leeuwen calls it—to pick up some soldiers from C Company. Van Leeuwen was feeling good, wind whistling through his headset and for once not in his face. "I was at home being a gunner, and at peace with myself and the world," he says. "Funny thing to say, being at war, a million miles from home."

Explaining what happened next, he says, is like explaining an entire life with a single gesture.

They were about halfway there, just before Highway 4 becomes a rutted track. He felt the noise more than heard it, saw glass exploding in front of him, sparkling glass popping in the air, and was sling-shotted forward in the G-Wagon. Then the turret rocked and tipped, tossed him out. As he saw the ground rushing up at him, he thought, "Ash, you're going to die."

He smacked onto the road and went skidding along it. Gagnon, also thrown out, almost chasing him and then overtaking him, followed by the G-Wagon itself, Adam Keen riding upside down on the hood, holding on to the steering wheel. The vehicle slammed into the ground before Van Leeuwen's eyes, then was behind him, still bouncing along the sandy highway.

He found himself lying on his right side, thirty metres from the initial impact, the inertia of the crash slowing within his organs. He was naked from the chest down, suddenly cold. He had no idea what had happened: IED, suicide bomber, ambush. "Ray was just ahead of me. You could tell it was him, just by his helmet, the way he wore his gear, the scarf around his neck." He was on his back, a hand in the air.

"My first instinct was to get to Ray," Van Leeuwen says. "He was maybe ten metres away. I saw him, I went to pull my body, and I knew I couldn't walk. My lung was punctured on the left side, I was pushing myself on my broken leg, my legs didn't move. I thought, 'Fuck, I'm paralyzed. Shit, I can't move.' Then I was wiggling my toes. Instant relief."

When he realized he couldn't get to Ray, he really looked at him. "I was laying limp, like a piece of meat in a frying pan, on a hot desert highway, and I saw for the first time that Ray was gone. I'm looking right at him. He's gone."

Keen scrambled toward Van Leeuwen, running past Ray to get to him. "Ray's gone," Keen said. "I know," Van Leeuwen replied. He told Keen he thought he had broken ribs on the left side and a punctured lung. What he didn't know then was that his right ankle was broken and his left leg torn open, that he was bleeding internally, and that his urethra was lacerated.

Keen took his hand. "To have him reach out for my waving hand," he says, "was the first time I felt safe." He could hear a medical team working on Gagnon. He saw someone put a blast blanket over Ray's body.

It was only when he was loaded on the chopper—"When they bumped me, I thought my vertebrae was gonna come out my ears"—that he could see the boot tips of his friend, and knew Gagnon was still alive. The two of them were rushed into surgery at the sophisticated hospital at KAF.

He phoned his dad, said, "Hello, Dad, it's me. Good news. I'll be home earlier than expected." His father heard the quiver in his voice and knew. Then Van Leeuwen saw Gagnon properly. "The nurses had flipped me onto my right side," he says, "and there, lying in the bed next to me was what remained of my friend." He had no hope of seeing him alive again.

That night, they weren't supposed to have any visitors, "but the boys, forcefully but respectfully, made their way in, and visited with unconscious Gagnon and me. I remember a lot of crying. I have no shame in admitting that; these were all family members." He fell asleep cried out, utterly spent, and crushed by Ray's death. "I still say that I would rather have suffered all my injuries and been there at that final moment with my friend than to hear it in orders."

The next day, they were flown to the U.S. hospital in Landstuhl. Van Leeuwen roomed with Jon Hamilton, the recce commander who was seriously injured in the August 3 firefight at the White School in Panjwaii.

"I went to see Gagnon," Van Leeuwen says. "I'm a spiritual individual. I don't conform to a religion, but I had a long talk with God that day, and I said, 'If he's not going to have quality of life, just do it now, do it now and don't let him suffer.'" He wasn't alone: Almost no one gave the tall, skinny kid, then just twenty, much of a chance.

By then, Linda and Dennis Gagnon were on their way to Germany, their assisting officer, John McCully, having achieved the impossible by getting someone to go into the Edmonton passport office on a Sunday to issue them documents. They'd talked to Dr. Will Patton, the base surgeon in Edmonton, before they left.

"He's a pretty straight shooter," Dennis says. "He described the injury and what a critical state [Jared] was in. Jared in fact lost a portion of his skull, and we'd have to wait and see." The neurosurgeon in Germany told them "the options were from him being in a vegetative state to maybe being able to look after himself one day."

Gagnon was in Germany for nine days, arriving at the University of Alberta Hospital two days after his folks. He'd had a tracheotomy, so now had a tube in his throat; the doctors tried removing it a couple of times, to see if Jared could breathe on his own.

Van Leeuwen saw him there shortly after. His description of Gagnon's progress goes like this: "I see him at the U of A, and he's tracking with his eyes one day, and the next day he gives you the thumbs-up or gives you the finger, and he knew who you were, the cheating bastard.

"Then he's sitting up and moving limbs, and then we go see him—it was the day of Master Corporal McFadzen's wedding—a couple of guys jump in the vehicle and go down to the hospital in our suits . . . and then he was getting words out. He can talk!

"And then you go to see him and he's not even at the U of A, he's at another hospital, he's improved so much. He can talk now, we go to see him and they say he's gone for a walk. 'What do you mean, he's walking?'" Van Leeuwen says, grinning at the memory. "I'm still on crutches, but *he's* walking?

"He's on a cane, he's outside in the pouring rain, he's talking with us. . . . That's Jared. Just a feisty bugger is what he was, he actually screwed death is what it was. Probably his greatest achievement, he literally spat in the face of death."

For Dennis, the hallelujah moment came in early September 2006. "When they took the neck collar off, his whole demeanour just changed, his whole attitude changed. At that point, you realized Jared was there, he was there." He calls it "getting him back."

Gagnon joined the Eddies for the adventure, when he was sixteen. At seventeen, he wanted to go to Bosnia. "We said no," says Dennis. When Afghanistan appeared on the horizon, Gagnon put his name in. It wasn't until the early spring of 2005 that his parents found out, and only then because Jared mentioned that he wouldn't be playing recreational hockey.

"Automatically," says Dennis, "I knew something was up."

What did his folks think?

"Can you turn the tape off?" Dennis jokes. "I thought it was probably one of the stupidest decisions he could make. He's nineteen years old, two years into university [studying general sciences]. Jared is a very, very level-headed young man; he's actually unique in that he plans for his future, saves everything he makes. He invests. As a nineteen-year-old, that's unbelievable." He'd even bought, and sold for a profit, a condo.

His parents tried to talk him out of going, and when that didn't work, they tried to trick him into not going. "If you want to hit Jared," says his dad, "hit him in the pocketbook."

They told him, "You want to be a man, you want to make a decision like that, fine, then you've got to live on your own, pay rent. Jared's very money-conscious; we thought it would be a way to get at him."

They wouldn't let him drive the car they'd bought for him and his oldest sister, Jenna, to share but which had become all his when she had bought her own. "They made me move out as of November 1," says Jared, cackling, "and I moved in with my grandma."

So he finished second year—"I was not doing well per se," he says, "but I passed"—and started workup training. His parents were at a loss.

"He's your son," says Dennis. "You love him. You try to make him realize what a stupid decision he's made. 'You could lose a leg, you could be paralyzed, you could die.' At the time, Afghanistan was quieter, and his rationale was, how do you defend against a suicide bomber? He said they were well trained, and he was nineteen years old and invincible, the odds are, with two thousand guys out there, it wasn't going to happen to him. There was no convincing him that if you were one of the few it happened to, the consequences could be life-ending or life-threatening."

"We said, 'Just wait a year.' We didn't tell him not to go," Linda says.

"I told him if you were in the military full-time, and going to school and were called up, that's a career choice, that's what you want to do. I have nothing against the military or their operation. I'm for it," Dennis says. "But not as a reservist, when you have a successful life going on outside. I thought he was basically playing at the military."

His parents' efforts had virtually no impact on Gagnon. They made him think "a little bit, but I still ended up going."

At no point, Jared says, did he ever think, "Holy shit, Dad was right," partly because the platoon's descent into the madness of Kandahar was leisurely from Gagnon's perspective. He still considers his decision to go "probably pretty good." He admits his dad is right, that in some measure he was playing soldier. "Yes, and I saw it as playing. But at the same time, I knew I was going to be called on to do something like this." Without the crash, he says, it all "would have felt pretty good."

Dennis says, "I like team sports. I see where they could love it. I was nineteen once. It's not mysterious."

By the time they saw him off, his parents were sufficiently resigned to Jared going that they could make jokes. "Before he left," Dennis says, "we were calling him Stumpy. We took pictures, as he's leaving, and said, 'Make sure you show your legs, while you still have them,' never dreaming . . ."

At the same time, Dennis says, they told him, "Okay, you're going. Just do your job. Don't volunteer for anything extra." Much later, they learned from Jared's platoon mates that whenever a volunteer was needed, their son was there.

The night before the accident, Linda was trying to email him, telling him, "Don't volunteer for anything. I've got a bad feeling. Don't volunteer." She was in tears, Dennis says, when Jared said he had to get going.

"I'm doing anything to keep him alive, anything to keep him alive," she says, "I'm checking DND [Department of National Defence] sites to see when he's coming back."

But with the same intuition, she knew after the crash that regardless of what the doctors were saying, Jared was going to be fine.

I interviewed Jared at his parents' home on September 29, 2006. He was still wearing a hockey helmet—to protect his head, with its missing piece of skull—and walking gingerly, with a cane. He had a scar. He'd lost a week or two of memory, but his acrid sense of humour was intact.

I saw him next in mid-November at a fundraising dinner for Fisher House, the residence where his parents stayed in Germany. He was in uniform, helmetless and handsome. In January 2007, I got an email from his mom: He'd had the surgery to replace his missing skull and was doing splendidly.

—

DARCIA ARNDT HAD TROUBLE, at first, with the notion that Ray had died in a car accident.

"I couldn't rationalize it in my brain," she says. "He could have come home and been in a motor vehicle accident, but I would have been able to have him for one more day. I couldn't wrap my brain around that. I was like, it would have been better if it was a bomb, a suicide bomber. I could rationalize it better. But now, any way you look at it, he was doing what he was supposed to be doing. He was still working, still doing what he was there to do."

The crash had been, in fact, a head-on collision with a civilian truck, one of the garishly painted and decorated jingle trucks, this one loaded with cattle, that often provide the only shot of colour in the drab south.

Darcia hasn't changed her mind, either about agreeing that Ray should go, or about the Canadian mission. "Sometimes I think I should have put my foot down at the very beginning and said, 'No, you can't go,'" she says, "because if I had said no, it would have been a big fight but probably, in the end, I would have won.

"And he would still be here.

"But on the other side of that, he was a soldier, and that's what he did, and that's what he wanted to do. And he did it well, and it's not very often in a person's life that they can say they absolutely loved what they did, that they would die for their career. But he believed in what he was doing, and because of that I have to believe in what he was doing and what the guys are doing out there.

"And yeah, it scared the crap out of me.

"I've got friends going there again [Grant Trudel, for one, is slated to go to Afghanistan in February 2008], and it scares the crap out of me. But if I didn't still believe in it, if I didn't still support it, I wouldn't have all that crap [Support Our Troops stickers, yellow ribbons, etc.] outside on my lawn, my windows, and my car.

"I never imagined that one day I'd be married to an army guy who'd be going overseas. Everyone always said the army guys are bad. But I haven't found many bad ones, that's for sure. All my army friends are wonderful. That would have been my life, you know?"

She's a bit haunted by something that happened in June 2006.

A cousin of Ray's had offered a bunch of baby stuff to them, knowing they were hoping to start a family soon, and had promised to hold on to it until they needed it. But the woman ended up selling her house, and couldn't keep it any longer. "She said, 'If you don't take it, I'm sorry, but I have to give it away, so if you want it you better take it.' So I said, 'I don't want it,'" Darcia says.

"Then I talked to Ray. Of course, the typical man—'Take it, it's free!' I said, 'I really don't want this in my house, the whole bad karma thing,' and he's like, 'Oh, nothing will happen.' But I was thinking in the sense of baby stuff, there will never be a baby if I take it," she says. "So, in essence, I guess that's what happened, isn't it?"

Ray's sergeant, she says, is suffering the same jinx pangs: "That morning, before Ray went out, he thought maybe he should pull Ray off the convoys, he's only got nine more days left and maybe he should relax, he was gonna pull him off convoys and that kind of thing. . . . 'Well, he'll just go and do this one, and I'll pull him off.'"

John Conrad, Ray's commanding officer, has the same wistfulness. He has a distinct memory of seeing Ray a week or two before he was killed. He was still wearing his black boots. "Master Corporal," Conrad asked, "where are your desert boots?" And Ray said the new ones hadn't come in yet. Almost to the end, the army institution was struggling to deal with this man and his odd-sized feet.

The desert boots arrived sometime in late July: Ray Arndt died looking like every other Canadian soldier.

When Ash Van Leeuwen thinks back on his tour, certain pictures remain unshakable in his memory. "We're driving on ground that's ripping our combat boots up and shredding our tires," he says, "and the kids running up to the convoy are barefoot, and they're not asking for chocolate. They're tapping their fingers on their palms and they're asking for pen and paper. Now, that's huge.

"I remember when I went to school, I got good grades and all, but I didn't *want* to go to school. These kids *want* to go to school. . . . I think that's where Canadians do rise above most of the other nations that are over there, we're fighting on a multi-level system. We're not saving Afghanistan so that we can do free trade with them after; I mean, you can import rugs to Canada, but it's not an industrial country.

"We build infrastructure, provide education for children. The girls never had it. And it's not taking away from their culture; it's kind of showing they're being empowered.

"Look how long it took to get women's rights in North America, and we're in a country [Afghanistan] that's back two thousand years. It's like walking with people out of *National Geographic*.

"There are people who have never had a Band-Aid, something every mother takes for granted when little Johnny scrapes his elbow."

Van Leeuwen is accomplished for his age: He played a summer of professional football; he's a legal surveyor by training; he's well-travelled even in his non-military life.

Grandpa Leeuwen, he says, "came to Canada because he looked at the world, he could have gone to the States just as easily, but Canadians helped liberate Holland. . . . I don't take this country for granted in the way that, I've been around the world and I've seen how Canadians are treated. It's not that we have a great hockey team or good beer; it's what our forefathers did for that country. Forefathers is an American kind of phrase, but it's what the generations before us did to establish the great tradition that people here don't even recognize.

"I was walking through Holland with my Canadian uniform on, and I think I had five cars stop me just to ask if I had a ride. One guy got out to talk, just because I had on a little red maple leaf.

"Other people throw it on their backpacks and think that they should be treated well because of that. And that aggravates me to no extent—no one fought for you to travel and get a cheap rate in a hostel."

When people ask him about his tour, he tells them, "Only the last forty-eight hours were bad. Losing Ray was the only bad part."

Ray Arndt was on his eighty-fifth trip outside the wire when he was killed. He was nine days away from leaving Kandahar, twenty-two days away from landing in Edmonton. Van Leeuwen was still at the U of A hospital the day his friend was to be buried. "They said I couldn't go unless I started getting into a wheelchair and got off morphine," he says. "I hobbled across the room, said, 'Take the morphine off.'"

Ray was buried, he says, in golden fashion. "When the burial party came over, I lost it hard. We all did. We're very much alpha males, very macho, but we were hugging each other. Master Corporal McFadzen was the last guy, I got no more tears left. I just hugged him, the heavy sign, acknowledge it's real and it was done right. We did him proud."

Afterwards, Van Leeuwen, the burial party, Darcia, her assisting officer, and all the Eddies went back to the sergeants' mess at the Jefferson Armoury. "We had a few drinks," she says. "We went and partied it up good for Ray, closed the bar down."

After all, the last line of Ray's in-the-event-of-my-death letter was, "Keep the beer cold."

From left to right: Cpl. Hugo Leblanc, MCpl. Daryl Presley, Maj. Bill Fletcher

9 July 2006

—

"We will never know those countless young men and women who went willingly into the heart of darkness, into the toxic, corrosive, destructive realm of combat. . . . The least we owe them is to understand the nature of combat and to truly understand what we are asking them to do."

—LIEUTENANT-COLONEL U.S. ARMY (RETIRED) DAVE GROSSMAN
IN *On Combat*

MAJOR BILL FLETCHER gave his company briefing for Operation Zahar late on the morning of Friday, July 7.

When I wrote about it later for *The Globe and Mail*, I described the briefing as "surprisingly literate," which amused him no end. "Did you think I'd just grunt or what?" he asked with a quicksilver grin.

Fletcher was the officer commanding, or OC, of the Patricias' Charlie Company, as opposed to the commanding officer, or CO, of the whole Canadian battle group, which was Lieutenant-Colonel Ian Hope.

There is no limit to the ways in which the army fucks about with the Queen's English in the hope that despairing civilians will bleed from the ears and give up trying to make sense of it. The briefing was held at the back of Charlie's BAT, or Big Ass Tent, so called because each of the three BATs could house two hundred soldiers sleeping on bunk beds, cheek to jowl, sweating miserably in the gaseous heat produced by the temperatures outside and air conditioners inside that only ever emitted asthmatic puffs.

As Hope once cheerfully told me, "I think the BATs were a good idea. I believe in unit cohesion. Cohesion is created by living together and suffering." Or, as he put it to his cadre of young officers: "Gents, I'm doing this so you'll hate it and be angry and want to get out," *out* being beyond the wire and security of the enormous base at KAF.

He was pretty much right, too, because for all that the troops always looked forward to a shower and a burger and a fix at the Tim

Hortons after being weeks in the field, within a day or so, whether out of boredom or discomfort or both, most were itching to do something, anything, even if that meant getting shot at. Besides, by training and inclination, if an infantryman isn't suffering physically, he begins to fret that something is seriously amiss.

Operation Zahar was a Canadian battle group operation, involving all three companies and recce platoon under Captain Jon Hamilton, two troops of artillery with their M777 Howitzer guns, a squadron from 1 Combat Engineer Regiment, and two companies of ANA and their American Embedded Training Teams (ETT). The ETT, like their Canadian equivalent, the Operational Mentor Liaison Teams (OMLT), are charged with professionalizing Afghan security forces, and though there are wide variations in competence and discipline, as a general rule the ANA is admired for courage that at its best is of the balls-out variety.

The operation was the direct result of a week of solid advance work by Bravo Company commander Nick Grimshaw. He had moved into the Pashmul area on June 24, after several U.S troops were killed there, and stayed to find out where and how big the Taliban groups operating in the region really were.

"He came to KAF to tell me that he felt we needed to try to isolate the cemetery/village cluster west of Payendi," Hope says. "His hunch was enough for me; I felt that he was right."

The battalion's operations officer, Major Mason Stalker, then had to plan how they would do it. "Mason controls all the moving parts of the battalion," Hope says. "He's the number one guy for controlling the fight." Hope calls him a pit bull, and says that after a couple of months of Stalker trying to get inside his head so he could better please or satisfy him, "He began to take control." Hope's RSM, Randy Northrup, says, "The Mace is a force unto himself. He thrived on challenge; he just fed off it."

Using aerial photographs, they determined the exact compounds they needed to target and search, "then drew lines around the whole lot and called it Objective Puma," Hope says, and assigned each company a slice. Then Stalker "added lots of route designations and coordination points at major intersections so that we could easily refer to these to coordinate the complex fire and movement."

The army always has an "objective," usually the piece of ground it wants to take, in this case those compounds (one of which was the infamous White School near Bayenzi, a klick from Payendi) and "a main effort," here the clearance of the Taliban from all the villages collectively known as Pashmul. In this instance, because the multi-national coalition, then headed by American General Ben Freakley, was convinced of the operation's necessity and the U.S. was providing an IED-detecting package of vehicles and air support, Op Zahar was also the main effort of the whole brigade, the southern Afghanistan branch of which was called Combined Task Force Aegis and led at the time by Canadian General Dave Fraser.

Op Zahar was phase one of what the brigade called Operation Hewad. Later phases saw the Canadians supporting the British and the Americans in Helmand Province, just as the British and Americans were supporting the Canadians in this phase in Kandahar Province by conducting "blocks" to prevent enemy from escaping. There would also be a significant psychological operation or "psy op" component, with commanders encouraging the Taliban to "surrender with honour as opposed to dying for a useless cause," Fletcher said. The whole shooting match fell under the ambit of Operation Mountain Thrust, which had started in May and continued until the end of July, its aim to put pressure on Taliban forces throughout the south.

The Canadians were to move into Pashmul, the western edge of the notoriously sketchy Panjwaii area just thirty kilometres west of Kandahar, and clear out the Taliban. Pashmul was and remains one of the worst and most dangerous parts of the Canadian-controlled area, particularly in summer, the Taliban's preferred fighting season. Though some of the villages have names, often with at least two different spellings apiece, some have none. To a non-military Western eye, their boundaries are as indistinct as those of the suburban sprawl of most big North American cities, and each looks like every other.

The area is a jigsaw puzzle: low mud walls over which grow grapevines so lush they look like they're on steroids and marijuana plants that at their tallest reach eight or nine feet, with rutted wadis lining either side of the mud compounds, or the freakishly aggressive greenery, or the branches of gnarled old trees. Here and there in the fields are two- or three-storey mud structures. Called *keshmeshkhanu* in the Pashtu language, these are easily the most substantial buildings in the countryside in this part of the south. They are used to dry grapes, but their metre-thick walls are also liberally laced with functioning gun ports and their roofs are usually topped by covered hidey-holes offering snipers perfect sightlines and sweeping views.

Afghanistan has been at war for so long, has been so regularly invaded, and is so steeped in centuries of tribal rivalries that virtually everything in the country, whatever its first function, is also purpose-built for fighting.

The briefing I attended—allowed because I was now "embedded" with Charlie—was for sergeants and section commanders and the leadership of the medics and engineers who would be accompanying the platoons. They in turn would pass on to the troops what they needed to know. In theory, I knew more about the mission than some of the privates or corporals. In practice, my head was swimming with indecipherable military jargon and terms. All that really sunk in was that this was potentially a very scary mission.

I was not the only embedded reporter along for the ride. Journalist Steve Chao and cameraman Tom Michalak of CTV were travelling with Bravo Company. It is testament to the complex ground we were on and the phenomenon known as the fog of war that though we were probably never more than a hundred metres apart, and sometimes much closer, the CTV crew and I have no memory of ever seeing one another over the almost three days we spent in Pashmul.

The area was familiar territory. As Fletcher put it, "Situation enemy: After having had their asses handed to them at Panjwaii the last six times, they've decided to come back again." Conservative estimates placed 100 to 150 Taliban fighters in the vicinity, most believed to have been operating in ten- to twenty-man cells focusing on IED placement and ambushes along Highway 1, moving mostly at night.

Experience had taught the Patricias that these Taliban would not be a ragtag lot. "Their ambushes are relatively sophisticated," Fletcher said, "employing cut-offs, machine guns, and RPGs, with cut-off teams to make sure no one can get out of the ambush. The enemy has a relatively sophisticated early warning network established throughout the area, both their own and tied into the local population. Local popular support is in fact in place, but it's unknown really whether it's coerced or freely given. Nevertheless, they'll do what they need to do to survive."

This was a soldier's version of what an official at the Indian consulate in Toronto had told me as I picked up my visa—on my first trips in 2006, I travelled from New Delhi into Kabul, and then to Kandahar by United Nations Humanitarian Air Services—a couple of weeks earlier. "Always remember," he said, half admiringly, "that you can never buy an Afghan, only rent him. And so long as you pay your rent on time, and no one offers a better rent, things will be fine."

"What we have are three rifle companies in a one-kilometre radius, all facing in the same direction," Fletcher said, "so imagine if you will what would happen if we all fired at once."

Such is the close-quarters nature of much of the fighting in Afghanistan—coalition forces and enemy squeezed into narrow battlefields, friends and foes dotted throughout the same small piece of ground, the front line a shifting and amorphous thing, and the potential for "blue on blue," or friendly fire accidents, omnipresent.

Of the fight that unfolded over July 8 and 9 in Pashmul, the A Battery Royal Canadian Horse Artillery commander Steve Gallagher, whose big guns with their astonishing thirty-kilometre range were so beloved by the soldiers, said that on the map of the battle—red pins showing the positions of bad guys, blue pins for the good guys—"there were so many pins . . . like ten at once."

Artillery has what they call "probable errors in range." At more than thirty kilometres, that range may be affected by meteorological conditions, small differences in the propellant that sends the projectiles so far, or even the spinning of Earth on its axis. "Here," Gallagher said, "80 percent of the bullets fall within that range. Twenty percent won't, and we have zero control over that. . . . We get a warning message if it's too close, but almost every time, we've fired anyway," because the alternative was to leave troops without fire protection.

I left the BAT clinging to something Fletcher had said. If attacked, the soldiers were to man the turrets "and start hammering the living crap out of where the contact initiated. We will always dismount and chase them. The overriding principle is that no one will ever shoot at us without being shot at."

Like most people, I'd never been anywhere near combat. With few exceptions, notably the 2nd Battalion Patricias' at the Medak Pocket in Croatia, neither had most Canadian soldiers since the end of the Korean War.

As Justin Kellehar, a twenty-nine-year-old corporal who drove the big trucks for the support and logistics arm, told me once, "Before Kandahar, the Canadian military was a nice safe place to be. The odds of you getting killed were scarce to none. No risk of layoffs or pay cuts, good medical for you and your family. And for a guy with a high school education, you get out to see places."

—

AT THAT POINT, the closest I'd come to danger was in Sarajevo in the summer of 1992. I was working for the *Toronto Sun* in those days, and went with Greig Reekie, then a staff photographer, to cover the Canadian troops who had deployed there that June. By the time we arrived in the region, Canadian Major-General Lew MacKenzie was in place at the Sarajevo airport, sitting in his lawn chair as though he were camping.

Word was out that the best way for reporters to get around was in a white car of any kind, because the United Nations Protection

Force (UNPROFOR) moved about in white vehicles. But none were available anywhere, so Greig and I got ourselves to Hungary and bought a beat-up black VW ragtop for about US$600, then drove down to Sarajevo from Daruvar in Croatia with the soldiers of the 1st Battalion, the Royal 22nd Regiment. There was no formal embedding process for Canadian journalists then, but Greig and I always believed that the soldiers were keeping an eye out for us and our silly convertible.

Virtually every day for the next four weeks, staying at the bombed-out Holiday Inn downtown, I drove Snipers' Alley out to the airport, dodging sniper fire real and imagined and ignoring Greig's pleas to slow down except at the half-dozen checkpoints, all of which appeared to be manned by quasi-drunken men in one quasi-uniform or another.

This was before cellphones and BlackBerrys had become ubiquitous tools of my trade, and when only the big U.S. networks equipped their reporters with satellite phones. I filed my stories to the *Sun* the old-fashioned way, yelling them over the one land line in the hotel that worked. That phone was at the front desk, and by 5 or 6 p.m. most evenings there was a long lineup of reporters waiting for it, taking their turns and shrieking in a half-dozen languages to their editors.

As I was dictating one night, the hotel was mortared on an upper floor. On another night, a colleague saw the infrared light of a sniper's scope—there were snipers in the shelled and abandoned apartment blocks across from the hotel—enter his room through its blasted-out windows. Shortly after arriving, I found places to sleep other than my own room, a couple of times even crashing on Greig's floor.

I took away three lessons. First, after being shot at, however peripherally, it is incrementally harder every day to go back out again. By the end of our stay, I was lingering over breakfast, having endless coffees and smokes (I'd started again after five years off), and searching for an excuse that would get us out of going to the airport that day and give us a graceful way to remain in the hotel.

Second, when you're afraid it's much better to have company, if only because it forces you to acknowledge the fear ("Why are you under my bed, Blatch?" leads to a frank conversation), which soon leads to joking about that fear, and the lessening of it. Third, you never feel so giddy as immediately after you've come through a scary time. After our daily adventures either in Snipers' Alley or out with the soldiers, Greig and I would always throw back a couple of fast gin and tonics in the Holiday Inn bar. We'd get back around 5 p.m. to this ludicrous ruin of a hotel with no power, no running water, holes in the walls, and not a single intact window, and there, in the corner of the lobby bar, a fellow in black tie would be playing the grand piano. It was so weird, and I would feel so gloriously alive, it was all I could do not to start dancing on the table.

On my first trip to Afghanistan in the spring of 2006, I heard the Patricias talk with reverence about a book called *On Combat*, by Dave Grossman. Some of the soldiers had heard him speak and many had read the book, so when I returned to Canada I ordered it and an earlier one called *On Killing*. They weren't what I had expected from books written by a guy who was the director of something called the Killology Research Group.

Grossman is a former U.S. Army Ranger, retired lieutenant-colonel, and West Point psychology professor. *On Combat* is subtitled "The Psychology and Physiology of Deadly Conflict in War and in Peace," which is a much fuller description of the contents. His bottom-line premise is found in a story he credits to an old and anonymous Vietnam veteran. This story is now in such wide circulation within the Canadian army that in a pub in Toronto in November 2006, a father whose son had been killed in Afghanistan the month before repeated it to me almost verbatim. Only he attributed the story to Mark Miller, now the RSM of the 1st Battalion, the Royal Canadian Regiment.

As that father, Errol Cushley, told it to me, "[Miller] said, what you've got to understand is that most people are sheep. And you've got your wolves that want to harm the sheep, and you've got the 2 percent of the people who want to be sheepdogs, and they stand between the wolves and the sheep. He said, now the people, they're frightened of the wolves, but the sheepdogs, they look a little bit too much like the wolves, so they don't really like them too much either."

The sheepdogs, of course, are soldiers and police.

Grossman says, "If you have no capacity for violence, then you are a healthy productive citizen: a sheep. If you have a capacity for violence and no empathy for your fellow citizens, then you have defined an aggressive sociopath—a wolf. But what if you have a capacity for violence and a deep love for your fellow citizens? Then you are a sheepdog, a warrior, someone who is walking the hero's path. Someone who can walk into the heart of darkness, into the universal human phobia, and walk out unscathed."

On Killing describes how armies have had to condition their soldiers to shoot. A Second World War study of American soldiers found that only fifteen to twenty of every hundred men actually fired their weapons, where in Vietnam the *non-firing* rate was down to about 5 percent. Grossman argues that the same techniques of depersonalization, desensitization, and what he calls inoculation to the stress of combat that ready a professional soldier to pull the trigger are being indiscriminately applied to the civilian populations of the modern West.

"In a kind of reverse *Clockwork Orange* classical conditioning process," he writes in *On Killing*, "adolescents in movie theatres across the nation, and watching television at home, are seeing the detailed, horrible suffering and killing of human beings, and they are learning to associate the killing and suffering with entertainment, pleasure, their favorite soft drink, their favorite candy bar and the close, intimate contact of their date.

"Operant conditioning firing ranges with pop-up targets and immediate feedback, just like those used to train soldiers in modern armies, are found in the interactive video games that our children play today."

I thought this a bit of a stretch until I had several young Canadian soldiers tell me that smack in the middle of a firefight, they thought, as Sean Niefer put it, "Oh yeah, I played this video game two months ago." But whereas soldiers learn to fire only under orders, and are taught to focus their aggression, adolescents playing video games have no such safeguards built into their conditioning.

Grossman has become a voice against violence in the media, an advocate of parental control and responsibility. In 1998, he was part of the crisis team at a school in Jonesboro, Arkansas, where two boys gunned down fifteen people, and he testified at U.S. Senate and House of Representative hearings held after the 1999 shooting at Columbine High School in Littleton, Colorado. Half advocate for soldiers and warriors, half activist against violence in the mass media, he's a complicated fellow.

On Combat is geared much more to helping a soldier prepare for the filthy realities of war. Grossman lays out in excruciating detail what happens to the body in a fear state: the adrenalin rush and inevitable crash when it's over; the way the ears shut out some noises and amplify others; the narrowing of the field of vision, or tunnel vision; the clever manner in which the nervous system dilates the bronchial tubes in the lungs and heart to increase their capabilities, but also shuts down such unnecessary-for-battle functions as digestion and salivation. As he puts it, the body reacts to combat by saying to the bowel and bladder, "We don't need no stinkin' digestion. You guys blow the ballast and get down to the legs where I need you."

The American Soldier, the official study of the performance of U.S. troops in the Second World War, reports one survey in which a quarter of all U.S. soldiers admitted they had lost control of their bladders, and an eighth admitted to defecating in their pants. Grossman's own estimate is that 50 percent of those who see intense combat wet their pants, and he quotes one Vietnam vet as saying, "I will go see a war movie when the main character is shown shitting his pants in the battle scene."

Grossman preaches, and his book teaches, the merits of tactical breathing before, during, and after a critical incident such as a firefight. It couldn't be simpler: Breathe in through your nose to a slow count of four; hold for a count of four; then exhale through your mouth to a count of four. Repeat until you've calmed yourself.

It reminded me of the breathing technique a respiratory therapist had taught my late father, who had chronic obstructive pulmonary disease and emphysema in the last decade of his life. My dad's guiding belief could have been framed roughly as "Never surrender," and he worked hard at controlling his breathing so that he could stay mobile for as long as possible. I can still see him slowly exhaling through pursed lips. It had worked for him; my parents were able to stay in their third-floor walk-up apartment for years after his diagnosis. I figured it couldn't hurt me either, so I practised it a few times on the long flight back to Afghanistan in July 2006.

—

WE WERE SCHEDULED to leave for Pashmul around 10 p.m. on July 7, 2006, the same night of Fletcher's briefing, and were to be gone for about three days.

I spent the intervening hours trying to pack my kit, loading water into the portion of my knapsack called the camel back that comes with its own built-in straw, forcing myself to discard the useless stuff and just bring what I'd really need, like box upon box of Nicorette gum. I didn't sleep.

Embedding rules prohibit us from telling our editors when we're rolling out, or where we're going, so I lapsed into the code my boss Colin MacKenzie and I had developed and which made us both feel ridiculous.

"Not going to be filing for a while," I'd say.

"Uh huh," he'd reply. "For about how long?"

"Oh, a while," I'd say.

I was travelling without a photographer and, as a technical klutz, decided to leave behind the satellite phone that would have allowed me to file stories from the field.

I can't remember if we left on time, though experience tells me otherwise. Rare was the convoy that left KAF on schedule, and my notes tell me there was at least some of the usual standing around and shooting the shit beforehand.

Being a smart young OC, Fletcher put me in his LAV, not wanting to inflict the reporter on anyone else. It was a lucky move for me, as I was soon being soothed by the rich Newfoundland accent of Corporal Keith Mooney, Fletcher's signaller—the guy who keeps the OC's communications up and running, carries the radio and phones, and goes everywhere the OC does.

From St. Mary's Bay on the Avalon Peninsula, Mooney is a strapping blond chatterbox whose stories blend seamlessly into each other. He is earthy and funny, and his rough and ready way of speaking reminded me of my favourite story from the Turin Olympics, which I'd covered just a few months earlier.

The Newfoundland curlers who won gold for Canada were out whooping it up after their medals presentation at Olympic Plaza. One was looking forward to his triumphant return to the bars of George Street in St. John's, where, he announced, he would wear his medal and get laid as he had never been laid before. "I may have a needle dick," he said, "but I've got an arse like a sewing machine."

Keith Mooney talked just like that. Like many soldiers, he swore all the time, but his use of profanity bordered on the artistic and never sounded crude.

I remember taking a last look at the sky before getting into the LAV. It was a typical starry Afghanistan night, with a three-quarters moon. The only view from the passenger compartment inside the vehicle is on the green-glowing thermal imaging screen, similar to a tiny TV set, or achieved by craning your neck such that you can get a glimpse of sky through the legs of the air sentries who stand in the two open hatches at the rear.

We rolled out of KAF in the dark, all vehicles in blackout mode but for the ANA, who needed lights. The crew commanders navigated by night-vision goggles (NVG). I'd already decided I was sticking close to Mooney, and for a while he talked my ear off and distracted me so I didn't cringe noticeably at every bump in the road. He regaled me with stories of the ups and downs of his career,

the firefights he'd been in already and how he'd punished the
detainees they'd picked up (by not talking to them, the brute). I was
feeling pretty relaxed when suddenly we heard that call sign One
Two (Alpha's 2 Platoon) was in contact. Since A Company was leading the way for the entire battle group, and it was only 12:30 a.m. on
July 8, this was hardly good news.

Kevin Schamuhn, the young captain who commanded 1 Platoon
and who was just a couple of minutes behind 2 Platoon, remembers
the moment vividly because it marked the first time that any of the
A Company soldiers had had a chance to fight back. They had
spent their tour up north, in two remote platoon houses, essentially
being IEDed often enough that the soldiers were frustrated and
tense. "So the possibility of actually going into live combat was
thrilling for us," Schamuhn says, "but yet it was scary too, because
all we had known was what it's like to get hit. We never got to feel
the satisfaction of returning fire and killing enemy . . ."

When 2 Platoon Warrant Officer Mark Pickford came on the
radio saying, "One Niner, this is 1–2, contact wait out" (One Niner
was Alpha commander Kirk Gallinger, and *contact wait out* means
"We're busy with enemy so hang tight"), Schamuhn remembers
"looking over to my driver and my heart was just racing. I said, 'All
right, this is it. Let's go.'" So 1 Platoon picked up the pace, but 2's
fight was over almost as soon as it began. "I don't think they found
anyone," Schamuhn says, "but they just returned a significant volume of fire, and then everything went quiet. So we kept advancing."

As Schamuhn's platoon headed south, they started taking fire
too, from what they assumed was an observation post, "just maybe
one or two guys with a machine gun shooting at our lead vehicle,
which was my vehicle. My Jeep [G-Wagon] was leading the way.
And we couldn't tell exactly where it had come from, because the
pucker factor was pretty high, and there's just a lot going on."

They continued to advance, and turned east to get into their
blocking position. Schamuhn sent Sergeant Quinn Beggs and three
of his soldiers out on foot to check out another road for 2 Platoon to
use. The platoon was starting to move down it when "all hell broke

loose and a huge gun battle ensued in which pretty much every vehicle in A Company unleashed a few rounds and the sky lit up."

There were so many vehicles firing, Schamuhn says, "that it sounded for a second like all of A Company was firing at the same target," so he called a check fire. "And then after that I got out and a couple of the other troops had gotten out of the vehicles, just to watch the firefight and fire a few rounds of their C7s [standard-issue Canadian Forces rifle] in the general direction of the enemy, because that's what you do when you're in the middle of the night in a firefight. Everyone wanted to get their first rounds off, and they were pretty excited."

He remembers going up to one young soldier, Private Jody Salway. "He was just, the adrenalin was just flowing through his veins. He was so happy. I remember him saying over and over, the whole fucking tour, everything we'd gone through up to that point, was worth it all now. This was why he joined the army and this was what he wanted to do. They were actually, for the first time in their lives, in their adult careers, they were given the opportunity to do what they had trained for years and years on end."

While the troops of A Company were eager for the experience, embracing their first time in combat, among the soldiers of Bravo, whose turf Pashmul was and who had been in too many fights already, the mood was sombre. "This was going to be our fourth fight in Pashmul," Nick Grimshaw says. "You could see it on their faces . . . sort of guarded optimism. We knew it could go one of two ways, a cakewalk and no one there, or we were gonna have to fight for every inch. It ended up being the latter."

As Bravo was getting ramped up, "We could hear A Company engaged in a firefight. The guys were saying, 'Here we go, it's Option B.' So the game face is on. But there was nobody who ever said, 'Sir, I'm not going.' It was just all business," Grimshaw says. "You can't ask for better."

Charlie moved through to the north bank of the Arghendab River, secured the first crossing at a little canal, then moved over to the White School. As Bravo began pushing through, "We started receiving fire." This was when Tom Michalak stuck his head out a turret and shot the remarkable footage—tracer fire and RPGs bursting in the night air—CTV viewers would watch on the news a few evenings later.

Alpha was fighting. Bravo was fighting. Charlie was fighting too. I was not as fearless as Michalak, or not nearly as aware. I understood the chatter on the radio well enough to know that large groups of women and children had been seen fleeing the area (a telltale sign that the Taliban is preparing to stay and fight) and that there were troops in contact (TICs) all over the place. But those radio voices were sufficiently calm that it was only afterwards I realized how hairy a trip it had really been.

Two things stand out. The first was a report that five or six men had been spotted walking along a tree line. "Significant movement in the trees," I heard Fletcher say on the radio. "They're wearing pants [rather than the typical *shalwar kameez*, loose pyjama trousers and to-the-knees tunic favoured by many Afghan men], they seem relaxed." He was afraid they might be dismounted ANA and ordered the soldiers to hold their fire until he had accounted for all of the Afghan troops.

The second, and I know the time because unbelievably I wrote it down, came at 2:39 a.m. "We have contact!" I heard. Then the boom-boom-boom of our LAV's 25 millimetre cannon firing. Then, "Got him! Got him!"

Beside me, Mooney, watching the thermal screen intently, grinned and said, "We engaged and destroyed two enemy." Our eighteen-year-old interpreter, who had been sleeping like a baby until now, suddenly woke up. As discreetly as I could, I was trying to make myself very small.

Then I heard, "You got movement, Suds!" followed by the boom-boom-boom of our cannon again as twenty-two-year-old gunner Chris Sutherland fired. At some point, I heard Bill Fletcher say, "Not sure where that RPG came from." At another, Mooney said, "Whatever is there is dead," then, "That's quite the battle going on there."

Some time later, probably close to 4 a.m., the shooting stopped, at least where we were. An hour later, Fletcher dismounted with some troops to do a battle damage assessment, and I went with him.

The river was to our right, a mud path in the middle, and there, in a ditch by a little irrigation canal on the left, was a dead Talib. Impossibly skinny, looking fortysomething the way Afghan men half that age tend to look, much of the back of his head had been blown off, and most of his clothes with it. One of the interpreters stepped away a bit and got down on his knees to pray. A few feet away was another man, seriously injured, unconscious, bleeding. He was treated by a Canadian medic and then choppered out.

We returned to the LAV, and though Fletcher, his lanky sergeant-major, Shawn Stevens, and Mooney soon went out again for most of the day, I stayed in the vehicle.

I don't recall being particularly shocked or upset. Yet I can see that I wrote almost nothing in my notebook. I have absolutely no memory of the rest of that day. I just sat there, alone in the back of the LAV, too afraid to leave.

I don't remember hearing about Chris Klodt, the young corporal with Bravo Company who was shot in the back of the neck during what Nick Grimshaw calls a significant close-quarter battle. "I didn't realize at the time how close things had really been," he says. "It was around corners and on tops of buildings. The enemy guys were pouring over those two walls, just pouring over the walls. They kind of caught the guys by surprise, they did an amazing job to keep the enemy at bay and extract Klodt without any more casualties." When he first crumpled to the ground, "Guys were going, 'Klodt, get up!' and he couldn't move." He, too, was choppered to the base hospital.

I didn't hear the bomb. I didn't even hear *about* the bomb for days.

Around the same time I was seeing my first dead soldier and the sun was fully over the horizon, Kevin Schamuhn was linking up with Alpha's 1 Platoon commander, Lieutenant Ben Richard, to go over the map and discuss the plan. "And then his platoon came under contact," Schamuhn says. "There are videos on YouTube of the platoon at this moment, getting in the firefight, and they were involved in some pretty intense, compound-to-compound, house-to-house clearing and trying to root out a couple of guys who had some machine guns and RPGs."

As they were battling, Kirk Gallinger decided to pull back and call in some air support. His Forward Artillery Controller, Bob Meade, radioed that an air strike was inbound, and that all troops were to move to a safe distance. Schamuhn checked the map and saw that everyone was clear, told the troops, "'All right, it's coming in about a minute, or thirty seconds, just get down.' But of course, troops being troops, a couple of them had cameras, because they want to get this on video, or want to take pictures of this massive, what we thought was gonna be a thousand-pound bomb explosion," though what was actually dropped was a five hundred–pound laser-guided bomb.

They heard the jet—an A-10 Thunderbolt American fighter plane—doing a dive. "He's dive-bombing, let the bomb go, and then from our platoon's perspective it just kept getting louder and louder and louder until BOOM! The bomb went off and it was, like, I wish I could explain how loud it was," Schamuhn says. "I'm surprised we didn't rupture our eardrums."

He picked himself up and found the whole area covered in dust. "And I was in shock," he says. "I didn't know what had just happened." His warrant officer, Justin MacKay, came tearing around the corner. "He's covered in dust, his helmet was blown off, he's pointing at my radio man, telling him to call it in, they got the wrong grid—they hit our platoon."

The signaller got on the air: "One Niner, it's One One. Wrong target. The bomb hit our platoon, wait out for case evac." The network went terribly silent.

Schamuhn ran over to the impact area. "I found this massive crater that's as deep as I am tall, just this huge thing you could fit a Volkswagen in, huge hole in the ground." Private Robert Adams, already nicknamed Danger and known thereafter as Danger Close, was "no more than six feet away from the crater, like six feet isn't even an exaggeration," Schamuhn says. Quinn Beggs, the section commander, wasn't much further away. "And I walked up, and I was calling out the names of Privates Adams and Beggs, yelling out their names, asking if they're okay, trying to get a response from them because we couldn't see anything. And my warrant officer, Warrant MacKay, he got mad at me. He said, 'No, they're not okay, Kevin, they're fucking dead!' Because we thought they must be in pieces because a bomb just landed right beside them."

Schamuhn went a bit further. "There they were, on their knees, covered in dirt. Their ears, they couldn't hear anything, their ears were still ringing. But they were fine." Schamuhn stood Beggs up. He looked at him, checked his body. "I checked his legs, because he thought he was in shock. He thought, 'All right, so where are my legs?' Like, what was going on in his mind was that he had either just lost his life and was kind of on the ship to the afterworld, or he had lost his legs or something. So I checked him over, I looked at him, and I'm like, 'Quinn, you're okay, buddy. Everything's exactly where it's supposed to be,' and we gave each other a big hug and we just kind of laughed. We're like, 'Man, that was fucking wild.'"

There were fourteen-inch-long shards of shrapnel in the crater, still too hot to touch. "So there were these chunks of metal, these huge pieces of jagged-edged, steaming-hot metal were flying around everywhere," Schamuhn says. He got back on the radio and told Gallinger there were no casualties. "It should have wiped out at least six to eight guys from my platoon, but we remained untouched."

Twelve days later, Ethan Baron of CanWest News had a piece in a couple of the chain's papers headlined, "Soft ground saves troops in latest friendly-fire incident: U.S. jet drops bomb on Canadians similar to one that killed four soldiers in 2002." Unnamed soldiers quoted in the story said the pilot had mistaken the Canadians for Taliban. In fact, the A Battery commander, Steve Gallagher, says that any mistakes made that day were made on the ground by the Canadian Joint Tactical Air Controller (JTAC), Meade's second-in-command.

The exhausted JTAC didn't have a piece of kit that was promised but never materialized—a simple laser target marker that shines a light on the target for the pilot to view on his screen in the cockpit. As a result, Gallagher says, the JTAC and the pilot had had to play a nervy game of "'Do you see me, I'm here.' 'I see you. I see a wall five hundred metres away, and a road intersection.' 'Yeah, that's it.'" The JTAC had also missed "a couple of procedures, not gross errors" that, done right, might have alerted the pilot to the mistake. The JTAC was decertified for about a week, retested, and remained in theatre. "He carried on and did further missions after that," Gallagher says.

As for Danger Close Adams, he was choppered out a little later because his ears started bleeding. Kevin Schamuhn later retrieved Danger's disposable camera from the lip of the crater. He grins at the thought of Danger sitting there, poised "for a sweet photo opportunity" when the bomb landed behind him.

One day in late July, I was hanging out with Adams' platoon mate, Jim Sinclair, and met the kid, who was still pretty deaf. "Danger wants to go back," Sinclair said, "but they won't let him." From his chair about three feet away, Danger Close yelled, "I'm good to go!" He had turned twenty-three the day after the bomb.

—

SUNDAY, JULY 9, I remember.

The night before, things had quieted down enough that the troops were able to sleep—albeit in shifts, because the observation posts had to be manned. They dropped around the LAV like pups around their mother, and seemed to start snoring the second their heads hit the sand. I followed their lead, or tried to, but then I started to get itchy—first my legs, then my back, then all over. Finally, I dragged my sleeping bag over to the LAV's ramp, which was down, and fell asleep for a couple of hours there.

In the morning, I was glad I had moved; the boys were covered, arms and legs, with small red bites from sand fleas. I had only a few.

God, it was a gorgeous morning, the sun rising in shades of purple over the foothills of small mountains you could see in the distance. It was still cool by Afghan standards. Reveille was at 4:30 a.m., and not long after, Fletcher told me they were going to sweep the grape fields and asked if I'd like to come along.

"Should I bring my backpack?" I asked.

He thought for a minute then said not to bother, we'd probably be back within an hour or two. I stuck my notebook in the pocket at the front of my body armour.

We stopped briefly in the cemetery—soldiers' graves, meaning most of them, marked by little flags, the triangular sort you see flapping at old-fashioned gas stations in Canada—where the troops of Bravo and CTV had spent the night, mindful of Grimshaw's direction to leave as light a footprint as possible.

We walked through the twisting, turning mud-walled maze, passing small compounds where people had been living just a day before. Through open gates, I saw in one compound two ancient black kettles sitting on a ledge. In the dusty courtyard of another was a group of lovely little tawny rabbits with jumbo ears.

Then we were in the fields, surrounded by clusters of tiny green grapes hanging fat on the vine, supersized sunflowers standing at attention here and there. The troops were spread out evenly in a line, walking through the bright greenery, occasionally poking under the plants.

It is unbelievable to me that I could have been so easily swept away by the pretty face Afghanistan was momentarily showing, but I distinctly remember relaxing and thinking, "Hey, this isn't so bad." I actually remember feeling the knots in my shoulders and neck start to loosen up.

Then the soldiers around me were suddenly running toward small-arms fire that was coming from a grape-drying hut somewhere in the distance.

"They're just saying good morning," someone said.

I spotted Keith Mooney and followed in his wake, scrambling over low mud walls when he did, falling into ditches when he did, stopping where and when he did. I have absolutely no sense of direction in the best of circumstances, and these were hardly those, so I suppose I was terrified of losing sight of him.

But I don't remember thinking that, or anything other than that I had to get out of there and simultaneously that I had no way out. So I ran where Mooney ran. My field of vision shrank to his blond head, sometimes just his sturdy legs and rear quarters. Once, he told me: "We're bringing in some 155 millimetre [the Howitzer artillery] to soften up the ground."

I thought I heard Ian Hope on the radio saying, "Come on, boys. Calm down. Be aware." Then, "Get your guys into some low ground if you can, we're calling in some artillery."

I could hear the snap and crackle of small-arms fire. I heard something louder and bigger and closer. Then, on the radio, someone said, "It's coming too close. . . . Check fire. Too close."

One minute Mooney and I were lying on our backs in a ditch, the next he was gone. I had lost sight of him, and feeling panic rise, I simply attached myself to another group of soldiers, none of whom I recognized.

Somehow, and I've no recollection of how we got there though we must have run, we were all lined up along a mud wall about five and a half feet high. We were on the other side of the grape fields now, near the grape-drying hut. Canadian soldiers were inches from me, some tossing grenades over the wall, others taking careful aim and shooting. ANA soldiers were further down the line, ducked down low like me. Once in a while, one of the ANA soldiers would throw his rifle over the wall and blindly fire off a burst.

I felt my bowels turn to water, and there, by the wall, in the presence of dozens of young men I didn't know, I squatted and did what I had to do, comforted only by the memory of Dave Grossman's explanation in *On Combat*: "We don't need no stinkin' digestion." I told myself no one had even noticed, but soon after I heard one of the troops warn others from the spot, saying, "Someone took a big crap there." I clung to the "someone," hoping they didn't know who the culprit was, but not caring much either way. I was indifferent even to embarrassment.

I spotted Fletcher and Mooney just as they were going in to clear one of the three—I could see now that there were three—grape-drying huts. I loitered outside the door, then went inside. It was cool and, up close, those thick mud walls were as beautifully and evenly perforated as pegboard, so the breezes would blow through and dry out the juicy grapes.

Abruptly, someone cried out that there was a casualty in the hut to the west of us. Someone was shooting from the roof. The first time I heard a name over the radio it was something like, "Tony Burdicki, reservist, Portuguese kid." Into my peripheral vision came Sergeant-Major Stevens, and then about six soldiers, struggling to carry a figure strapped onto a black rubbery stretcher over the rutted ground, fire still coming down behind us.

It wasn't even 8 a.m. yet; Stevens was now running behind the boy on the stretcher. I was just behind him, trying not to step in the blood that was falling onto the dirt in front of me.

The boy was Anthony (Tony) Joseph Boneca of the Lake Superior Scottish Regiment, the Lake Sups, in Thunder Bay, Ontario. He had the plug of an airway tube visible in his mouth; it looked like a baby's soother. A medic was running alongside him, giving first aid, and Stevens was barking out, "Careful, boys! Be careful! Easy, boys!" A couple of times, the soldiers stumbled off the mud ruts, scrambling to hold the stretcher upright and keep their balance.

Boneca's section, Sergeant Matt Gaulden says, had just cleared the bottom half of the compound. "Everything was going good, our drills were really tight, and all of a sudden we heard a weapon cock from the roof." At the sound—"a frigging gut drop," Gaulden says— the troops backed off. Some headed for the protection of an over-hang; Boneca was off to the other side, behind one of the walls. He was yelling at the Talib to drop his weapon "and all of a sudden the guy just stood up and sprayed. And it wasn't a good shot. Honestly, I think it was a ricochet off one of the walls that hit Tony, because he was squared off to him."

It was a fluke shot, the round catching Boneca in the throat just above the plate of his body armour. He was twenty-one years old, and he was dying.

They got him to a casualty evacuation point, nothing more than a Bison ambulance in a clearing with one LAV for protection, where other medics worked on him with increasing desperation. They knew it was futile but they never stopped.

"I did my best," Corporal Gord Creelman, from 1 Field Ambulance in Edmonton, said later. "I wanted to be able to tell his mother I did everything I could."

Boneca was choppered out at 9 a.m.

I ended up back at the same wall near the grape-drying huts, following Stevens, only because I could think of nothing else to do. There, hours passed, and then more hours behind some smaller walls, where the heat stroke casualties were taken, and then more time down by a stream. I wasn't a heat casualty but I badly wanted to be one, would have done anything to get somewhere safer.

We ate grapes, broke open watermelons. No one seemed to have any water.

The Predator, an unmanned U.S. air vehicle, dropped Hellfire missiles; American Apaches, attack helicopters, repeatedly strafed the rooftops of the compound where Boneca had been shot.

Around 4 p.m., I told Bill Fletcher I had to leave to file my story—accurate enough, but hardly the whole truth—and he led me back to the casualty evacuation point, where with an older ANA soldier and a couple of heat casualties, I hitched a ride back to KAF.

Only later did I learn that in the short time they were out of my sight—I think when I was dogging it with the heat casualties—Mooney and Fletcher were by that same wall again when a bomb was dropped on the compound. There was a secondary explosion as a Taliban weapons cache blew up, and Mooney thought someone had whacked him hard across the knees. When he looked down, he saw blood pouring out of the tops of his legs. He'd been hit by shrapnel from the secondary blast.

He started shaking, was suddenly very cold. He began yelling, "Are they all right, boys? Are they all right?" For a few minutes, the soldiers around him thought he was asking about his mates.

Given the location of his wound and the amount of blood, Mooney was in fact inquiring about the health of his balls, as

Fletcher soon realized. The OC was drafted to personally ensure that Mooney's penis and testicles were intact.

"That's my worst story ever," Fletcher says, groaning.

Once reassured, Mooney buoyed up immediately, and in fact grabbed his own replacement. "And all the while still putting pressure on his wound, [he] goes, 'Here's the radio, here's the frequency, here's what you gotta do.' He was phenomenal."

I saw Mooney again the very next morning. He was in a wheelchair on the tarmac at the air field, his big blond head bent over, trying not to cry as Tony Boneca's casket made its way from a LAV, past the rows and rows of soldiers, and into the belly of a green-grey Hercules aircraft.

The next time I saw Mooney, he was lying on his cot in the Big Ass Tent. Unsolicited, grinning, he raised the leg of his cut-off sweatpants to show me his scars.

Sgt. Derek Thompson in front of Capt. John Croucher's burning LAV

22 April 2006

—

"Human bodies aren't supposed to look like that."

—WARRANT OFFICER JUSTIN MACKAY,
AS QUOTED BY CAPTAIN KEVIN SCHAMUHN

As the sun was setting on February 9, 2006, the soldiers of Alpha Company's 1 Platoon moved through the village of Pada. They were then still so new to southern Afghanistan that they were on their inaugural trip "outside the wire" of the big coalition base at KAF. The platoon was en route to the remote compound, about 130 kilometres north of Kandahar, that with sunny American optimism the soldiers of U.S. Task Force Gun Devil had named the Gumbad Safe House. The Patricias were doing a handover with the Yanks, who had established the rudimentary base in the fall of 2005 and were now yielding it to the Canadians.

Located on the rolling brown terrain of the Gumbad Valley and bordered by the improbably stony hills that are part of the Hindu Kush mountains, Gumbad was to serve as home base for 1 Platoon and headquarters for company operations.

"We were travelling at dusk," says platoon commander Kevin Schamuhn, who was riding in a U.S. Humvee with his American counterpart. Soldiers were navigating by night-vision goggles.

Just outside the village, where the path splits into two, one fork rising and the other dipping, the last LAV in the convoy rode up on the higher path, tipped over, and rolled on its side. No one was hurt, but the vehicle was disabled, which meant troops had to stay with it until it could be recovered.

On a tight schedule to relieve the Americans, Schamuhn left behind enough soldiers under Warrant Officer Justin MacKay to secure the scene and pressed on with the rest of platoon. They got about four kilometres further north and were driving in complete blackout conditions when, Schamuhn says, "There was this enormous CRUMP!, explosion, right behind us. And I remember the American sergeant knew exactly what it was right off the bat, and he yelled out 'Mother bitch!' and he just jumped out of the Humvee with his machine gun and started running toward the mountains after these guys by himself."

It was an IED, and as Schamuhn ran back through the dust to the LAV that had been hit, he saw the crew commander, Scott Proctor, yelling to the driver, Private Danny Hoidas. "He thought the driver was dead," Schamuhn says, "because the hatch had been blown open" in the blast.

Hoidas was fine. Everyone was fine but for mild concussions. Only Trevor Greene, the Civil-Military Co-operation (CIMIC) officer, had a sore enough neck that he was evacuated as a precaution the following morning. "So that," Schamuhn says, "was our first welcome into Afghanistan."

The soldiers of Alpha were the bomb babies.

From February 9 to the glorious day in late June when they bid Gumbad farewell, A Company's 120 troops were IEDed another five times, to much more devastating effect, and discovered another four bombs before they blew. They saw friends suffer gruesome physical injuries. They raced to the rescue of others. They stood in the bloodied remains of still more. And they fought, all of them, the constant psychological stress of waiting, 24–7, for the next bend in the road, the next bump, the next bomb. For almost six long months they were the sitting ducks of the Canadian battle group, driven near to madness by the frustration of rarely even catching a glimpse of the enemy.

Lieutenant-Colonel John Conrad, the logistics commander who went out on at least one convoy a week with his troops and was significantly involved in a major suicide bombing, says that being hit by an IED is akin to having a chair suddenly break under you in that no graceful recovery is possible. "Getting IEDed is like having a bruise.

Once you've got a bruise, you're always kind of favouring that leg a bit, or trying to not get it rebruised."

Early on in the tour, Conrad saw an IED's effects play out on one of his most beloved soldiers, a sergeant named Paul Jones, "a guy I've known almost all my career . . . a salt-of-the-earth Canadian. He loves to hunt, loves his ATV [all-terrain vehicle], he's a very physical, big strong bull of a man."

On March 3, a suicide bomber attacked a Canadian convoy returning to Camp Nathan Smith, as the Provincial Reconstruction Team (PRT) office in Kandahar is called. It is out of the PRT, essentially a self-sustaining satellite, that most of the Canadian military's small reconstruction and development projects are run. Ironically, the convoy that day was carrying members of the army Board of Inquiry (BOI) investigating the January 15 suicide attack that had killed Canadian diplomat Glyn Berry and seriously injured three soldiers. The BOI members wanted to go out at the same time and travel the same roads that Berry's convoy had taken, which is what they were doing when their own convoy was bombed.

Ian Hope's LAV was hit, though the CO wasn't in it that day, and his first crew commander, Master Corporal Mike Loewen, was the most seriously hurt, his right elbow shattered and shredded. Loewen kept his arm in the end—still on the mend months later, he joked it might look as if he were giving Hope the finger when the CO returned to Edmonton and Loewen saluted him—but it was very much touch and go at first.

With Loewen's arm hanging by a thread, Jones drove the Bison at breakneck speed to the sophisticated base hospital at KAF, going so fast that he burned out the engine just at the gates of the base. Loewen then had to be cross-loaded onto the roof of a G-Wagon, with Jones, medic Shaun Kaye, and a couple of other soldiers holding on to him the rest of the way.

Conrad visited Loewen and Jones in the little hospital later that night. When the Bison engine had burst into flames, the fire extinguisher system in the vehicle had gone off, and Jones had inhaled some Halon, a fire suppressant. "He had some Halon in his lung," Conrad says, "which is not good. That's why they were keeping him."

But that wasn't what was alarming.

"I could see in his eyes that he wasn't home, that he was trauma-tized," Conrad says. "Mentally, he was vacant, and shaken, and trying to figure it out, and you know, very despondent. As a CO, looking at one of your salt-of-the-earth stalwart sergeants, on day four of your mission, that rocked my confidence."

Jones stayed in Afghanistan and got his mojo going again.

"He regained his confidence, and I would say within a week he was back to his old self, as much as possible," Conrad says. "He recovered, he got over his mental bruise, and he went on to do a full tour, but I know it took a toll. At one point in the tour there," he says, "he told me he was tired of seeing dead people."

IEDs, or roadside bombs, now account for more than half of the combat deaths of U.S. servicemen in Iraq. Afghanistan, with almost a third of combat casualties inflicted by IEDs, is only slightly behind. Though all of the devices have a firing mechanism, initiation system, and detonator—and what British Major Jim Blackburn, for a time the coalition staff officer who spoke about bombs to the press, once called "murderous intent"—they vary widely and are limited only by the bomber's ingenuity and the materials at his disposal.

As fast as Western militaries develop better, tougher vehicles, the bombers build bigger, meaner bombs. Some are activated by vehicle weight; others are set off by a human being sitting nearby, coolly watching and pressing a button at a time of his choosing; radio signals, often from a cellphone, activate Remote-Controlled IEDs (RCIEDs). Some are jerry-rigged with accelerant, while others are built with ball bearings to broaden their kill zone. The military's new family of acronyms barely hints at the variety—there are VBIEDs (Vehicle-Borne IEDs), BBIEDs (Bicycle-Borne IEDs), DBIEDs (Donkey-Borne IEDs), and even FCBIEDs (Food Cart–Borne IEDs),

That first bomb, Alpha Company commander Kirk Gallinger says, "helped mature 1 Platoon very quickly. . . . It definitely allowed us to cut our teeth, in terms of getting IEDed, so we definitely learned some valuable lessons off of that."

It also saw them pretty quickly find a more accurate label for their new home. "Colonel Hope kind of prompted us to switch names," Gallinger says, "because ironically the Gumbad Safe House was never really safe and it was never a house." The Gumbad *Patrol* House was born.

The soldiers loved so much about being there.

Unprepossessing at best—inside the mud walls and behind a huge wooden gate was one building with a series of simple doorless rooms and a firepit; outside the walls were a plywood shitter, a long piss trench, and the company vehicles—Gumbad had no water, intermittent and unreliable electricity, and dubious charms. The men lived exclusively on hard rations, and most slept in or by their LAVs, with some of the small rooms used for briefings and the remainder able to house only a handful of people.

In other words, for infantrymen who thrive on hardship even as they love to bitch and moan about it, it was perfect.

Gumbad was 130 kilometres north of KAF, sufficiently far away that the troops enjoyed enormous independence. They were subject to little of the garrison mentality that prevailed on the big base, where sergeant-majors are on the constant prowl, much as they are back in Canada, for the soldier who hasn't shaved or isn't wearing his boot bands.

The rules police don't stop at telling soldiers what to do, either.

Several times, one or another of my newspaper colleagues was called out for tucking an ID badge in a shirt pocket or for feeding the plump orange tabby, Steve (named after CTV's Steve Chao), who hung around the Canadian press tents and was prone to dozing off on our laptop computers.

I was grateful this never happened to me, though I probably broke as many inconsequential rules as anyone else. If I sometimes fantasized that I might have made a good soldier, the truth is that the incendiary temper that erupts whenever someone tells me what to do would have seen me flame out fast. I would have had a brief and undistinguished career.

Jimmy Sinclair, who because of an excess of Jims in his platoon was nicknamed Reggie Dunlop after the hockey player/coach played by Paul Newman in the 1977 movie *Slapshot*, treasured those early days, when it was only him and the men of the 1–3 at the patrol house. At dawn, the sun rising in pinks and yellows, Sinclair would hear the distinct click of the local muezzin down the valley flipping on the power to his microphone. Then he'd hear the rasp of the man flicking a finger once or twice on the mike, testing it. And then came the muezzin's singsong voice, calling the faithful to prayer for the first of five times. Hardly a dreamy romantic—Sinclair is a tough son of a bitch with a front tooth that he takes out and puts in depending on what he is doing and who he is doing it with—he nonetheless relished these moments.

I thought I knew why. In the test-test-test ritual familiar to concertgoers everywhere in the world, Sinclair could practically feel the planet shrinking around him. He had experienced some of that same sharp recognition when he saw his first dead Taliban, and the platoon found drugs in their routine search of the bodies.

A reservist with the Royal Regina Rifles and in his civilian life the owner of a campground at Regina Beach, he once told me how, before he went to Afghanistan, he had studied up on the country and what he believed would be a disciplined enemy. "I thought they were very fanatical and religious," he said, "that they would fight to the death. And then you see the truth, how poor they are, that they fight stoned, that they're drugged out of their minds."

If he was not alone in loathing KAF, Sinclair was one of a very few to cut short his leave. He jokes that it was because, during a visit with family in Scotland, "I was helping relatives move sheep at night and discovered they were rustling." Besides, "my liver couldn't handle it. I was drinking alcohol like I was going to the electric chair."

He really did return a week early, after harassing the leave NCO and the leave RSM to get him on a flight. "I missed being here," he said one day over coffee at KAF. "I didn't come on tour to go on leave. I'm a reservist. I love what I'm doing here. No soldier wants to go to war, but when you get the mindset, you don't want to stay away too long, or you can't get back in the game."

"For the first part of the tour," A Company commander Kirk Gallinger says, "which kind of completely baffles a lot of people back here [in Canada], a lot of times I would talk to the platoon commanders [at Gumbad] just on the radio, and say, 'Tell me what you did the last twenty-four hours, tell me what your plans are for the next twenty-four, and let me know what your concerns are.'" Such was the quality of his young officers, NCOs, and the troops, Gallinger says, that they could manage the freedom he gave them and just go out and make it happen.

Hope had given them a very clear vision. "We weren't initially fixated on destroying the enemy," Gallinger says. "We were very much trying to work along the lines of the operation—security, governance, development. But we wanted to build a picture of information first, so we could assess where we would put our resources."

The platoons would leave Gumbad and head out for nine to twelve days of living rough, walking and sleeping in the mountains, meeting the neighbours, identifying village leaders, and then having *shuras* with them. *Shura* is an Arabic word that roughly translates as "consultation," but the word's lexical meaning—"to get the honey out of its sources"—far better captures the leisurely pace of the process.

As Gallinger says, "The problem was, we put so much effort into doing leader engagements, and visiting all the different villages, and development moved so slow over there. You just have to be so patient. It was very much a battle for the leadership to keep the troops sharp and keep them motivated."

The upside was that with events unfolding in this stately manner, absolutely the norm in Afghanistan, the troops had time to get their mountain legs and build up their stamina.

They certainly had both of these in spades when *Globe* photographer Louie Palu and I got to Gumbad in mid-March, just as the company was spreading out into the famous Belly Button, the area called Sha-e-Mardan-Ghar where for centuries Afghans have been repelling and generally beating the hell out of foreigners and invaders.

Within an hour or so of our arrival, there were sudden shouts to "stand to!" and soldiers began tearing about in a way that appears chaotic only to civilians. An IED had blown about four kilometres away, smack in the middle of a convoy of 2 Platoon, led by John Croucher. The platoon had gone out to pick up the men of the 1–3 who were coming off a lengthy overnight foot patrol in the hills.

As it turned out, the bomb blew between the fifth and sixth LAVs, missing the former by about twenty feet, or all of two seconds. Although no one was seriously hurt, the blast ripped the watch off one driver's wrist, tore off three tires on the LAV, and left Master Corporal Sam Demopoulos half-deaf in his remaining good ear, the hearing in the other already gone after his vehicle had been hit by an anti-tank missile in Croatia in 1992. Deafened almost completely as he was by the explosion, Demopoulos didn't miss a beat. The big cannons on the LAVs laid down suppressing fire, and he was out the ramp in a flash, getting off seventy rounds with his C7 assault rifle as men cleared the hills and fired into caves. They found a blood trail and searched for the bomber—to no avail.

It was a stark introduction to the all-bombs, all-the-time reality that was about to become A Company's world, though not even the soldiers fully realized it yet.

It certainly didn't register with me, because two nights later, when Louie and I headed out for a couple of days in the hills with Captain Sean Ivanko's platoon, in my mind I was still framing the exercise as a sort of extreme form of camping, not as travel over ground that had already proven dangerous.

Once, when Ivanko clambered over the rocks and almost lost his grip on a boulder, dangling perilously over a canyon for a few seconds, I shrieked, "Jesus Christ!"

From his perch in mid-air, he hushed me with a pointed, "Shhhhh."

Like much about the army's ways, this made no sense on the face of it. There were about forty of us, schlepping along in single file up a mountain. If there were bad guys around, I thought, surely they would be alerted to our presence by the sound of forty pairs of boots, not one silly woman shrilling? It was another illustration of how discipline is instilled: If troops are taught to be as quiet as possible, even in preposterous circumstances, they will be quiet when it might matter.

We were part of Operation Solo Kowal, which in Pashtu means "peacemaker," a scheme designed to find out if, as the CO's intelligence suggested, there really were hundreds of Taliban hiding in those stony hills. Hope sent three hundred soldiers into the mountains—we went as high as 6200 feet—on seven different routes to discover the truth of it.

They found "not a sign of the supposed six hundred Talibs hiding there," Hope says. But the mission had been fruitful. Almost every path in the Belly Button was now catalogued, every village registered, and as important, it confirmed for the CO "my suspicion of the numerous human intelligence reports of imminent attacks" from the mountains.

He spoke to them that night standing by the firepit, an oil lamp beside him, his men sitting around his feet in the flickering light, others up on the roof, their legs dangling over the edge. He reminded them that Afghans have been abused for thirty years by soldiers who looked much like they did. "They fear us. We roll up in a LAV, kitted up like *Star Wars* troopers, we inspire fear. We need discipline and we need to keep up our professionalism—that's what distinguishes you from every other guy with a gun in this country."

He also warned the officers that after an IED, they better make damn sure the soldiers involved sit down and talk. "If tears are shed," Hope said, "good. A soldier who does that will be fine. The guy who thinks he's tougher will degrade, degree by degree, and in three or four years will be useless."

There would be plenty of time for tears, and plenty of occasions when crying wouldn't be nearly release enough.

The one thing about Gumbad that no one in Afghanistan ever mentioned—not in the week I was there, not in the soldiers' discussions in the aftermath of various bombings, not even when I talked to those who had been blown up and gravely injured—was that the place was made to order for bombers.

Only after everyone was back in Canada late in August 2006 did I learn for the first time that there were only two ways in or out of Gumbad. One route went north of the platoon house for four or five kilometres to Tangay, then swung east a bit, and then went down into the wadi where, unusually, there was actually a sliver of flowing stream. The other route went pretty much due south, with a choice of going through either Pada or Shinkay.

The soldiers did what they could to mix things up, were careful to avoid routines, moved in the middle of the night and at different times of the day, went blackout drive, made themselves a "harder" target by adding more LAVs to the convoys, switched up the length of time the platoons stayed out of the house, went dismounted as often as they could. But the one immutable, unalterable thing they could do nothing about was geography: One way in; one way out. Even the dumbest bomber had a fifty-fifty chance of getting it right.

"We were just ringed, eh?" Gallinger says. "Really, no matter what we were doing, no matter our tactics, no matter how good our vehicles were. . . . It was a case of luck, and you only get lucky so many times."

As the One Two commander, John Croucher, puts it, "That A Company thing at Gumbad, two roads, every day it was getting worse." It was almost comical, he says, like "being in a huge crowd of people, someone punching you, you turn around and that person is not there anymore, and there's nothing you could do about it unless you wanted to beat everybody up, and that was something we couldn't do."

Ivanko, who turned thirty in Afghanistan, says that not long before the One Three got there, the local ANP was IEDed near the platoon house. "They went into the villages and beat everyone up and all that, so [the villagers] thought we were going to do the same. All the villagers were afraid of that. They're still people, they can relate and have empathy; they knew we were upset about it. But the fact is that we, our platoon and the Canadian army, didn't take it out on the villagers. I think that was a turning point in gaining more support from them."

Still, he says, there was an enormous amount of anger. "When we did the handover with the Americans, they said there will be times, because of the IEDs, you'll feel this rage, because of this faceless enemy, this unseen force, that attacks you and kills you and your peers and there's nothing you can do about it. You feel impotent to change anything."

Ivanko says he thought, "Okay, understood," but only in the aftermath of one particularly lethal bombing did he learn that "it's nothing that can ever be properly explained. I'd never experienced anything like that in my life. Literally, I was consumed with rage, every single cell of my body was screaming for vengeance, was screaming out with this blind rage.

"Obviously," he says, "at the end of the day, that's what separates us from the bad guys, that we understand that it wasn't the villagers who did it, we understood that most of the people in Afghanistan want us to win, most of them want to help us. So it's not like we took it out on the villagers."

He was gripped by that blind rage for the first time on April 22.

To set the stage, in early March one of A Company's CIMIC officers, Trevor Greene, was chopped in the back of the head with an axe while sitting in a *shura* in Shinkay, just a bit south of Gumbad.

The CIMIC guys, reservists all, are the ones who lead most of the village engagements. It is they who, in a considered gesture of respect and trust, remove their helmets and sit cross-legged with elders on blankets in dusty village squares, drink chai, and try to learn how the Canadians can help, without, as another CIMIC officer, Matt Kirkpatrick, once told me, "creating a sense of dependence and that sense of entitlement that Western countries tend to give people in poverty-stricken areas."

Because CIMIC officers are generally of this thoughtful stripe, because they make themselves so vulnerable, regular soldiers tend to feel protective of them. Kirk Gallinger certainly did about his CIMICs, Trevor Greene and a lanky Canada Post letter carrier from Edmonton named Bill Turner.

When Greene was attacked—he suffered devastating head trauma, and is still recovering in Vancouver, the prognosis unclear—it was a huge shock to the entire company. Gallinger listened to the first reports on the radio, feeling helpless and full of angst and guilt. "I don't think any degree of experience, any degree of time, really will take that away," he says. "That was one of the worst times we had."

Under the circumstances, with Turner now the company's only CIMIC officer, Gallinger says, "You could understand a person saying, 'I don't know if I'm up for doing this job, it's dangerous.' But Bill went back out and did his job, and CIMIC is such a frustrating and unrewarding job at times, but no, he did his thing."

Gallinger has a vivid memory, after Greene had been hurt, of standing at the sink in one of the bathrooms back at KAF, Turner beside him.

"We were doing our ablutions and shaving, and he stopped and said, 'Sir, I just want you to know, I'm going back out there to do my job and I have complete faith in the soldiers. I know they'll protect me, they'll keep me safe. You don't have to worry about me.'"

So Turner carried on, cheerfully and with a quiet confidence. In late March 2006, Louie and I spent our last day in Gumbad with him at a *shura* in Pada. It was mostly about trying to arrange for the village to be compensated for a mud wall the Canadian convoys had dinged on their constant travel in and out of the village. Turner sat, helmet off just as Greene had done, cross-legged for more than an hour without flinching, not bad for a forty-five-year-old guy.

He was immensely agreeable, with a big grin that ate up most of his face, but he wasn't a fool, and when elder Haji Mohammad Nabi suggested that what Pada really needed was better irrigation for the fields, up Turner popped, asking Nabi to show him. The fields were bursting with poppies, of course, about a month away from blossoming. Turner made the point, softly, that if Pada wanted Canadian money for irrigation, the village had better grow something other than opium-producing poppies.

Later, as we waited in the sun for the convoy to pick us up, Turner peppered his interpreter, Zee, with questions about local plants and trees, each time repeating the Pashtu names—*zardalu* for the white flowers, *shaftalu* for the purple ones—making sure I wrote it down in my notebook for him so he could copy it later, which he did. He was gentle and curious.

As April wore on, he was also getting tired, *shura*ed out.

"Poor Bill was getting skinnier and skinnier as each day went by," Gallinger remembers, "and between myself and Warrant MacKay and Sergeant-Major Pete Leger, we all kind of agreed we should probably get Bill out of the platoon house and get him back [to KAF] for some well-deserved rest. And we thought we had a cunning plan to get him out of there, fly him out in a helicopter, but that didn't pan out."

General Dave Fraser had come to visit Gumbad, travelling by chopper but with his close protection team moving in a convoy on the ground in case things went south while he was at the platoon house. It was decided that Turner would jump in with the general's team, in their G-Wagon, and return to KAF with the convoy.

Kevin Schamuhn was on leave at the time, but his LAV sergeant, Scott Proctor, told him later that at some point during that day, he and Turner had been up in one of the observation posts, having a smoke. "And he told Sergeant Proctor that he had a bad feeling about the road move and that he didn't feel safe rolling with anyone but 1 Platoon. And that really stuck out in Sergeant Proctor's mind. I remember it really hit him."

The rest of the company was out in the field, in the east in Mianishin district, when the first call came over the radio that the brigade commander's protection party was in contact.

"And we were, again, glued to the radio," Gallinger says, "listening to what was going on, and then it was identified that there were some casualties, and then it came across that they had Priority 4 casualties."

In the military system, a Priority 4 means non-urgent, but it can be for one of two reasons: either the wounded are walking and in no immediate need of help or they are dead.

"None of us at first believed they had casualties that were dead," Gallinger says. "You know, in our minds we pictured that they were maybe just cut or scraped or something. It wasn't too long before my signaller said, 'Sir! Sir! I think they're dead by some of the traffic that's coming on the radio,' and it just hit like a sledgehammer."

Then came the dreadful wait as, one by one, the zap numbers—the army ID numbers on the soldiers' dog tags—were read on the radio: Matthew Dinning, twenty-three; Myles Mansell, twenty-five; Randy Payne, thirty-two. And then Gallinger heard "the fourth number, oh no, it's Bill Turner. Just dumbfounded, completely shocked."

They abandoned their mission and headed straight to FOB Martello, a brand new base the company had just occupied, only about twenty kilometres from Gumbad as the crow flies, though over several prominent mountain ridges.

Back at the platoon house, Justin MacKay, in charge because Schamuhn was away, heard the same confusing reports on the radio. They were made by headquarters staff from the brigade, neither extensively trained nor practised in calling in contacts. Believing the men to be under fire, MacKay ramped up the 1 Platoon Quick Reaction Force and raced out of the platoon house in a convoy.

The ordinary trials of getting around Afghanistan do not cease simply because men are dead or dying: Just as MacKay's convoy reached the wadi on the other side of Gumbad village, one vehicle got stuck and another blew a tire. "His mobility was completely down," Gallinger says.

MacKay grabbed section commander Sergeant John May and said, "John, our vehicles aren't moving, there's troops in contact, you gotta get to them!"

May was the first soldier I met at Gumbad, a sort of infantry version of the streetwalker with the heart of gold. He is tough and tattooed and a bit brusque, but with a tangible sweetness. "I'll talk to you," he told me with a grin when we met, "but don't ever quote me and never take my picture." Within a few days, he was borrowing my iPod and cheerfully subjecting himself to an interview with Lisa LaFlamme of CTV.

He and his men, all wearing the usual seventy pounds plus of weaponry and kit, sprinted across the mountains on foot, running toward—into—what they thought was an ongoing firefight.

"John tells the story afterwards," Gallinger says, "that there's the commander's protection party, given the absolute worst horrors you can imagine, but they're not in contact, they're just securing their scene, and here comes a handful of 1 Platoon soldiers, running up the wadi full tilt, they thought their guys needed them. They did need them, but they thought they were in a firefight, and our guys got to the scene, and some of our boys were throwing up because they'd just run their guts out, but it's just an example of the level of professionalism and drive the soldiers have. True warriors. There's just no other word to describe them."

The IED, Kevin Schamuhn was told, looked like "two sets of double-stacked anti-tank mines," more than enough to take out a full tank. Instead, it had hit a little G-Wagon. "The Jeep itself had been blown apart, essentially blown in half, and the guys who were in it were also blown into pieces."

Schamuhn got the story from Justin MacKay, when he returned from leave. "He was very quiet," he says of MacKay, "a lot more quiet than usual, and he smoked a lot more cigarettes, and he just had a stare, like he would just stare off into the distance a lot more? And I asked him if he was willing to talk about it, and he told me just a little bit about what he had seen."

MacKay hadn't been far behind May and his section.

"When they got there, there were three of the guys in the Jeep who were obviously dead, and then the fourth one had very, very serious injuries but he was essentially still in one piece," Schamuhn says. "So on the radio, they were communicating that they had one Pri 1—Priority 1 casualty—and then three Pri 4s, which is vital signs absent. And I remember Justin saying that he had caught flak from whoever was operating the radios in the headquarters back at KAF, saying that they can only pronounce them dead once a doctor basically says, 'Yeah, this is KIA [killed in action], he's dead.' And Justin was really upset about that, because he was standing there, surrounded by body parts, and it was pretty fucking clear that the guys were dead."

MacKay recognized immediately what a catastrophic effect the scene would have on his young soldiers. As Schamuhn says, "Justin thought it best that as few people from the platoon as possible actually be involved in the scene management, so they spread the platoon out in an all-round defence to provide security, and then he took it upon himself, with the assistance of a couple of other guys, to clean up the mess."

Most of the troops were facing out, away from the carnage.

The convoy carried five body bags; it took all of them to package up the three broken men. At one point, the soldiers put an arm in a bag without knowing whose it was.

By the time Kirk Gallinger arrived from FOB Martello with 3 Platoon in tow, "They were just completely, they were fried, they were burned out. We relieved them and got them movin' back to the platoon house, and we spent the rest of that day cleaning up the wreckage. We made the decision that after the bodies had been evacuated, we [were] not going to leave anything but the crater, [nothing] for the enemy to have a public relations victory."

They combed through bushes, finding scraps of metal and other debris. "We cleaned everything up, and put it on the back of this vehicle, and wrapped a tarp around it, and we drove ourselves back to the platoon house," Gallinger says. "I tell you, they recognized Warrant MacKay for his leadership on that scene [he received a Mention in Dispatches] because you know there's no [way to understand], you literally can't imagine the difficulties and the things they had to deal with, and the level of control and the forethought that he had. He was just amazing. He was a rock, getting that site secured and cleaned up, and taking care of the troops."

Sean Ivanko and his 3 Platoon arrived two or three hours after Warrant MacKay. He knows they were lucky, getting there after the first awful cleanup was done. He knows enough to know what he and his troops were spared. It was hard enough to perform the final sweep of the area and then get back into their own G-Wagons, having just seen first-hand what a bomb could do to the lightly protected vehicles.

The worst for him came a couple of days afterwards, "as we went into the villages and talked to people, how they were saying they knew about it [the IED], and they didn't tell us. That was a lovely challenge to deal with as well."

Ivanko understands the reasons for the villagers' silence: fear of the Taliban; the complex terrain that would have required the villagers to walk or cycle five kilometres to the platoon house to tell the Canadians; fear of being spotted, if they risked making the trip, by people in rival villages who might tell the Taliban. Nonetheless, that was the first time Sean Ivanko, with his university degree in environmental science and his big brain, felt the fury and the primal need for vengeance that the Americans had warned him about. "It was a little startling, actually, that people are capable of such raw emotion," he says.

I think he means that he was startled to realize that *he* was capable of it. This was the dark side of Jimmy Sinclair's favourite time in the morning, when he'd hear the muezzin tap the microphone and with a flush of recognition think, "Hey, they do that too."

Justin MacKay and 1 Platoon remained out in the field, at Gumbad and FOB Martello, for another month. "They didn't really have the opportunity to get back and talk to anybody about it," Kevin Schamuhn says, "so it just started eating away at them."

—

KIRK GALLINGER SAYS it's hard to describe the period after Bill Turner was killed. "There was lots of support from peers and a lot of support from leaders, but a lot of people were really quiet, just contemplating life and doing a lot of thinking. It was a hard night in the platoon house. I still had guys coming up to me, months after the tour, saying, 'Jeez, I can remember [Turner] was saying he almost had a premonition he might not make it out, and he was telling guys, you know.'"

Gallinger and Schamuhn have divided the tour into two in their minds: the first long frustrating part, and the last part, when they were in combat almost daily. They talk about it sometimes as though it were cleanly divided, each piece lasting a little longer than three months.

But A Company's "first" tour lasted until the end of June, their fighting compressed into little more than four fast and furious weeks. For so long, for three-quarters of Roto 1, they had at best fleeting engagements with enemy on the mountains, occasionally chasing them through wadis, rarely even seeing who they were hunting let alone catching anyone.

Once FOB Martello opened, Gallinger rotated troops through both places. Martello was Canadian-built and purpose-built too—to act as a pit stop for the Dutch to move into Uruzgan Province, their area of operation, and get them there safely during the NATO expansion at the end of July—and ended up being a significant strategic and political accomplishment. John Conrad, who had a maintenance detachment and a diesel team there while the engineers were building the base, calls Martello "a real demonstration of Canadian resolve." Everyone was acutely aware—most of all the Dutch troops themselves—that if they suffered even some casualties getting in place, their government's will might have weakened.

One late July day, I jumped on a Canadian C-130 that was flying a contingent of Dutch soldiers to Tarin Kot, the Uruzgan provincial capital. "How's public opinion back home?" I asked the Dutch warrant officer, Hans Kievith, who was herding the troops into the belly of the plane.

It was fine at the moment, he said, adding, "There are no dead or injured people. That's when it changes. . . . It's the same in all the countries."

"Because we had Martello," Gallinger says, "the Dutch had enough confidence to make their way up north, and in fact they were able to move their whole task force up north without any incidents, without any losses. That was obviously a combination of a lot of things. For almost every convoy, at least at the start, we were providing intimate support for them. They had our reconnaissance troop escorting them as well. They had lots of support, and we were there [at Martello] essentially as a way station effectively securing the road, and it worked. The proof is in the fact they got up there safely."

The route to Martello is much safer than the route to Gumbad ever was. It's just off the Tarin Kot highway, paved almost the entire distance. That makes it significantly harder for the enemy to plant IEDs, usually buried in soft ground. But in the early going, the base was even more primitive than Gumbad—as Gallinger says, "just a dip in the ground" with vehicles keeping watch from the hills. It was a grim spot to be stranded.

For a time in May, there was intelligence that Gumbad was about to be attacked by large numbers of enemy; Ivanko and 3 Platoon were similarly stuck at Martello for a month, again under supposed threat of imminent attack and unable to leave. It was only because of his strong NCOs and his troops, Gallinger says, "that we got through it. But it was not what we [imagined], because at that point we didn't feel like we were having a huge impact in terms of convincing the local population about all of our themes and working with our Afghan partners. We were having an effect," he says, "but it was just so slow compared to Western standards that it was frustrating for us."

And all the while, the bombers were still at work, of course.

John Croucher's LAV was hit on May 25—cruelly, while 2 Platoon was out on a mission to look for IEDs and pronounce part of the route safe. "I called the sweep short of our last objective," Croucher says, "and switched to an exit route out of the wadi. We had been hit here before, and I thought it a great opportunity to confirm it a safe route again."

That done, just short of the platoon house, the troops mounted up and headed home on a route that had been swept just days before and pronounced secure. "Not two hundred metres into our return trek, the lead car, my car, got hit."

It was a remote-controlled, pressure-plate IED, which means the bomber would have had a couple of minutes to melt into the hills after activating it. With the plate buried slightly ahead of or behind the bomb, the IED would arm itself and blow within fifteen seconds of a vehicle's front tire hitting the plate. There was also a can of fuel beside the bomb, so with the explosion came a huge fire.

As crew commander, the thirty-three-year-old from Fredericton, New Brunswick, was the only one travelling at what he calls "blood level," his head and upper body out the turret. In that position, the LAV couldn't protect him, but its armour saved the seven soldiers inside.

"The explosion was incredible," he says, "and if it wasn't for the headset I had on and the protective goggles, injuries would have been a lot worse." Fire, dust, and smoke were everywhere. "My first words were, 'Oh shit, oh shit.'"

Feeling his legs burning, he tried to get out of the turret. "My first push with my arms told me that I was getting no help from my legs," he says. He managed to get out onto the back deck of the LAV, by now on fire "from toes to mid-body." He rolled himself off the vehicle and onto the ground so the troops would see him; they did.

With a broken fibula and tibia, a shattered ankle and heel, a huge puncture wound from shrapnel, and first- and second-degree burns on his right leg and hand, Croucher underwent emergency surgery at the base hospital, four more operations in Landstuhl, and another three when he got back to Edmonton.

Once again, Gallinger learned about the explosion over the radio net. He knew that Croucher had become engaged over his leave, knows the woman—now his wife—Nikki, and was tortured, thinking, "Omigod, the poor guy's not going to get a chance to get married."

Three or four days after Croucher was hit, Sean Ivanko and 3 Platoon were heading up to Gumbad to relieve the soldiers who had just lost their OC. A Company had by now developed an IED proto-col. It was almost etiquette, a matter of sheer good manners: When troops are coming in, you go to meet them and make sure the road is safe. So 2 Platoon was out clearing the route into Pada for the men of 3 Platoon when they spotted a couple of guys walking ahead of them, one carrying a brown sack.

At the sight of the soldiers, the men dropped the sack and started to run. Young Alex Wooley and a couple of his buddies jumped out of their G-Wagon and gave chase. One man got clean away, but Wooley and his pals stayed with the other, following him into the wadi. They spotted a pair of shoes sitting outside a small hole, no bigger than five feet by three feet.

"He's in there," Wooley said.

They called over their interpreter, had him tell the man to come out. Nothing. They threw smoke grenades into the hole. Nothing.

"It came down to someone had to go in there," Wooley says.

At that moment, Ivanko and 3 Platoon arrived.

The hole was so small that it was a matter of picking, as Ivanko says, "the ones whose Afghanistan Weight Loss Program" had worked really well. Master Corporal Billy Sesk from 3 Platoon and Wooley from 2 Platoon, the two skinniest guys, had to strip off their body armour and gear to squeeze in. Wooley had a fragmentation grenade and a magazine for his weapon in a pocket, and took a C8, a compact rifle. Sesk, armed only with a pistol, went in first.

They got in a metre or so when, Wooley says, "All I hear is this guy talking Pashtu. He's talking, he's coming closer." He and Sesk backed out of the hole, and out came their man after them, wires trailing from his pockets. Sesk and Wooley went back into the cave, and the further they went, the narrower it got, until they were on their knees, crawling in water. They went in about 125 metres, found a storage area, shot off a couple of rounds (temporarily deafening Wooley in his left ear), and were so scrunched up their shoulders were touching the walls, their heads pressed tight against the roof of the cave.

Outside, soldiers took the man to the ground, searched him, and found one thousand Pakistani rupees, a spider device for an IED, and a radio.

There was, Ivanko says, some of that dark fury. "We finally found someone who'd been doing this to us, and a few of the soldiers on the ground were becoming very aggressive. You could see [it] from both sides—2 Platoon, they'd been up there for a month, they were tired, and you could see some of the frustrations building up—and 3 Platoon too.

"I mean, did they do anything untoward? No, they didn't. Yes, they were angry; yes, they were yelling, but that was pretty much it. They got some fresh guys in there to take over, and then we brought the guy back with us, and ultimately, I hope, they were able to get information out of him."

I first heard about the kid from the Royal Regina Rifles—Wooley turned twenty-one just before he went to Kandahar and is that contradictions in terms, a full-time reservist—who had chased an IED bomber into a cave from Jim Sinclair. Coming from almost anyone else, I might have thought the story apocryphal.

"He had the balls to go in that dark little fricking cave," Sinclair says. "Takes a lot of courage." For Sinclair, the lesson was that "Canadian soldiers still have the get-up-and-go and the aggressive nature to get up and face the enemy."

About three weeks later, the company was hit again, this time resulting in two serious casualties. One was Martin Larose, the francophone exchange officer from the VanDoos, the Royal 22 Regiment of Canada (the PPCLI and the 22nd regularly exchange officers for two-year stints) who was Gallinger's second-in-command. The other was Ryan Elrick, a popular soldier adored by Gallinger as "always a pleasure to work with" who was grievously injured in the blast and ended up losing both legs.

Larose, whose ankles were basically smashed to pieces, was conscious the entire time, and is a remarkable and, if only about himself, bemused eyewitness.

He was freshly back from leave in Edmonton, where he'd met his new baby girl for the first time. He had scheduled leave around her anticipated birth, but she had arrived three weeks early. Larose and his girlfriend had been trying for three years to have a baby, and he was so delighted at the prospect of being a father that when his girlfriend told him, over the phone, "She has the face of a Daphne," he didn't even think about arguing the name.

He was returning to Afghanistan when Croucher was hit, and felt his absence keenly. Larose had extended his exchange stay so that he could be part of the Kandahar mission, and had worked with the big man for three years. Operation Mountain Thrust was still going on when Larose returned to KAF on May 31, with most of the company regrouping in FOB Martello and about to start missions in the north. As the company second-in-command, Larose was responsible for all things administrative, including replenishment, and he fretted about the guys at Gumbad. He wanted to get them resupplied because he didn't know when he'd next get the chance, and he didn't want them running short.

"So that's why we decided I had to go Gumbad and resupply them," he says. "It was just going to be like going in, and get out, the same day." He loaded up the convoy and left Martello, but en route they had a rash of the usual minor problems—flat tires and the like—and pulled in late. "It was getting really dark," Larose says. "The OC told me, 'Stay there, relax, it's not urgent you come back tonight.'"

They left early the next morning, were still in Pada, when Larose felt more than heard a huge bang. "I kind of felt myself going up," he says, "and after that, going down."

It was another enormous IED, two or three stacked anti-tank mines. Larose had been on the radio, talking to Gallinger, when it blew, and at the other end, the OC's heart sank. "I had about five seconds, I had Martin on the radio, I was just talking to him and he was on the radio and then he's no longer there," Gallinger says. "And I had the engineer sergeant come up on the radio and scream, 'One Niner Alpha!' and that was Martin's call sign, 'One Niner Alpha's been hit! He's been hit with an IED!'"

He lost communications with Larose completely then—the blast had fried the LAV's electronics. Playing in Gallinger's head were the pictures of the beautiful baby Larose had shown him. There wasn't a medic travelling with the convoy, which was now forty-five minutes from Gumbad.

Larose tried to get out of the LAV "to find the enemy and destroy it," realized his feet were hurt, and pulled himself out of the turret with his upper-body strength. "I looked at my feet, my right foot I thought was kind of done, that there was nothing to be done, there was so much blood. The boot was open, I was seeing the bones and all this stuff."

He looked for Corporal Elrick, "and I was not seeing anything, there was so much smoke inside the vehicle, I wasn't able to see anything. I was just hearing him, 'Ohhhh, my legs' and 'I don't feel my legs' and kind of screaming."

Troops from other LAVs rushed up and took Larose out, and he told them to go to Elrick. "They went in and removed Corporal Elrick and at that time I saw he was in really bad shape." A section from 2 Platoon under Master Corporal Chuck Prodnick secured the scene and then went on the offensive with guns blazing, allowing Prescott Shipway, a section commander with 3 Platoon, to do what he could for Elrick, by now unconscious.

"It was Sergeant Shipway," Gallinger says, "who had the presence of thought to get on a satellite phone and talk back to KAF and talk to a doctor, basically saying, 'This guy's dying on us.'" With the doctor talking him through the procedure, Shipway, who received a Mention in Dispatches for his leadership, and a couple of soldiers managed to get tourniquets on Elrick's legs.

"There was a lot of heroism," Gallinger says, "and they basically saved Corporal Elrick's life."

With the helicopter seeming to take forever and radio calls growing ever more frantic—"Blood pressure dropping, it's dropping, he's not gonna last!"—unable to rationalize staying put while Larose or Elrick was fading, Gallinger snapped.

"I finally had enough," he says. "I said, 'All right, that's it, we're gonna make our move to them.'" But Sergeant-Major Leger, whom Gallinger calls "my conscience," prevailed. Bill Fletcher was already racing to the scene from the south with an ambulance. He was closer, and Gallinger realized, "We couldn't have got there quick enough in the end" to help.

Less than a week later, the Canadians left Gumbad for good.

"Did you have a big fucking party?" I asked Gallinger once.

"We left in classic Canadian style," he said. "We threw one hell of a party."

Visions of the platoon house burning, as the soldiers gaily danced around it, maybe shooting off a few celebratory rounds as they bid farewell to the place that had done them such harm, ran through my head.

But no.

What Gallinger meant, of course, was that the day before the Patricias pulled out, they had a giant Village Medical Outreach (VMO) at the Gumbad District Centre. Warrant Officer Chris Thorne, the acting 3 Platoon commander because Ivanko was on leave, brought in a whack of medics and dentists, as well as an American veterinarian from Bagram. These doctors then saw and treated 469 local Afghans (men and children only; despite pleading, no women were allowed to go) and 136 animals.

The notes of Captain Marilynn Chenette, the medics' OC, show one unusual thing. Some of the locals who were treated then asked to help; they were posted at the polio vaccination and deworming stations, where they stayed for the duration of the clinic.

That was June 26, and then the medical folks left by chopper.

On the morning of June 27, the Patricias departed the platoon house. They were travelling with one of two American "route clearance packages" then on the ground in Afghanistan.

The package is an IED-buster.

The lead vehicle, called a Husky, is equipped with ground-penetrating radar and metal-detecting plates that raise and lower according to the terrain. The second vehicle is a heavily armoured Buffalo, which carries the explosives ordinance disposal guys, those brave souls who disarm and then blow up bombs. The rest of

the convoy are usually RG-31s, the South African anti-mine carrier, and Humvees.

On the way out—on the very route Kirk Gallinger would have
used on the day Larose and Elrick were hit—they found an IED.

Capt. Kevin Schamuhn

4 March 2006

—

"In general, and in contrast to the average member of Canadian society, soldiers answer to a higher calling . . . they tend to believe that duty and loyalty are important. They do not place the pursuit of happiness above duty. . . . They are even willing to sacrifice family life, to a certain extent . . ."

—FROM THE RESULTS OF THE ARMY'S
ORGANIZATIONAL CULTURE SURVEY, 2004

KEVIN SCHAMUHN and the men of Alpha Company's 1 Platoon had been on the ground in Afghanistan for almost a month when they headed out of their base at Gumbad for a village engagement, or *shura*, in Shinkay.

Especially in early March, Gumbad is all of a drab brown piece. The mountains around it are bald, treeless, and dun-coloured, with surrounding terrain to match. The platoon house itself, no longer in use, consisted of a low, long mud-walled compound and a big wooden gate. John D McHugh, an Irish photographer who spent some time at Gumbad when embedded with Canadian soldiers, refers to it simply as "the shithole."

So when a small element of the platoon, with the usual complement of ANA, pulled into Shinkay—their CIMIC officer, Trevor Greene, aboard as usual—they were gobsmacked.

This place, though only a few kilometres south of Gumbad, was gorgeous.

"It was a beautiful day," Schamuhn says, "and I remember the troops and me talking about how beautiful it was when we first showed up, because it was the only place up to that point in the tour that we had seen green grass, and there was some actual running water in the river, which is a novelty in that part of the country. Just a really nice river, green grass, blue sky, birds flying around. One of the troops said it was like Shangri-La, just a really nice peaceful spot, an oasis in the middle of the desert."

The introductions done, Greene and Schamuhn sat down on a blanket with three elders—"three white-beards," as Schamuhn calls them—with about twenty other men and boys looking on. Schamuhn noticed, peripherally, that some youngsters were playing with one of the ANA soldiers; one of his men was aware of a teenager moving the children away from the meeting.

"We thought it was cute how the ANA soldier was just interacting so well with the kids," Schamuhn says. "Didn't think anything of it."

Greene was a reservist, his regiment the Seaforth Highlanders of Canada. And like many reservists, at forty-one he was already an accomplished man. Rangy and good looking, six-foot-seven, he was a gifted athlete and rugby player, a business journalist, and the author of two books (*Bad Date*, about Vancouver's now-famous missing prostitutes, and *Bridge of Tears*, about the homeless in Japan, where he worked for a time). He had plans to do much more in Afghanistan.

Also, Greene was a new father: Baby Grace, then about fourteen months old, was back in Vancouver with fiancée, Debbie Lepore.

"So as Trevor was talking," Schamuhn says, "he had just started asking the villagers where the nearest medical station was, and if they had a school, and I remember him asking if they *did* have a school, if they would allow girls to go. And the [Afghans] just got a good chuckle after that, because they couldn't really understand why you'd send girls to school."

They were sitting cross-legged, Greene about six feet from Schamuhn on his left, in between them the interpreter. Sergeant Rob Dolson was to Schamuhn's right, a little behind him. As Greene talked, one of the young men standing behind him moved forward. He was wearing, as do many Afghan men, a blanket over one shoulder. Schamuhn heard him scream, "Allahu Akbar! [God is great!]," and for a second looked up at him, looked him square in the eyes, "big, golf ball-sized, bloodshot eyes."

"I didn't see the axe," Schamuhn says. "I don't think anyone really did, because he was holding it behind his head. And there was just the sound of the river kind of flowing in the background, and birds flying around chirping, and kids playing off to the side. It was just such a peaceful, calm place, and then that was just ripped away with this guy's scream, and we just didn't know what was going on.

"And then he just sunk the axe right into Trevor's head and it was like, I remember it was probably more like a yelp than anything else, but something, my vocal cords just kind of flexed and some weird sound came out. I was just fucking horrified."

He saw Greene's eyes roll back in his head.

"And then I remember looking down at my C8, my weapon, and picking it up and kind of stumbling backwards and staring at the safety, trying to get the fucking safety off as fast as possible, but it seemed like it took a minute. And as soon as it was off, I just pointed it at that guy and just fired three rounds before I was even on my feet. Sergeant Dolson, who was to my right, had already fired a couple of shots, and one of the other troops, Private Matt McFadden, was also shooting at the same time."

The attacker took fourteen rounds in about a second and a half, two at most, and was dead before he fell. The young man flopped to the ground, the axe dropped, and suddenly everyone scattered. Rockets started to go off.

"I had no fucking clue what was happening," Schamuhn says. "I could barely breathe. I remember my chest was really, really tight, and my gut was just twisted. I just had a hard time breathing. I kept saying, 'What the fuck! What the fuck!' I just said that over and over and over, just trying to make sense of what I had just seen."

He walked past Greene, saw his head split open, saw pieces of his brain, small bits of brain matter, on the ground. "And I'm just like, 'Holy fuck, man!' I just started yelling out, 'Medic! Medic! Medic!' He came running and I just basically gave him a quick, 'All right, he took an axe to the head, do what you can, he's right over there.'"

Schamuhn ran back to his G-Wagon to call in the contact report. "I was breathing so heavy and I could hardly catch my breath and I would just stop, take a deep breath in, and then transmit. And just pass on as much information as I could in one breath, and then just end the transmission, and then start gasping for air again."

Listening to this, much further south in the district of Khakrez, was A Company commander Kirk Gallinger, suffering, not for the last time, the powerlessness of not being there.

"I was scared shitless, I'll be honest with you," Schamuhn says. "I was so deathly afraid—just because there were bullets flying around, and it's one thing to get into a gunfight, but it's another thing to have a gunfight initiated by seeing one of your friends take an axe in the head, six feet in front of you, so it was just panic, like I was just panicking."

He did the smartest thing he could have done under the circumstances: went over and talked to Dolson. "It was probably the most helpful thing," Schamuhn says, "to bring my nerves back down. Because he was processing really quickly what he had just done, like we just wasted a guy and his dead body was lying ten feet away from us, and he was just really processing that. And it helped me kind of bring myself back into the present moment, and try and figure out what the hell was going on, if we were getting ambushed or if it was the ANA firing at the civilians or what."

It was not an ambush by a crazed loner. The soldiers later found a line of machine gun fire from an AK-47 along the side of one of the ANA trucks, and a tire on one of the G-Wagons was hit by a bullet and flattened.

They were still under attack, bullets were still flying, but Schamuhn and Dolson soon realized "they weren't hitting us, they weren't hitting our vehicles, and we weren't in any grave danger." They wouldn't have to move Greene to a safer area to have him evacuated by chopper.

"In the chaos that ensued," Schamuhn says, "I remember thinking very clearly that this is it. This is where all of your training comes in. This is where everything is important. This is real, this is actually happening, and these are the moments where you shit or get off the pot, especially as the guy in charge of that situation."

He talked to the medic after that. He did it as a matter of protocol, almost as a pro forma inquiry, never imagining Greene could be alive. "And to my surprise, he told me that the vital signs were stable. His breathing was I think about fourteen breaths a minute, and his pulse was at sixty beats per minute, and I was dumbfounded. I thought Trevor was dead for sure."

But the medic, Corporal Sean Marshall, also told him: "Yeah, he's fine, he's alive, but we gotta get the medevac in here *now*, we gotta get him evacuated as soon as possible because this could sour really quickly."

Two choppers were coming in, a U.S. Black Hawk under escort of a U.S. Apache gunship. Schamuhn had a soldier on standby to pop a smoke grenade, to mark the landing zone, as soon as he saw the choppers; he did, but the grenade was a dud. A second one was also a dud.

In the meantime, Schamuhn and three soldiers were carrying Greene on a stretcher, heading for the landing zone. Greene had begun to vomit, and with his jaw clamped shut so tight the medic couldn't pry it open, the men were frantic. "He's choking, he's on his back," Schamuhn says. "He could die from just lying there."

The third smoke grenade worked, "but by that time the helicopters had pretty much determined their own landing spot and they went about two hundred metres, maybe one hundred to two hundred metres, further away from us than I had planned for, so we had to pick up the stretcher with Trevor and then run down the river valley as fast as we could to get him on the helicopter."

In the din of the choppers, they got the stretcher on the Black Hawk. "The Canadian stretchers don't fit on Black Hawks," Schamuhn remembers, "and that's not exactly the time that you want to find out something like that. So we put him on and the fucking door wouldn't close." Over the roar of the rotor blades, Schamuhn yelled loud enough that the on-board medic understood, and immediately began to get Greene's jaw open and clear his airway.

"So I don't know if they got the door closed or they chopped the handles off or what they did. I remember just feeling like, 'Holy fuck, can anything else possibly go wrong?'"

The story reminded me of something I'd seen twenty-six years earlier, when Terry Fox learned that his cancer had returned and was forced to stop his cross-Canada run in northern Ontario. At an impromptu press conference in the downstairs meeting room of a Thunder Bay motel, before he was flown home to British Columbia, the young man I'd seen just a week earlier—who had looked so strong and beautiful I thought he would surely live forever—was carried in on a stretcher to tell a small knot of reporters what we already knew.

Fox's stretcher wouldn't fit either; the doorway was too narrow.

The message was the same: No tragedy, however enormous, however heart-busting, is ever big enough to do away with the ordinary humiliations that life dishes out.

"After that, things got quiet," Schamuhn says, "and I went to jack up the locals. I went up to talk to them. And there were about seven old men, really old men, and a whole bunch of women and children that had been rounded up by the ANA, and I just laid into them. I just didn't care. I was yelling at them and swearing at them and I told them that if they wanted to make sure that they never see a hospital again, if they wanted to make sure their kids never went to school and were always in a war-torn country, then they should keep up exactly what they had just done that day, which is either being a part of the attack or knowing about it and not doing anything to prevent it."

Schamuhn's public description of what had happened, given shortly after the attack, was as calm and lucid as his radio transmissions were that day, despite how rattled he thought he sounded. He also had a perfect audience—back at the platoon house at Gumbad was veteran journalist Mitch Potter of the *Toronto Star*, who with photographer Rick Madonik had been embedded with A Company for the previous week.

The *Star* team had accompanied Greene, Schamuhn, and 1 Platoon on most of the dozen engagements they conducted with villages in the area, watched them, as Potter wrote in a moving story that appeared in the March 5 edition, begin to develop "a bond, however fragile" with the locals.

At Gumbad on the very day before he was attacked, as they sat around the fire that soldiers call caveman TV because of the way everyone inevitably stares mesmerized at the flames, Greene told Potter that he hoped "I still have some naïveté that hasn't been beaten out of me. I want to work with the United Nations for a few years, not because I have great faith in the UN, but just so I can learn how the system really works." Then, he said, he planned to strike out on his own. "I have friends out west who are on the same wavelength. We want to start an organization that can really get to the core needs of Afghanistan."

I read the story and watched the coverage from Canada; I was leaving for Kandahar for the first time, via New Delhi and Kabul, on March 6. It was an assignment I was iffy about: I had no particular interest in Afghanistan and knew just enough to be apprehensive. But Potter's compelling piece, with its portraits of Greene and Schamuhn, did away with any ambivalence. For the first time, I think, I had a glimpse of the complexity of the mission, the country, and the Canadian soldier.

Schamuhn's frankness, with Potter and in a phone interview he did with other media, including CTV's Lisa LaFlamme (the audio of which was still available on network websites early in 2007), garnered enormous attention in Canada. It also quickly came to be regarded by army public affairs officers (PAOs) and their bureaucratic masters in Ottawa as a mistake.

I know that by the time I got to KAF less than ten days later, the conventional wisdom was that the twenty-six-year-old captain—raised on the Prairies and in Chilliwack, British Columbia, and a graduate of the Royal Military College in Kingston, Ontario—had been too forthcoming. At least one PAO told me directly that never again would a soldier involved in an incident be so immediately available to the press.

This was couched in concern for Schamuhn and his psyche, of course. The spin was that he should have been debriefed and counselled before being put in front of the reporters—shades of the view prevalent in the Canadian Forces in the late 1980s through the 1990s of the soldier as a creature of delicate mental constitution. The concern may have been genuine, but I thought it showed a patronizing misreading of the man—as well as the Canadian public—and, as important, was indicative of a corporate reluctance to trust the judgment of the soldiers who were actually on the ground.

Who better to determine if Schamuhn was fit to speak about what he freely admits was probably the worst day of his life than the men who most loved and knew him? I've seen soldiers protect their own when they need protecting, whether from their own folly or from reporters. If NCOs like Rob Dolson and Justin MacKay saw no need to slow Schamuhn down that night or keep him under wraps, there was none. In fact, Schamuhn had spoken to Major Tod Strickland, Ian Hope's second-in-command, before talking to the press, and Strickland had encouraged him to shoot from the hip.

As for the effects of his raw accounting upon Canadians, I thought it was precisely his naked honesty (and the careful and intelligent way that Mitch Potter wrote about the attack, thus establishing, as the first major newspaper story often does, the tone that subsequent coverage would take) that marked a significant turning point in the court of Canadian public opinion. Suddenly, a couple of things seemed to come clear to the back-home audience. One was that Afghanistan was a place where danger did not always arrive by conventional means but could come from any quarter at any time. The second was that whatever one's view of the mission as an expression of Canadian foreign policy, those young soldiers were pretty damn impressive.

Schamuhn found speaking out helpful. "It may seem insignificant," he says, "but something as minor as hearing a female voice [Lisa LaFlamme] on the other end had a very soothing effect on me. We've been told numerous times by mental health staff that often the best remedy for dealing with traumatic events is talking through the details with others who were there." Speaking to reporters, while not the same thing, was useful for him.

"I can understand the effects of the public affairs types, though," he says. "I imagine that having front-line solders give unedited accounts of military actions could be a bit nerve-racking. That being said, I'm definitely glad I slipped through the cracks."

Much trickier to work through was the effect of the incident upon him—or as he puts it, "inside of me"—and how to make sense of the tacit acquiescence of the locals who knew or suspected the attack was coming. "I feel like the wrong that was done was immediately and remorselessly answered with an equal, opposing reaction," Schamuhn says. "That is, our bullets. I have never felt even an ounce of guilt or uneasiness about having taken that guy's life."

But the experience forced him to go deeper than just feeling betrayed, and set him on a complicated journey: "Why Trevor, and not me? Was the young guy who hit Trevor part of something bigger, or just a local headcase that was paid off? Why was it so difficult for the locals to understand that we were there to help?"

Schamuhn knew, from the get-go, that "the country was messed up and would take more than a quick fix to resolve itself. I knew that it would take a lot of energy—more than we were capable of giving—to help undo the wrong in that country."

That view was solidified by his interior examination. "We, as a Western society, want to stop terrorism, so we try to kill as many Taliban as possible before they kill us," he says. "The fact is, if we want to stop terrorism, we should start by avoiding whatever it is that sets these guys off in the first place. The idea that soldiers fight to resolve the problems of their fathers rings true.

"Also, the concept of soldiers providing aid to the masses is difficult enough for Canadians to wrap their heads around, much less a local Afghan who has associated foreign occupation with turmoil since the day he was born. We never really help, so why would they trust us? All we really do is ask them the same questions they've been asked for decades. Do their crops get better? No. Do schools get built? Rarely. Do living conditions improve at all? Hardly.

"We ought to try to come up with a little more incentive for the locals to side with us rather than accuse them of siding with terrorism.

"After that horrible day, my skin got real thick real fast, but it didn't prevent me from trusting again; I just had to rely on my intuition a lot more. We also learned to remove as many variables from the equation as possible; that is, only engage in situations in which we had the upper hand. Unfortunately, the more comfortable we made ourselves, the less comfortable the locals inevitably were—a delicate balance, to be sure."

Schamuhn and his wife, Annalise, a logistics officer in the military, have formed a business. They plan to earn enough capital (mostly from small real estate investments they have begun making with the proceeds from the sale of their house in Edmonton) to become self-sufficient, then they'll begin establishing aid projects around the world. The business takes its name from the Parable of the Talents described in Matthew 25:14–30.

In the story, a man going away on a trip called in his faithful servants and entrusted each with a number of talents, a talent in Biblical days being a weight of precious metals such as silver. Two of the servants invested or traded their talents, and were able to return more to the master, but a third, fearful, effectively just crossed his fingers. He buried the talent and was able to give back the master only what he'd been given.

The message is that as God's stewards, human beings have the responsibility not only to grow their own gifts but also to help others grow theirs.

"In a nutshell," Schamuhn says, "[we plan to] make tons of money, quit our day jobs, and live out the rest of our lives helping people—and surfing every now and then."

—

JUST HOURS BEFORE Trevor Greene arrived at the Landstuhl Regional Medical Center on Sunday, March 5, Tim Wilson's casket was loaded onto another aircraft at the large U.S. air base at nearby Ramstein, a ninety-minute trip from Frankfurt on one of Germany's speedy autobahns, for the journey back to Canada.

The day before, the same day that young man had buried his axe in the back of Greene's head, Wilson was formally pronounced dead at 2.50 p.m. Frankfurt time. The machines had kept him going only long enough for his organs to be harvested. His organs helped save the lives of seven people who were strangers to him, and his cornea and soft tissues benefited still others.

Wilson suffered devastating head trauma on March 2 when the LAV he was crew-commanding was T-boned by a taxi in Kandahar, caught the shoulder of the road, and rolled over three or four times, tearing the turret from the vehicle. Corporal Paul Davis, the gunner who was in the turret with Wilson, was also fatally injured. Several other soldiers were injured, though less seriously. All were with the 2nd Battalion, Princess Patricia's Canadian Light Infantry, Bravo Company, now based at Shilo, about thirty kilometres east of Brandon in southern Manitoba. Twenty-eight-year-old Davis died at the base hospital at KAF shortly after the accident, but Wilson stayed alive.

Cruelly, when the 2nd Battalion, which was then the army's reserve battalion, got word that it would be supplying the third company for Kandahar and Bravo was chosen, both Davis and Wilson had an easy out if they wanted it. Davis already had put in for an occupational transfer; deployment would stall that. Wilson, due for promotion to sergeant, was slated to take a necessary section commander's course, and there was no promise as to when he'd get another chance.

B Company commander Nick Grimshaw sat down with both men and put it to them: "What do you want to do? Stay in Canada, or deploy and no guarantee?"

Neither hesitated: They would deploy.

Sergeant Guy Britten had known Wilson for five years. He was the second person Britten had met when he arrived at the 2nd Battalion, when it was still located in Winnipeg, and "right from the get-go we hit it off." Originally, both were signallers—the communications guys—though Wilson was always an infanteer who also handled the radios, while for Britten coms was his specialty and trade.

It seemed they were always tasked together: They were on Operation Apollo, the Canadian military's first mission to Afghanistan, for five months in 2002; they roomed together; they had leave together in Dubai; they were on the same crew commander course and later taught it together; they fought fires together. In off hours, they'd play squash and socialize at the junior ranks' mess.

They ended up in Kandahar at the same time too, Britten arriving on February 12, four days after Wilson—just enough time for the considerate thirty-year-old to lay down some flooring and get Britten's quarters nicely set up for him. But whereas Britten's job with the National Command Element at brigade headquarters kept him tethered to the base at KAF, working in the building adjacent to the media office tents, Wilson was now a section second-in-command with Bravo Company's 4 Platoon, the long-range patrol platoon, and so was outside the wire all the time, regularly travelling those demented Kandahar streets and beyond.

The platoon was in the process of moving to the smaller Canadian Provincial Reconstruction Team base in Kandahar, but while still at KAF, Wilson's and Britten's tents were only about five hundred metres apart, and they saw each other frequently.

A day, maybe two, before the accident, they grabbed an iced cappuccino at the Tim Hortons and shot the shit. "We sat down and talked a bit," Britten says. "He was getting his hair cut. His last words to me were, 'Fucking quit smoking.' I told him I would on the twenty-first, it was just the day I picked, and I did."

The day of the crash, word got around KAF, as it always does. Britten heard there had been an accident, that it involved B Company, but "I heard it wasn't a G-Wagon and I was relieved."

Until then, Wilson had travelled exclusively in a G-Wagon.

Britten knew he had no need to know, didn't want to go poking his nose in, "so I just say, 'I came from Shilo. Those are guys I know, so when it's released . . .' I kept working."

After an early dinner, he went down to the Bravo Big Ass Tent and saw Jamie Leck, who pulled him aside and told him that Davis had been killed, and that Wilson was seriously injured, though he seemed better now. Britten went straight to the hospital and asked to see his friend.

"I just hung out with him," Britten says.

Darren Haggerty and a couple of the other less gravely injured soldiers from the crash were also there, and they took a lot of smoke breaks, and talked. Britten phoned his fiancée, Mandy.

"When I first walked in there," Britten says, "there were tubes and stuff everywhere, but he looked strong and healthy. His vitals were good. I'm sure others have gone through this, it's a common thing to see the machines and everything, the crash team. It's intricate, to get someone wired up like that."

He and Wilson just talked, Britten says, then corrects himself: "Well, I talked. I told him he was probably sick of me talking. I joked around . . . you know how you run out of things to say, so you joke around, and sometimes you say serious stuff to him. You don't know if it's helping or not, but if there's even the smallest chance [he can hear] . . . it can't do any harm."

At some point, he saw the doctors perform tests to assess the severity of Wilson's brain injury, and got a better look at his unconscious friend when the sheet was pulled down. It began to sink in how gravely hurt Wilson was. Realizing he might have to be flown to Landstuhl, Britten spoke to his CO and RSM and told them, "If he goes to Germany, I'd like to go, make sure he's good to go, and then I'll come back."

While escorts are always sent with dead soldiers, they are rarely appointed for the wounded. A medical escort goes on the plane with the soldier, of course, and sometimes his family is flown from Canada to meet him in Germany, but almost never does a fellow soldier escort him.

Britten spent a panicky few hours trying to make arrangements, not sure when Wilson was going to be moved, because for a while he wasn't stable enough to be moved. When the docs gave the go-ahead, it all happened quickly. It was Grimshaw who finally cut through the last of the red tape and got Britten on the flight.

Britten was terribly anxious as Wilson was loaded onto the Boeing C-17. "It was hard to see him be moved . . . it's precise, like firing the space shuttle. It's a pretty intense procedure." He sat beside his friend throughout, occasionally nodding off from sheer exhaustion, knowing the crash team was right there.

"Tim was on a stretcher," he says. "I just hung out with him. There isn't a person who wasn't helpful, it was embarrassing, everybody coming up and saying, 'Do you need anything?' You don't want anything. You just want to hang out."

At Landstuhl, there were CAT scans, and then a major and a neurosurgeon came out and told Britten that Wilson was brain-dead.

"'Tim's brain-dead,' he says. "You don't know and you hope for the best. Daphne [his wife] and Jane [his mother] were flying in. Meeting the next of kin," Britten says. "I was just so worried about it. It wasn't a burden, it was a huge sense of making sure you do everything right, a huge sense of responsibility." He knew it would comfort them to see someone they know. "It was tough, tough meeting Jane. Jeez, they were good about it—good isn't the right word. But they were strong."

He tried not to let himself feel it. "There are times when it hits you," he says. "There are things I saw that would make the hardest people [cry], but what overrides that is the responsibility. You have things to do for them, what Jane and Daphne need, and what Tim would want."

Daphne and Tim had discussed organ donation before, she says. It was a no-brainer for her, and "Tim was kind of ambivalent about the whole thing. His attitude was, 'I'm not going to need them anymore, so whatever.'" The idea was first broached when she was still in Shilo; she agreed immediately. "That Tim's death could bring hope to someone else's family has been one of the few tangible comforts that has come out of this," she says.

Britten went in to see Wilson as he was formally pronounced dead, said his own goodbye, and was there when Jane and Daphne said theirs. "Jane was reading a letter she'd written to Tim, and Daphne was reading letters from Jesse and Sheralynn [they were then nine and thirteen]," he says. "I felt like I was in a movie or something. I was very detached from what was happening, but even in that state could not stop the tears. I was thinking more along, 'Jesus, is this really happening?'"

Britten's work began in earnest. From now on, Wilson was solely his responsibility. Every time his body was moved, examined, touched, dressed, carried, or regarded, Britten would be with him.

He, Master Corporal Alonzo Hampton, and the others practised how they would carry him onto the plane for the flight back to Canada. Britten was furious that when the time came, it didn't go as smoothly as he wanted, if only for an instant—when the pallbearers went to lift the casket, they found it was still strapped down. "Tim would have found it funny," he says, "but I was pretty pissed off. It was one of the few times I sort of broke down. I was pretty pissed off it wasn't perfect."

As he explains, for the Canadian military, caring for the dead isn't "something that happens a lot. We're not experts at this. The Americans are very precise; they've had a lot more practice. They're better at it. They're more proficient, but less personal."

The aircraft came from Kandahar and was already carrying Paul Davis: The two men who had been mortally injured in the same crash would go home to CFB Trenton together. Thus began a whole new worry for Britten: The soldiers' caskets were identical, and he was tortured by the thought that they somehow would be switched and returned to the wrong family. "It sounds stupid, but it could possibly happen, and this is why you're overly anal about it. You gotta keep checking—This is Tim; this is Paul.'"

At Trenton, Britten says, they emerged from the plane to bright sunshine, crowds of dignitaries, cameras flashing. "Tim didn't like cameras," he thought to himself. "Tim I doubt would ever sit down in this environment." After the repatriation ceremony, Britten accompanied Wilson to the coroner's office in Toronto for the requisite post-mortem.

"I had a need to tell this story afterwards," Britten says. "Soon after, I had a compulsion to tell the highlights and the horrors. I'm not usually much of a talker," he says, unnecessarily, because if there is a man as rent with sorrow and twisted with constraint, I've not yet met him.

"When you move a body, you have it on ice," he says. "That's just the way it is. They're very heavy. It's why when you see troops struggling, it's because it's a metal casket full of ice and the body itself. If you're watching TV and it looks like they're having a tough time, it's because they are."

By the time Wilson's casket had travelled from Germany to Trenton to the hearse that took the body to Toronto, much of the ice had melted. Whenever the driver touched the brakes on the highway, Britten heard the sound of water sloshing. "It's like a cooler full of beer, water going back and forth. I'll never forget the sound of the water shooting back and forth. I'll never forget that."

Then came the flight to Winnipeg, the Air Canada crew bumping him unbidden to first class, "the stews almost in tears." He was in his desert camos, a Canadian flag (it had flown in Germany at the small ramp ceremony for Wilson at the airport) neatly folded on his lap, Wilson's name on the flag.

"I'll never forget the hurt I saw in the eyes of the lady sitting next to me," he says. "You know they knew what the flag meant, and some people just didn't know what to say. It's hard to see people's sympathies or hear them. It makes you face what you are really doing, which is taking your dead friend home to his family."

As he walked off the plane—"from the dark of this place into the light"—again there was a crowd of people. He met Wilson's dad, Dale. He watched the pallbearer team, got into another hearse, and went with Wilson's body to the funeral home.

"Officially, that's the end of it," he says, meaning the end of his official escort duties. But Daphne and Jane had asked him to give the eulogy. "I was honoured by it, but it scared the shit out of me," he says. "I'm not someone who likes public speaking."

When the time came, he felt as if someone was there with him, calming him down. "Tim was there," he says. "Sort of." By everyone's account, Britten did a sterling job. Among the things he said was that "Tim was about truth."

He was a pallbearer one last time. "All those times, and all the little ones like from the morgue to the funeral home, we tried to make it as formal and respectful as possible. We paid him and Paul full compliments. That's saluting, standing at attention."

Even after his official duties were over, he was around, helping out. "There comes a point when your responsibility is not just to Tim, but to the people around him, a point where things tend to be for them." Many times, people would ask him, 'Are you okay?' or tell him they were proud of him. "It was shameful to hear them say that," he says. "It was a drop in the bucket compared to what Tim would do."

Britten found such kindness almost unendurable. "It's hard," he says. "Like it taps in directly to what you're really feeling for some reason. It goes down to the grief or whatever. I found that weird. I've never experienced that before."

He had a few days at home, with his wife, Mandy, and their children, six-year-old Brady and Caiden, their baby girl of almost a year. These were difficult days, awkward. "You get so good at having something to do," he says, "and not dealing with it." He was anxious to get back to theatre and was also riven with guilt. "I'm doing this, Tim's dead, and I'm sort of at home, and Mandy wants to spend some time as a family, but is it bad to sit there and smile with your son you won't see again in however many months and your daughter, and lay with your wife?"

Britten returned to Kandahar, and was home on leave when I met him at Mandy's mother's house in Winnipeg. The day after my visit, he suffered what appeared to be a heart attack. It wasn't, as it turns out, but rather cardiomyopathy, an inflammation of the heart muscle. The fit thirty-four-year-old had picked up the virus in Afghanistan. He was unable to return to theatre, though he has since fully recovered.

"When you can see and feel the effects of a loss of a soldier on yourself and his family and friends," he wrote me in an email later, "you see the cost of what we are doing. I'm not here to decide if what we are doing is worth that price, but I wonder how many people would support it if they had to pay that price first-hand."

I know reasonably well another soldier who was Wilson's friend, and who learned what sort of man he was. The two trained together for

Joint Task Force 2 "selection"—JTF 2 is Canada's elite special operations force, and selection is the brutal weeding-out process held
every September to which only 1 to 2 percent of Canadian soldiers
even dare subject themselves. Fewer than 10 percent of the few who
try out make it through to the end of the seven-day test.

Now with another elite unit of the Canadian Forces, the soldier
can't be identified. Jokingly, he suggested I call him by his porn name.

"By proper protocol," he said, "my porn name should be the name
of my first dog, combined with the name of the first street I lived on.
So in that case, my name should be Tipper Taylor." It is not, as he
says, the greatest porn name, but it will do.

Taylor first met Wilson at the track behind the gym in Shilo.
"There aren't many people who get out at 6:30 to hurl themselves
around in circles in the cold fall air, or to tread water in the pool
with a ten-pound rubber brick," he says. The few who did gravitated
to one another. Wilson didn't talk much, but genuinely listened, and
over the course of a few weeks, "we got to be pretty good friends,
sharing experiences and anxieties."

Taylor had been on JTF selection before, and the one thing he'd
learned was that the process is so tough you have to be able to ask
for help from the men on your serial, and be willing to help them, to
be the best team player you can be. "It doesn't mean you're weak,"
Taylor says. "Everyone is weak at some point. They help you get
through, and it's almost guaranteed you will have the opportunity to
return the favour. Tim really took that to heart."

Taylor had drawn the last seven-day serial of the year, with
Wilson going before him. He'd injured his knee just before his serial
started, and Taylor was worried about him. "You can't go into that
process wounded," he says. "You have to go in 100 percent."

Sure enough, Wilson's bad knee ended his attempt early and he
returned to Shilo after only a few days. "It's tough to come home like
that," Taylor says. "It's exhilarating to get to the big show, but after
investing all that time and effort it is a big letdown to come home
early. What makes it even worse is that so few people go through that,
so how can anyone relate to how hard it is?" They went out for coffee.

Taylor's turn came, and just before he left, Wilson showed up with some expensive and valuable kit: a Gore-Tex stealth suit to wear under combat gear and a softie, a warm and highly compressible jacket.

"It was a big deal to me, and helped out a lot," Taylor says.

This time, Taylor survived the full seven days, but still wasn't good enough to make the team. "I came back feeling pretty down," he says. "It was by far the hardest thing I'd ever done, physically and mentally. It was even tough emotionally. Essentially, it was seven days of being told, and having it demonstrated, how stupid you are. If you get picked up, it's easy to dump all of that and say it's bullshit, but if you're not, well, that makes it pretty damn difficult to sort it all out."

Worse, Taylor had signed up for Search and Rescue Technician selection, a comparable ordeal, and had to prepare himself to go out and do it all over again in a matter of weeks. "This time," he says, "it was Tim's turn to make me feel better."

They went out for coffee again. Wilson helped him gather the shreds of his confidence and introduced him to two fellows from 2nd Battalion PPCLI who were also trying out, and who cheered him up.

When they arrived in Edmonton, one of those men handed him Wilson's stealth suit. "Tim knew I was too shy to ask for it again," he says. "He was absolutely right. I had wanted it, but didn't want to impose. Once again, he was saving my ass."

Taylor made it through the two weeks, was deemed an "acceptable" candidate, but again wasn't selected. "It was a really heavy blow," he says. "I came up short—again."

Wilson took him for coffee in their now familiar ritual and "I got one of the best compliments of my life. I remember he told me that nobody could look me in the eye and tell me I was a failure after having survived two selections back to back." As Taylor proceeded to put himself back together, he kept replaying in his head what Wilson had said.

On March 2, 2006, there was still snow on the ground in Shilo. Taylor was trudging through the field behind the gym where he and

Wilson used to hurl themselves around the track. As soon as he got to work, he checked the Internet for news from Afghanistan, as he always does, and learned about the crash.

"I don't have a lot of friends," he says. "I have a lot of acquaintances, and people I know, but only a select few people that I really make an effort to keep in touch with. Soldiering is a peripatetic lifestyle, and that makes it easy to drift in and out of friendships. Tim was a keeper."

———

DAPHNE AND TIM WILSON were married for almost five years, and never had an anniversary together.

On their first anniversary, he was in Afghanistan on Operation Apollo; on their second, in Wainwright; on their third, in Shilo (they still had a house in Winnipeg, and Daphne and the kids were there); on their fourth, in the field on a three-day exercise. "We joked that his leave from Afghanistan might fall over our fifth anniversary and that he might come home," she says. "Tim felt that might be bad luck."

They lived on a farm about twenty kilometres southwest of Shilo, where Daphne still operates the horse sanctuary they started in February 2005. It's not an anti-slaughter organization, she says, but rather a charity that gives horsemen another option when the time comes to give up a horse.

She works at a daycare centre in Souris, exactly fifty-one kilometres away, and on the day of the crash there was a storm. She tried to leave the house at 6 a.m., made it only a little way down their road and had to turn back. "Right before leaving the house, I had heard the report on the radio of persons being killed and injured in Afghanistan," she says, but believed Tim was safe because she hadn't received a phone call.

When she returned to the house, she poured another coffee and turned on the computer to see if she could learn more about the accident. "Nothing had been posted on any of the news sites yet," she says.

"I remember seeing vehicles at the end of my driveway. They were stopped, and I assumed it was one of my neighbours who had seen my tracks going in and out of the drive and was checking to see if I was okay; rural people do that. Even when the vehicles turned into the drive and came up to the house, I still thought it was either a neighbour or someone looking for a phone who had pulled in because the house lights were on.

"I couldn't see what kind of vehicles they were, so I went to open the garage door. The padre was standing there. I don't remember seeing his face, only his uniform and the cross on his rank patch. I remember saying something like, 'You can't be here' or 'You can go now.' I never imagined I would see the padre at my door."

Every morning now, as she gets up in the dark, she hears the two gravel trucks that drive down the road toward her house. She knows where they're going; she knows they are not coming for her. "Every morning," she says, "I relive that moment until they pass my house, and I remember they can't deliver that news twice."

She and the kids are doing okay. All of the firsts—birthdays and Christmas, particularly—without him were difficult. "We've tried to set up small remembrances," she says. At Christmas, one of their traditions is that everyone picks out one new and special decoration for the tree; last year, they each picked one and then added one for Tim. Tim's brothers have been a terrific support, she says, as have their parents. "Guy [Britten] has also taken the time to give Jesse some 'man time' and do some of the things that girls just don't understand," she says. "I think this mainly involves *Star Wars*, but I'm not sure."

The loneliness, the missing him, hits her at the oddest times. She had to buy flannel sheets: "My cats don't create the kind of body heat that he did." The worst time is late at night, "when married couples have those lying-in-the-dark conversations. . . . I miss him when I'm grocery shopping and I still automatically want to buy Gatorade and cottage cheese, two items that were exclusively his. I miss him when I see a couple that has obviously been together for many years, and I know we never had a chance to get to that stage."

Some of the soldiers and wives in Shilo set up a fund after the crash. Originally established to show solidarity for the Davis and Wilson families, it soon morphed into a broader vision. In April 2006, when the organizers had a social at the Brandon Armoury to raise money, I attended to write a story for *The Globe*.

Yellow ribbons were tied to the tables and yellow sashes were around every slender waist. There was a bar and music, and despite the evening's sombre purpose, the dance floor soon filled with young couples, all dressed up and naturally irrepressible. I couldn't imagine a worse place, a harder place, for a brand new widow to be, but Daphne came, of course, because she knew the sight of her would comfort the others.

Nineteen days later, when Tim Wilson had been dead two months to the day, she celebrated her fifth wedding anniversary.

Shura *in Maynard at the district centre*

24 June 2006

—

"I thought, 'Well, there you go—the highway police are shooting at us now.'"

—MAJOR NICK GRIMSHAW, OFFICER COMMANDING,
BRAVO COMPANY, 2ND BATTALION PPCLI

WHEN NICK GRIMSHAW FLEW out of Afghanistan for leave on May 17, 2006, the countryside of Kandahar Province was still so safe that the long-range patrol element of his company, not to mention his own small headquarters group, was able to travel about with relative abandon. Most of the time, his headquarters—which consisted of two LAVs and two G-Wagons—would roll out with the patrol element, but not always. "Sometimes they'd go off on their own, and I'd link up with them later," Grimshaw says. "And that was quite fine at that point. We were still driving around with four-vehicle convoys and it wasn't a big deal."

A good thing, too, because Bravo had such a mixed bag of assignments the company was spread pretty thin. They had one platoon dedicated to what's called "force protection" at the small Provincial Reconstruction Team (PRT) base in Kandahar. They regularly ran security patrols on city streets that, except for the madding crowds, resemble the post-apocalyptic. These soldiers also escorted the Royal Canadian Mounted Police (and, at the time, one Charlottetown, Prince Edward Island, officer), who are involved in training the Afghan National Police (ANP), as they travelled to various stations.

Another platoon had three distinct responsibilities. One section acted as a personal protection party for the PRT commander. Another section was at the Joint Coordination Centre, responsible for ensuring that the various Afghan and coalition security forces worked together during emergencies and incidents. The third section

Sgt. Patrick Tower

Sgt. Vaughan Ingram

Cpl. Keith Mooney and behind him Maj. Bill Fletcher

Darcia and Ray Arndt in Mexico, May 2006

Taken early in the tour at the ANA 530 Compound in the village of Senjary. B Company Weapons Detachment and HQ soldiers relax at the end of a long day.

Capt. Jon Hamilton addresses recce platoon.

Capt. Jon Hamilton (left) and Sgt. Willy MacDonald clearing the roof of a known bomb cell compound.

Members of C Company 1 PPCLI take a break. Pte. Burke, Sgt. Tower, Cpl. Rachynski.

Capt. John Croucher was seriously wounded on May 25, 2006, in an IED strike. He credits the cool-headedness of Senior Section Commander Sgt. Derek Thompson with keeping him alive.

Maj. Bill Fletcher and Capt. Ryan Jurkowski

Combat operations in Zhari district. Left to right: Pte. Woods, Capt. David Ferris, Capt. Jay Adair, Capt. Konrad von Finckenstein, Capt. Sean Ivanko.

Recce on patrol. Front to back: Sgt. William MacDonald, Capt. Jon Hamilton, their interpreter, MCpl. Matt Tibbetts.

Near the village of Pashmul during a dismounted patrol. One of Maj. Nick Grimshaw's interpreters is standing with him. Grimshaw called the interpreter Mike.

Sgt. Tower's platoon. Front, from left to right: MCpl. Perry, Cpl. Joe, Pte. Mahlo. Back, from left to right: Cpl. Rachynski, Pte. Rustenburg, Pte. Dusyk, Pte. Leitch, Pte. Bayliss, Pte. Barker, Sgt. Tower

formed the Quick Reaction Force, which responded to suicide bombings from the coalition base at KAF.

And then there was the long-range platoon. "We'd go out for three or four days," Grimshaw says, "and leaguer up somewhere or go into a patrol base in the middle of the Arghendab River or the desert, and we were fine."

Leaguer is an alteration of the word *laager*, an obsolete Afrikaans word itself taken from the even older High German word for bed, *leger*. A *leaguer* is the original circle-the-wagons formation, a temporary defensive position of armoured vehicles usually set up for a speedy refuel or resupply. A patrol base is different in that it offers all-round defence and better protection from attack. Some are temporary, but others, like Patrol Base Wilson (PBW), which is named for Master Corporal Tim Wilson, may become relatively permanent fixtures. Leaguers work fine in reasonably secure, wide-open terrain like a desert, while patrol bases are better on more dubious turf, and in tighter quarters such as a valley.

That young Canadian troops still pepper their speech with terms that date to the Boer War is an illustration of how far back the collective military memory goes and how broadly it plumbs its diaspora. As the soldier who can be known only as Tipper Taylor once told me, "We've got traditions that go back past any living member. . . . We remember the lessons learned by the organization in the hardest of the hard-knock schools—the battlefield. You may have heard the guys talking about getting a chit, or camouflaging their vehicles with hessian. You know where these terms come from? The British Army in India. *Chit* is Sanskrit for paper; *hessian* is Urdu for burlap."

Thus, the leaguer.

By leaguering up and patrol-basing throughout Panjwaii, Grimshaw's soldiers could stay out in the field long enough to meet the locals, visit district leaders, attend *shuras*, and generally get a feel for the neighbourhood. In April and May, they also had a number of gunfights—including the first Troops in Contact (TIC) in the whole battle group—as, at the request of the local governor, they were drafted to support the local ANP.

While Canadian soldiers never had any role in the Afghan government's controversial poppy eradication scheme, they were there to support local security forces. For Grimshaw, during that time, that meant providing extra troops in the Zhari-Panjwaii area.

"They were trying to weed out the non-Panjwaii personnel because they were afraid all these foreigners were coming in and were going to cause trouble," he says. "The ANP and the governor's plan was to provide security in the districts by going through the villages. The Taliban was in the villages. The basic plan was to surround them, with us in support in an outer cordon and the ANP going in and rounding up the fighting-age males. We thought, 'Hey, this is how they do business. We're here to support them. This is the Afghan way, so be it.'"

But as he soon learned, the ANP's way of doing business in this particular part of the country was to run roughshod over the villagers.

"They were alienating themselves from the local population because of the way they operated," Grimshaw says. "Not only were they rounding up fighting-age males, but they were extorting money, stealing food, stealing motorcycles, without any regard for any ounce of professionalism, without any investigations. It was completely by discretion of the ANP commander on the ground or the district leader or the district chief of police. There were significant problems with corruption in the ANP, and as a result the locals became very distrustful of them, and then we became guilty by association."

All this, Grimshaw says, was "part of the reason things kind of went south during our tour, I think."

Still, as he headed off on leave—he was en route when he learned that Nichola Goddard had been killed, and so went reluctantly and sorrowfully—he had no real sense that things were about to shift dramatically. He met Jo, his wife, and their two little girls in London and spent a few nights there before heading to Spain and a rented villa. A military friend with children had warned him how difficult it was to go home to Canada and try to slip into the dynamic of a family that had grown used to him not being there, only to pack up again so soon. Grimshaw took his advice to take his leave elsewhere and was glad he did, though, "It was harder to say goodbye to these guys [his family] after that leave than it was to leave in the first place."

Halfway back to Kandahar, he stopped at Camp Mirage, the base in that friendly Middle East country that must never be identified (though it is, irregularly), and ran into some of his guys going on their leave. "I could see in their faces they needed the break," Grimshaw says. "A guy like Warrant Officer Darren Hessell had said, 'Sir, if I don't get in another firefight for the rest of my life, I'm just fine with that.' Guys like that were telling me, 'Hey, it's pretty crazy. We've been ambushed, we've cleared compounds, we engaged a lot of guys. Everyone's fine, but we're now living at Patrol Base Wilson, 2 Platoon is out there, and company headquarters, things are changing.'"

Grimshaw was stunned. "I didn't sleep for three days, because I just couldn't believe what was happening in an area where we had been able to operate with impunity," he says. Apprehensive and concerned, he was eager to get back to see for himself. He didn't have long to wait. Shortly after landing at KAF on June 7, he was in the thick of it, in Pashmul, with Bravo acting as a block for the ANP and Charlie Company, who were then involved in some pretty hard fighting.

For the rest of the month, as the area filled with people looking for work in anticipation of the grape harvest, Grimshaw met leaders in an effort to get a handle on who and where the Taliban was. He no longer moved in vulnerable mini-convoys, and now most of the *shuras* were held at the government district centres. Ultimately, on the basis of intelligence produced by Grimshaw's work, Operation Zahar was mounted, and in early July the battle group moved into Pashmul in force. As Ian Hope told a symposium in Calgary in the summer of 2006, the notion that high-tech geegaws—such as drone aircraft, which can take surveillance photos from the sky—can ever replace eyes on the ground in a counter-insurgency is bullshit.

By mid-June, B Company had already done a couple of VMOs in Panjwaii, one in particular that Grimshaw found rewarding. Medics had treated a little girl with a badly rotting foot—it had been burned, then riddled with infection—so useless that her big brother was carting her about in a wheelbarrow. The Canadians arranged for her to be brought to the PRT, had a doctor have a good look at her foot, and then provided the funding for it to be amputated.

"We were able to go back to the village to see her, to check up on her," Grimshaw says, "with a view to saying to her family, 'Hey, we're not heartless people; this is not an occupation.' They seemed to be grateful, but again, it's very difficult to tell. Some things are lost in translation."

It's the same with maps, he says. "They don't have the same understanding of a map. We talk about north, south, east, west; they talk about where the sun rises and where the sun sets." In a country where most people are illiterate, and Kandahar Province has one of the lowest literacy rates, Afghans still rely on easily recognizable landmarks and directions that are more likely to be of the "by the graveyard near that big stand of trees" or "where the two roads meet near the wadi" variety.

But everyone on both sides of the cultural chasm can understand VMOs. They are the feel-good exception to the general hard-to-read rule: Sick Afghans come to be helped; soldier medics and doctors care for them while others keep watch; everyone leaves a little happier and with hope surging in the heart.

I went on a VMO once, on March 24, 2006. I know the date because, long afterwards, in one of those six-degrees-of-separation moments, I got an email from Darcia Arndt, a young widow I'd interviewed in Edmonton. Nine months after her husband's death in a crash, she had finally received his effects from Afghanistan, among them his journal. And in the entry for that day, she said, he had written that he'd been out on a VMO and that a *Globe* journalist had been there. When I checked the date of my story, I realized it had been me. Over the course of many months, I'd spent hours in interviews hearing about a man I thought I'd never seen, and as it turns out, I'd once spent five hours under his protection.

The VMO on which Ray Arndt and I crossed paths was held because the week before, when a Canadian vehicle got stuck on the road, a group of villagers emerged to help dig it out. The grateful soldiers wanted to say thanks, so they returned to Ghani Kalacha, a dot of a village just south of Kandahar. It was a joint Romanian–Canadian venture, as VMOs were in the early days of Roto 1, and the doctors expected to see about 150 people. They ended up seeing twice that many—including, to widespread delight, a large number of burka-clad women who patiently waited, eyes cast downward, until all men and children had been treated, but who dared to come nonetheless.

There were some patients in serious pain or distress. A thirteen-year-old boy named Mohammad Naim had a badly infected tooth pulled by the Romanian dentist, a bloody and muscular procedure that took thirty minutes, with no anaesthetic. Yet he never flinched, and when I asked how long the tooth had been hurting, the boy serenely replied, through an interpreter, "Two years."

There was a fail-to-thrive baby, so weak she could hardly hold up her head, the sight of whom reduced almost everyone to tears. "It's like holding nothing," Master Corporal Liz Churchill, a medic with five kids of her own, whispered as she picked the baby up. Afghanistan has one of the highest infant mortality rates in the world, and most who saw this little girl had the sinking feeling she would soon be counted on the wrong side of that grim ledger.

It seemed to me that many people also came to the VMO for the same reason people in Canada, especially the elderly, often go to the doctor—for a little human contact, a gentle touch, the feel of another's hand on a weary brow, and a reminder that there is kindness in the world still.

Everyone loved VMOs and, as time went on, got better at them. "We learned from the first few," says Marilynn Chenette, the OC of Edmonton-based 1 Health Services Support Company, whose sixty medical technicians not only looked after the ordinary health concerns of Canadian soldiers in two separate clinics and provided extra hands for the Canadian-led hospital at KAF in cases of mass casualties, but also went daily outside the wire with the combat platoons. "Wherever the battle group was," Chenette says, "we were there too."

Chenette began asking local Afghan doctors to participate in the VMOs, and eventually included ANA medics. For the bigger VMOs, she would call on the Americans at Bagram Air Base north of Kabul, who would contribute more medics and veterinarians.

Behind concertina wire and a minimalist security cordon thrown up in a dusty square, they would set up stations for a dentist and polio vaccinations for the children, privacy curtains for Afghan women, and deworming stations for the animals. And they would hand out what the military calls "material assistance"—foodstuff such as rice and beans, tools, clothing, first-aid kids, radios, towels, and the like. Chenette also began to buy VMO medical supplies locally, the idea being to "provide the locals with their own types of medication, with instructions in their own language, rather than providing them with North American medicine they wouldn't see again."

By the end of the tour, the Canadians treated 3800 Afghans throughout the south—from the villages within spitting distance of Kandahar to those in the Panjwaii area, as far south as Spin Boldak and as far north as Gumbad—in a total of fifteen VMOs. That final number should have been seventeen.

"I told Mason Stalker and the CO at the PRT that I would do a VMO every week if I could," Grimshaw says. He had two large ones planned for June 24 and 25, in the villages of Mushan and Talukan, tucked a few klicks apart in the furthest southwest corner of Panjwaii district about seventy kilometres from Kandahar. Mushan was reportedly a hotbed for the insurgency. It had a school. Talukan had a clinic. Both had been torched by the Taliban. "We thought, 'Hey, good location. Walled compound. We can do VMOs there,'" Grimshaw says.

It was meant as an in-your-face expression of determination, to show the Taliban that they could burn down whatever they liked, but the Canadians would not be so easily deterred. Chenette got involved. "I had planned for an ambulance, four med techs, one Canadian military doctor, three U.S. doctors, nurse-midwives, local doctors, ANA medics, a veterinarian, a deworming team, health educators, and interpreters," she remembers.

On the afternoon of June 23, Grimshaw drove to the dried-up riverbed near Mushan, an area he'd been to before, and there in the low sandy bottom of the Arghendab, the troops set up a patrol base. "The intent was to secure a helicopter landing zone for the following morning," Grimshaw says. The VMO team was to arrive by Chinook first thing on June 24.

The troops set up their defence as they routinely did: ensured that the machine guns had interlocking arcs of fire so that coverage would be 360 degrees, went through the stand-to drills, figured out that the most likely ambush spot was from a small tree line. "Luckily, we had learned, and it had been reinforced many times, so we applied the basics, the fundamentals we know and love so well in terms of our defensive posture," Grimshaw says. He and Warrant Officer Marcel Schuurhuis even walked the positions to be sure everyone was good to go. "It's certainly not a joke," Grimshaw says. "This is what we do."

Grimshaw also wanted an early warning in the event of an attack, and decided to send out Sergeant Jeremy Silver, a section commander in 6 Platoon, and his soldiers at around 2 a.m. on June 24. They would check out the school in Mushan, and secure it for the VMO.

"I was sleeping by the back of the LAV," he says. Corporal Josh Purc, a light sleeper, was in the turret. Grimshaw was awakened by the sound of Purc telling Jay Boyes, the weapons detachment commander, "You better have a look at this; there's something out there." Boyes had a look and saw "four or five people, moving in single file. They appeared to be carrying something and moving toward our location, at two in the morning."

Grimshaw knew Silver and his section had just left their makeshift base to go on patrol. They'd stopped at something like map grid 945; the men Purc and Boyes were now watching were at grid 954. There were eight men in Silver's section and, as it turned out, not five or six but eight men in that ominous single file.

"I just wanted to make sure someone wasn't reading their grid wrong," Grimshaw says, "because we were looking at six guys, now seven, it turned out to be eight that we could see carrying something, but we couldn't tell if they were wearing, because of the distance they were at, Canadian uniforms or not. I wanted to be sure we weren't going to shoot up our own guys."

He got in the back of the LAV and looked through the thermal imager. "And then I saw, it was very clear to me, when the guy came up and put a machine gun with a bipod [a two-legged support for the weapon, so it can be used by someone lying down] on the berm, and you could see his turban flowing in the air. And I went, 'Okay, that's enemy.'"

Most of the men were awake by now, so Grimshaw issued a silent stand-to and made sure Silver would stay put. "We always thought, where there's one, there's more, and we don't know who's out there."

He watched as the column of men started to fan out in the classic ambush position, setting up at equal distances along the length of the berm, about three hundred metres away—a good range for the LAVs, but an equally good range for the enemy weapons. "I was just about to issue the open-fire to Master Corporal Boyes to engage the enemy," Grimshaw says, "when they initiated contact."

At first they were hit with PKM fire [a general-purpose machine gun still in production in Russia], and then with RPGs. The Patricias returned with a heavy volume of fire, Master Corporal Tim Fletcher lobbing in about sixteen mortars. In about two minutes, the enemy guns went quiet.

However, the Canadians thought they'd also taken fire from the north side of the river, and Grimshaw was concerned that they were surrounded. He called for aircraft or helicopters, and was told there were none available. "I expressed my dissatisfaction with that reply," he says. "Said, 'You know, we may be surrounded in this patrol base and I need someone to confirm that that's the case.'"

It was just after 2 a.m., with three more hours of darkness ahead. They had won the firefight, taken no casualties, silenced the enemy. "What we didn't know at the time," Grimshaw says, "was that the

enemy had withdrawn from the position because they were surprised as hell we'd been able to return fire, and they'd pieced up
their casualties and egressed toward Sergeant Silver's section."

Silver and his soldiers, hunkered down in an irrigation ditch, had
listened to the gunfight and then heard movement. The fleeing
enemy were heading right for them. "They quickly fanned out into a
defensive position," Grimshaw says, "and realized that there were
only eight enemy guys, dismounted, by themselves."

The soldiers had their night-vision goggles on. They watched
the men draw closer and could actually hear them talking among
themselves. The firefight that followed, conducted with the two
sides only about twenty-five metres from each other, again saw no
Canadian casualties.

"It was extremely close," Grimshaw says. "It would have been
extremely difficult if we had received casualties at 2:30 in the morning at two different locations, isolated in Panjwaii, on our own."

They counted Silver and his section back in to the patrol base,
and Grimshaw and Schuurhuis looked at each other, wondering,
"Do we stay or do we go?" They decided to sit tight, and there,
adrenalin buzzing, nerves jangling, they waited for dawn.

The scheduled medical clinic was just hours away and, at this
point, Grimshaw says, "I was recommending we don't do the VMO.
We're not sure there are any civilians here, but more important, they
don't deserve it." He was furious.

The VMO hadn't been widely advertised in advance—word of
mouth is usually all that's needed for throngs to show up—so the
Canadians wouldn't lose face publicly.

At first light, Captain Dave Ferris took two sections of 6 Platoon
in to do the usual battle damage assessment. "They came across
damaged chest rigs, paraphernalia from RPGs, and AK magazines,"
Grimshaw says. "It was obvious we had inflicted casualties on a few
positions."

As they were clearing an area along a canal, looking for falling
bloodstains, a van pulled up. "There were two injured little girls,"
Grimshaw says. "We don't know if they were injured by our fire, or

Taliban fire, but automatically there was a medic there, and we treated these two civilian casualties."

One child had a shrapnel wound in her shin; the other had shrapnel in her backside. The Canadians offered to take the girls to Mirwais Hospital in Kandahar, but the adults with them said they would do that themselves, so the medics patched the girls up.

"We don't know if it was our mortars, or us, we don't know," Grimshaw says. "At the time, it didn't matter: We were there to help. [The girls' injuries] were very unfortunate. We helped. We followed up later with the district leader at the next *shura* and he informed us [the girls] were fine, they were back with their parents, there was no further concern there."

This incident is so telling of the soldiers' strange, schizophrenic existence—one minute bursting with good intentions, the next immersed in all-out combat; full of righteous rage, then stricken and chastened. "It was totally that," Grimshaw says. "We'd dial it up to eleven for firefights, and back down. That's one thing we did extremely well, that I believe Canadian soldiers do extremely well."

But it was emotionally draining. "That firefight in Mushan," he says, "that feeling of, we drove down here with the intent to help, and while we were getting squared away, there were groups of people out there plotting against us. And actively manoeuvring against us, to kill us. And that to me was just like, wow, this is nuts. We're here to help you and why didn't anybody inform us, why didn't anybody come and say. . . . But of course they won't, because they're afraid for their lives as well. You know, it was a very strange place."

Part of him was becoming very cynical, Grimshaw says. "Because you're there to help people, to help the Afghan people make their country better. It's so frustrating to be in that position. You want to say, 'Don't you people realize what you could have?' That's all we want. There were days, like after that firefight particularly, when I came back and said, 'Screw it, it's not worth it. This place is fucked. They don't deserve our help.'" But for every day like that, there was the other sort, when "you drive around a corner and you see little kids and you say, all right, we have to be here."

Kevin Schamuhn, an Alpha Company platoon commander, told me something similar once. He'd just returned to KAF after an extraordinarily long and dangerous time in the field that had culminated in his troops arriving at a school that was still smouldering after the Taliban set it afire. They had trashed the place, broken children's desks, burned their bright drawings, smashed the chalkboards. "It was just this horrifying scene of just complete destruction," Schamuhn said.

The soldiers found those universally familiar class sheets, with names and one-inch pictures of each child, that are usually hung on classroom walls. The sight, he said, "ignited something else in me. . . . Those kids can't do anything about it, but we can. It makes it easier to fight them [the Taliban]."

Yet sometimes determining who to fight, who exactly was the enemy, was the trickiest part. Grimshaw says that on occasion his troops were in *shuras* where they recognized people they had detained earlier, who had been identified by villagers as Taliban. "And now they're representing the village, attending the *shura*. . . . Has he denounced the Taliban, or is he here to see what the leader is up to? We don't know, and it's so hard to tell."

Captain Jay Adair, Grimshaw's second-in-command, describes an occasion on May 24 when after a day of on-and-off fighting they'd stopped a Talib and six of his friends at a checkpoint. "While we had him in custody," Adair says, "his phone rang. So I had my interpreter pick it up, and it was the Taliban at the other end, wondering when our friend was coming to meet them and pick up the wounded."

At the Canadians' insistence, the ANP detained the man—but only for a New York minute, it appears, because three days later Adair was at a *shura* and there was the same Talib. "He wanted money from us," Adair says, "because we had fired artillery at his house! I couldn't believe it!"

Grimshaw found his patience growing very thin. "It was very difficult to know if they were telling you the truth or not."

On an earlier visit to Talukan, he says, they stopped at the local bazaar. "I said, 'Let's stop, let's ask what's going on, what concerns they have.' They wanted the school rebuilt, and we knew the clinic had been burnt, and I wanted to compare the replies of the locals and the answers of the district leader. I wanted to hear from the people in the villages. The Taliban burned your clinic; is it a good idea to rebuild it? What about the school? Is it important to you now? What about the roads? The road to Zhari-Panjwaii is a dirt road and the ANP are afraid to travel on it because of IEDs, but roads are the key to everything in Kandahar. If you can rebuild the roads, you can rebuild that province."

They walked into the bazaar, Grimshaw says, and saw there were plenty of fighting-age men around. "Don't your sons go to school?" he asked, and the men replied that the school was damaged and that "the governor has to fix it."

"The governor can, to a degree," Grimshaw replied, "and I can talk to my commander about rebuilding the school, but not if it's going to get burned again. I need something from you.

"I said, 'What do you need today?' And a man said, 'I'm just a farmer. I need a shovel.' I turned around to my LAV and I said, 'There's a shovel in there. I will give you that shovel right now; you tell me where the Taliban is right now and I will give you that shovel.' And he's, 'Oh, we don't know where the Taliban is.' Yeah, right. We got shot at the next time we went in there."

After Operation Zahar in Pashmul on July 9 and 10, the rest of the battle group was sent west to Helmand Province, in support of British forces, and Bravo was left to hold the fort in the Zhari-Panjwaii area.

"We were getting reports that the Taliban was moving back into Pashmul," Grimshaw says. "We had been told that, you know, the villagers would come back in. We were hoping we'd go in and do that, that the governor and district leaders would encourage their villagers to come back, and that, I guess naively, there would be incentive for them to go back and they'd be in a position to tell the

Taliban they were no longer welcome there. And, in fact, none of that happened.

"We created a vacuum and the vacuum was filled by the Taliban, by insurgents once again. But this time they changed, improved their defences, brought in more guys, and realized the coalition are using these roads and we're now going to put IEDs on them. And we got reports, we could hear them, destroying the bridges on Route Vancouver and Comox." (The Americans first and then the Canadians gave names to the otherwise nameless roads they used.)

For the rest of that month, Grimshaw says, they saw an increasing number of ambushes along Highway 1, which links Kandahar and the Panjwaii area and leads west to Helmand Province. "It became almost a daily event, whether it was against us or Afghan security forces or USPI [U.S. Protection and Investigations, a private security company], those types of organizations. . . . And if it wasn't an ambush, what started to occur in July was indirect fire engagements onto the patrol base [Patrol Base Wilson]."

As part of trying to secure the highway, the soldiers started visiting various Afghan National Highway Police (ANHP) checkpoints, and one day headed to one west of Howz-e-Madad, near one of the villages where they had earlier done a humanitarian assistance visit. It was July 12, Grimshaw thinks, at ANHP checkpoint No. 6.

"I got a report that there's something very strange going on at this highway checkpoint." Dave Ferris and 6 Platoon were there, Grimshaw says, and Ferris told him that he suspected the police were in fact Taliban. What Ferris described went as follows, Grimshaw says.

"There were two guys. Neither one of them was in uniform. And inside the checkpoint were all these bloodstained clothes that looked like they'd been shot up, and a whole bunch of medical equipment that doesn't exist at any of the other highway checkpoints, and a hole in the back wall, and tire tracks leading up to it. And it appeared that they had helped treat the wounded we'd engaged two days previous to that."

As part of the background, making the troops doubly suspicious, were the reports they'd been getting from villagers, that the Taliban had stolen ANP vehicles and been spotted wearing ANP uniforms.

Ferris told Grimshaw they'd seized a cellphone, with numbers matching those of a Talib they'd detained just two days before. "So something's going on," Grimshaw says.

Ferris had already called the Joint Coordination Centre and asked them to inform the highway police that some of their officers appeared to be in cahoots with the Taliban, that they needed to send fresh troops to the checkpoint, pronto, "because we can't trust these guys anymore."

Grimshaw rolled out to the checkpoint himself.

Two trucks full of heavily armed highway police showed up.

"They're armed to the teeth," Grimshaw says, "and they look like they're ready for a fight." He and his men were out of their vehicles. "I look for their commander, and I say, 'What's going on with you?' And he says, 'I hear the coalition are firing highway police.' And I say, 'We're not firing anyone, but I'll tell you what this looks like. And by the way, I haven't seen you before. Where are you from?'"

The commander told Grimshaw he was from Helmand Province, and Grimshaw replied, "What are you doing in Kandahar Province? You should be in Helmand."

Grimshaw laid out how he saw the situation: "There's a whole bunch of medical supplies here; it looks like someone's been treated, and the numbers on his cellphone match Taliban numbers. So you tell me what's going on."

Grimshaw tried to bluff the commander, told him he hoped he would report all this to his boss, as he would do to his.

"So they took off," he says.

Then a second group showed up, led by a local ANHP commander whom Grimshaw had met many times before and knew as a hothead. His men were wearing various states of quasi uniforms, and he immediately accused the Canadians of occupying their checkpoint.

"Okay," Grimshaw says he told him, "We've met before. I know you, let's have a talk and sort this out."

The commander abruptly "opens up his shirt and says 'You've dishonoured me. I have no reason to live. Shoot me now.'"

Grimshaw tried to calm him down, but the man insisted he had been dishonoured in front of his soldiers. "I said, 'The only one who's dishonoured you is you,'" Grimshaw remembers, "'because you're acting like an idiot.'

"At that point in the tour," he says, "I had very little stomach for any histrionics."

The Canadian Military Police officer with the platoon was seizing evidence, including used drug packets, medical equipment, and the cellphone, and taking pictures.

"I said, 'This is what my policeman is doing, what are your police doing?' And I said, 'I'll make a report. I hope you make a report,' and then we left. If I knew they were all Taliban, I would have rounded them up," Grimshaw says, "but you don't know. And to get in a gunfight with the highway police would be [disastrous], so I tried to calm things down. Everyone mounted up and [said,] 'Let's get outta here,' but if there's a single round that's fired, we will deal with this."

They left unscathed, but that night two RPGs flew over Patrol Base Wilson. Grimshaw thought, "Well, there you go—the highway police are shooting at us now."

After that, PBW was regularly targeted. "They gradually got more accurate, and the munitions became larger too," Grimshaw says, "to the point where we were engaged by 100 millimetre rockets and 82 millimetre mortar rounds."

When I saw Grimshaw at PBW one day in early July, Bravo had been in more than twenty major firefights, and as he would tell anyone who asked and some who didn't, "We didn't start one." He was so frustrated.

Weeks earlier, on June 22, one day before the troops had moved into Mushan to prepare for the VMOs that were aborted by the ambush, Afghan President Hamid Karzai had made a tearful speech complaining about the rising death toll, noting that "even if they are Taliban, they are sons of this land."

Grimshaw had heard about that much-publicized speech. Of how he felt at the time, he says, "You tell your Afghan sons to call off their dogs."

He remembers a conversation he had with Habibullah Jan, an opposition member of the Afghan national parliament. Never entirely sure of the man's allegiances—he was always quick to point fingers at other tribes or governors—Grimshaw nonetheless found him honest and passionate about his country, the only individual he met who was. "He's the only bigwig who ever said, 'If we can't make Afghanistan work this time, we will never make it work.'"

Grimshaw is uncertain about how far he and his men may have helped push the country toward that end. "It's hard when you're there to say, 'Are we really making a difference?' And you know, treating those small kids at VMOs. It's difficult sometimes, when it appears that all you're doing is driving around, whether in convoys through Kandahar city, or driving people from the PRT to meetings and back, when we're out conducting ops without the ANSF [Afghan National Security Forces] beside us.

"Yeah, you ask these questions. But I always think about the alternative: What would Kandahar Province be like without the Canadian military?"

He still wonders if he did the right thing by cancelling those VMOs in Mushan and Talukan. "That was my feeling at the time," he says. "It was a trade-off. But we talked afterwards that there would have been value in doing [them]: 'You can shoot at us all you want and we're still here.'"

Capt. Nichola Kathleen Sarah Goddard, Forward Observation Officer

17 May 2006

—

"Most of great literature is about the nobility of the warrior.
We need people who will fight to the death for things. It's important."

—VICTORIA GODDARD, ON SOLDIERING

MAY 17 was shaping up as a huge day for Nichola Kathleen Sarah Goddard, Forward Observation Officer.

FOOs are the artillery officers at the front end of the front lines. Their job is to watch the enemy in its positions so they can call in and coordinate the big artillery guns, 81 millimetre mortars, and attack helicopters. As a former gunner, retired Colonel Mike Capstick, once told me, "You can't engage stuff you can't see. You have to know what you're shooting at, and to do that, you have to expose yourself." More poetically, Capstick says the FOO is the "orchestra director," the person who decides "which weapons system is best for the job, and orchestrates its delivery in concert with the manoeuvre force."

As a result, the FOO's job is considered to be one of the most dangerous jobs in the artillery, and among the most dangerous in the entire army. It has always been that way.

Steve Gallagher, Goddard's battery commander (BC), remembers going to Vimy Ridge, the site of the most storied victory in Canadian military history, with a gunner friend. Already steeped in gunner lore, they were nonetheless struck by how many of the seven thousand Canadians buried in the immaculate graves of the thirty war cemeteries within fifteen kilometres of the Vimy Memorial were artillery, almost all of whom were FOOs.

The 1st Regiment Royal Canadian Horse Artillery (1RCHA) is the oldest unit of the Canadian Forces, the descendant of the original batteries of artillery that were formed in 1871, when guns were carried about by horse-drawn carriage. In Kandahar, its A Battery had three FOOs, each of whom was attached to a particular infantry company—Goddard with Charlie and Major Bill Fletcher, Mike Smith with Bravo and Major Nick Grimshaw, and Bob Meade with Alpha's Kirk Gallinger.

In May, the battle group's main effort was still up north, so Meade was at FOB Martello, then brand new, and Smith was at the Gumbad Patrol House. With Bravo Company under acting OC Jay Adair slated to go into the Panjwaii area, Goddard was the only FOO readily available.

Originally, the company was supposed to head further south to a village on the Arghendab River called Kadahal, Adair says. But as they were approaching it, Ian Hope got on the radio and told them to turn back to a place called Pashmul, where local intelligence said the Taliban were massing.

That morning, Hope remembers, the people in Bayenzi village complained to the local Afghan National Police in Bazaar-e-Panjwaii that "Taliban had slept in the school and turned children away." This was the same White School where so much Canadian blood would be spilled. But at that time, neither it nor Pashmul—which isn't a single entity, but a series of villages and compounds—were particularly well known.

The troops turned around and headed back toward Bazaar-e-Panjwaii. As they crossed the Arghendab River, they saw a large number of women and children fleeing—the usual harbinger of the Taliban preparing to make a stand and fight.

Goddard, whose call sign was Golf One Three, was attached to Captain Konrad von Finckenstein's 5 Platoon. By 11 a.m., she had already called in the first artillery firing in direct support of troops in contact.

"She was the first FOO to call in bullets since Korea," Gallagher says, using the term *bullets*, as gunners invariably do, for the enormous shells fired by the M777 Howitzers. (With a diameter of 155 millimetres, or about six inches, and weighing in at between 43 and 46 kilograms, or 95 and 100 pounds, they're not bullets as most people know them.) "Not the first woman," Gallagher says, "the first FOO—and she was ecstatic."

Or, as Adair puts it, "She was enthusiastic, but still calm."

It was not the first time the M777s had fired in support of operations; that had happened early in February, when the Gumbad Platoon House was attacked by RPGs, and again in support of Fletcher and Charlie Company when they were in Helmand Province. But it was the first fire mission in support of soldiers who were actually under fire—in this case, Jon Snyder's 8 Platoon, who were attacked from Haji Musa about eight hundred metres west of the White School.

The fire mission was quickly cancelled, and Goddard called in U.S. Apache attack helicopters. FOOs can call in attack helicopters, which inexplicably aren't classified as "close air," though they certainly can come in close and low. However, the range of fixed-wing aircraft are instead handled by Forward Air Controllers (FACs).

"That afternoon," Adair says, "Nich was doing two things: controlling Apaches, very effectively, and calling in the artillery."

Then things seemed to slow down, Adair remembers. "Throughout the afternoon, we were playing this cat-and-mouse game. We had a little bit of contact, but nothing serious."

Later still, the troops were able to search the area, where they found at least a dozen Taliban hiding in the grape fields. "You'd look down a vineyard and see their feet," Adair says, "and they'd hidden their weapons, and you'd drag them out." They also searched the nearby compounds and found firing positions, weapons, blood trails, and thirty bags of nitrate fertilizer.

As all this was coming to a close, Adair says, gunfire suddenly erupted along a frontage of 1200 metres—a coordinated enemy attack that ambushed von Finckenstein's platoon and Goddard as they were preparing to move south. Goddard was in the turret, in the right-hand seat, her head up even higher than usual as she directed the LAV to back up along a narrow road. Master Bombardier Jeff Fehr was beside her in the left-hand seat.

"He says he saw a big white flash," Gallagher says, "and he was knocked down into his seat, and he got on the cannon and starting whaling with the 25 millimetre cannon. The cannon jammed, from the dent, so he went to the Coax [the coaxial machine gun, mounted on the same axis as the 25 millimetre cannon] and that jammed too. So he hopped on the machine gun [a pintle-mounted weapon] and that's when he looked over and saw Nich slumped down."

The LAV had been hit with RPGs at the front and rear left side. Shrapnel had torn into the back of Goddard's head.

"Immediately, over the radio," Adair says, "I hear, 'This is Golf One Three, my sunray's down.'" (*Sunray* is a generic term that means commander, either a platoon or company commander. FOOs are the commanders of their LAVs.)

Gallagher was sitting on the highest hill in the area with Ian Hope. "The last thing I heard her say on the radio was, 'I'm just backing up, we've got some ANA behind us, I'm gonna get turned around,'" Gallagher says.

He remembers hearing Fehr say only "'One Three, Sunray's been hit.' He didn't say Golf One Three, he just said One Three. I could hear Colonel Hope, talking to himself [on the radio], saying, 'Slow down, slow down.' I knew the only One Three was Golf One Three."

Adair knew only that Goddard was down. "I don't know she's dead," he says. "We race over, we now recognize that this platoon and her have been ambushed and we have to somehow get them out. I have to make a decision very quickly, have to decide, do I go up and get them, on that narrow road, or do I fire to their flanks and suppress and have them come back?"

Adair stayed put, his troops laying down suppressing fire so the others could clear the area. "It was the worst feeling ever," he says, "because there was panic on the radio, it's getting dark, there's lots of smoke, lots of noise, and quite frankly, I don't know if I've made the right decision. I see people running and jumping onto the sides of vehicles, just to get out of there. It was crazy."

The troops pulled back to the White School, 5 Platoon the last to arrive. "They'd reported they had casualties," Adair says, "but they were back and could account for everyone. . . . Then Nichola's vehicle came back, we got her out—and she was dead."

Hope had heard that there was a Priority 4 casualty, then that the casualty was vital signs absent. "Then I was given the ZAP number," he says, the four-digit code that allows soldiers to identify casualties without naming names on the air. He always carried with him a list of his soldiers, about six typed pages, with each soldier's ZAP.

He walked over to Gallagher and Battery Sergeant-Major Paul Parsons and told them it was Goddard. "Tears flowed instantly in their eyes," Hope says.

He got the grid references for the Taliban group that had ambushed Goddard and 5 Platoon and called in the second fire mission of the day. It was followed quickly by a thousand-pound bomb dropped by a B-1.

The troops couldn't return to the area until the next morning, by which time the Taliban had done a thorough job of policing up their dead and wounded. But Hope remembers that "we had evidence—numbers of blood trails, body parts, and witnesses of enemy being hit—to suggest that between twenty and twenty-five Taliban were killed or wounded" that day. Another thirty-two were detained by the ANA.

"I knew it was Nich before they told me," Hope says. "I knew because on all ops up until that point, Nich was a constant on the radio, giving me incredible detail about what was happening, and coordinating all the arty [artillery], air, and other support assets. That evening, her silence warned me of her fall before I was told."

The next day, caught in yet another TIC, Ian Hope was bereft: "There was no one to give me my sitreps [situation reports]," he says. "She could synthesize everything."

—

IN EARLY APRIL 2006, the reporters embedded with Charlie Company heard Nich Goddard on the radio. She was with Bill Fletcher, as usual. On a twenty-four-hour trip to FOB Robinson, about one hundred kilometres north of Kandahar, it was her voice we heard most often.

It was a hellish trip. Almost everything that could go wrong, short of an attack or bomb, did. Vehicles broke down or got stuck. A suicide bomber tried desperately to make his way through the ruined Kandahar streets to get to the convoy. And to cap it all off, a civilian truck side-swiped the LAV I was in, spinning the 25 millimetre cannon to squarely whack and badly injure the two young air sentries standing in the rear open hatches. One of them, Private Daniel Mahlo, bloodied and moaning, tumbled back through the hatch into the LAV and almost into my lap. Both he and Private Dawson Bayliss had to be choppered out.

By the time we got to the FOB—a naked patch of powdery desert ringed by a row of Hesco Bastions, the container system that looks from a distance like ordinary sandbags but is more durable and much stronger—the sun was coming up. Exhausted, nerves frayed, we all dropped to the sand by our LAVs to grab a little sleep.

The soldiers were there to secure the base, where just a few days before one of their own, Private Rob Costall—as well as U.S. Army Sergeant John Thomas Stone, a medic—had been killed in a fierce three-sided Taliban attack. When we awoke around 10 a.m., already drenched in perspiration from the heat of the spring sun, Fletcher agreed to show us the area where the battle had taken place.

As we walked over, the first question Rosie DiManno of the *Toronto Star* and I asked, almost in unison, was, "Who was that woman on the radio last night?" We had been in different LAVs for the long trip, but both of us had been comforted by the sound of her voice, so calm. I distinctly remember thinking that as long as her voice didn't quaver or rise in inflection, nothing really awful was happening.

"Oh, that's Captain Nich," Fletcher replied with his trademark lopsided grin. She was fabulous, he said, and he'd prefer never to go anywhere without her.

Much later, months after her death, he told me, "She was my FOO, so she was always right beside me. And she was phenomenally good at what she did, to the point where we leaned on her pretty heavily. [Her death] was real hard on the fellows."

As it turned out, DiManno and I, the *Globe* photographer, and another journalist were all choppered out of the base within the hour on General Fraser's orders. We weren't around long enough to meet Goddard. Rosie and I would have sought her out, I think, if only to thank her, and to meet one of the few women we'd encountered in the combat arms end.

The artillery wasn't Goddard's first choice, says her husband, Jason (Jay) Beam.

Recruits joining the military are given a list of jobs and asked to select their top six. "I'm not sure if they do this still," Beam says, "but back when we joined, a common sales pitch at the recruiting centre was that if you liked the outdoors and things like camping, then you'd love the infantry. Nichola thought this was a good choice, and put infantry down as her first choice, with artillery as her second."

When she was accepted at the Royal Military College (RMC) in Kingston, Ontario, she got her second choice and was enrolled as an artillery officer. "At the time," Beam says, "she had no idea what the differences between infantry and artillery were, but eventually was very happy that she was a gunner."

Beam and Goddard met during their first week of basic training at Saint-Jean-sur-Richelieu near Montreal in June 1998. One of the things recruits had to master was assembling the various bits of their kit. They'd be sent running down the long halls to get their boots and then be shown how to lace them. It was during one such mad dash that Goddard introduced herself.

"Goddard," she said.

"I'm Beam," he replied, clueless in the way of young men that she might be interested in him.

They were in the same platoon, her room across the hall from his. Though they became friends right away, he was sufficiently blind to the signals she was sending out that she finally had to sit him down and squarely raise the subject of their dating.

As her father, Dr. Tim Goddard, put it at her funeral, "Dear Jay . . . she knew right away he was the one."

Three weeks after Goddard and Beam met, they were a couple, and they dated throughout their four years at RMC, marrying on December 28, 2002, in the same Calgary church where her funeral was held.

Beam is a thoughtful and cheerful young man, a self-described computer geek born and raised in Niagara Falls, Ontario, whose parents divorced when he was a teenager. He joined army cadets at age twelve, and was so sure the military life was for him that RMC was the only university he applied to and wanted to attend.

During a mandatory training course, while attacking a hill, he dislocated his right kneecap. It was the twelfth time in four years he'd dislocated it, and finally in the spring of 2001 he had surgery. It was successful, in that Beam hasn't dislocated his knee since, but he couldn't run anymore. The operation launched him down a long road of physiotherapy and specialist appointments.

He and Goddard graduated in 2002, Beam with a degree in software engineering, she on the Dean's List with an English degree. While he stayed behind at RMC, working as a lab assistant in the school's electrical and computer engineering department and waiting for the first round of medical paperwork to go through, Goddard was commissioned as a second lieutenant, sent to Gagetown for specialty artillery training, and then posted to 1RCHA in Shilo, Manitoba, as the gun position officer (GPO).

When Beam was ruled unfit for the army and it appeared he was headed for a career as an air traffic controller (ATC), he was posted to Winnipeg, a two-hour drive from Shilo. He was due to start the ATC course when someone noticed on his paperwork that he couldn't run and wouldn't be able to complete the mandatory physical training test. According to the "universality of service," everyone needs to be able to fight as an infantry soldier, regardless of their trade, so the paperwork for a medical review was restarted.

"Everyone thinks it's kind of funny that I needed to be able to run in order to be an ATC," Beam says. "I joked that I'd need to be able to run to grab a fresh coffee between planes landing."

Only in the spring of 2004, when it was clear he would be let go from the Forces because of his knee, was he posted to Shilo to wait out his release. After seven years of trying to make the military work for him, his medical release finally went through in November 2005. He is remarkably without bitterness or regret.

"People have often asked if I miss the military life, or if I wished I was still in. My views are that it isn't an option at all," he says with the very pragmatism that would have served him so well in the army, "so I don't really think about it or miss it. I enjoyed my time in the Forces, and was sad to leave, but that was just the way things were."

Major Anne Reiffenstein had just taken over as A Battery commander when Goddard arrived in Shilo in August 2002. Almost immediately, the battery was out on exercise, and the two officers shared a tent.

"We just clicked," Reiffenstein says. "I'm her boss, and it's not a small separation. It's fairly significant. But it was so easy . . . we must have spent an hour and a half just laughing inside the tent."

Finally Goddard said, "Ma'am, we have to stop," aware that the men would think they were laughing at them.

Almost fifteen years older than Goddard, Reiffenstein joined the military in 1989 after dropping out of university. She was one of the first of the new wave of young women full of piss and vinegar, convinced they could do anything—and everything. The one thing she was sure she didn't want to do was be a "loggie," a logistics officer, because that's what women so often did in the Forces.

In those days, there was something called the Combat Arms Officer Selection boards (CAOS) where, at Gagetown for a week, recruits got to see first-hand what each of the trades did. Reiffenstein saw the infantry, as she puts it with a grin, "attacking the top of a hill, as they always do."

Her brother is a tanker with Lord Strathcona's Horse, and she thought that being a tanker would be fun until she saw the confined inside of one for the first time: "It stunk of dirty socks," she says. "No way."

And then she saw the guns fire, thought it magic, and made her decision.

After that first brave group of which she was a part, Reiffenstein says, "there weren't any more women officers for a long, long time. I sang solo for a lot of years."

Yet finally, there before her in Shilo was this smart, switched-on, charismatic young woman. "She had everything," Reiffenstein says of Goddard. "But I'll tell you the one thing she didn't have, and it's unusual for female officers—I have one. She didn't have a chip on her shoulder."

That chip is nothing you ever want, or cultivate, Reiffenstein says, but as one of a handful of women in the band of brothers, it just develops. It comes from the constant gnawing need to prove you can beat a man at the game.

And there was Goddard, so at ease in her own skin and so damn nice, and "she saw the military as a worthwhile career option. . . . It proved a point to me in my head. Yes, it was worth it, all those years wondering if I'm just blowing smoke. I opened the door to people like Nichola coming in, so that was really good."

It's one of the main reasons, Reiffenstein thinks, why Goddard's death hit her so hard. Another is that they were major and junior, boss and rookie, and that meant "she died before we could be friends. I'm always going to regret that."

The Gun Position Officer (GPO) is a big job in an artillery battery. Responsible for the firing of the guns and the attendant logistics support, the GPO works with about sixty soldiers, and two or three other officers.

"When things go for a dump on the gun line," Reiffenstein says, "the battery commander calls for the GPO to 'explain' the situation. In my case, it usually involved a lot of profanity, both as a BC and muffled under my breath when I was a GPO."

The job is done at a frantic pace, and is perfect for the sort of people who overcommit themselves, complain about it, and then do it again and again. Goddard didn't complain, at least not to Reiffenstein, but she was "really good at it. I ran her ragged, and she was great. I pushed her really hard. I pushed most of my officers really hard. There are generals who squished me too, to get the most possible out of me."

They had a lot of fun, too, and had a superb crew, Reiffenstein says. Every day, they'd gather at the front counter in the battery and inhale gummy bears and tell stories, Goddard contributing long, convoluted ones about her and Jay's two mangy and enormous mutts, Sam and Bill. "I miss it terribly," says Reiffenstein, now the chief instructor at RMC.

Once, when she gave Goddard "extra duties"—there'd been a screw-up on the gun line and, as the GPO, she was responsible so "in the end she bore the punishment"—almost every senior NCO and the Warrant Officer himself came to Reiffenstein's office to plead Goddard's case. She didn't change her mind—"extra duties build character and make you a better judge of when to hand them out if you've done some yourself," Reiffenstein says—but it was a measure of the sort of rapport Goddard had struck with her men.

In the spring of 2005, with Afghanistan on the radar, Reiffenstein knew her young charge was ready to move on. "She had planned major exercises, fired the guns on tricky and complex fire plans, and proven that she understood artillery fire from the gun line end," she says.

Goddard was promoted to captain, and began her FOO course.

It is a very different job with very different demands. The FOO's life is less hectic, akin to the fireman's, with incredible bursts of adrenalin punctuating long stretches of quiet. A FOO has multiple masters, from the battery commander to the infantry company commander, and competing loyalties, and lives cheek-by-jowl with a crew of four (sergeant, gunner, signaller, and driver). "It's a closer, more involved relationship with your crew, and one, I'll be the first to admit, I never mastered," Reiffenstein says.

Goddard made productive use even of the down time common to a garrison-bound FOO. Whereas Reiffenstein says that as a FOO she "just hung around, shot the shit, and smoked cigarettes," Goddard took a French course.

But Reiffenstein's favourite Nich Goddard story dates back to the late summer and fall of 2003. The Canadian Forces were helping fight the fires then devastating the British Columbia interior, and A Battery was bugged out to go.

Reiffenstein was still a brand new BC. Her husband, Major John Reiffenstein, a Patricia, was deployed in Bosnia, and they had two youngsters at home. She had a backup plan, of course, but had hoped never to have to use it. She had thirty-six hours' notice to get it in gear. Her friends and family rose beautifully to the occasion, she says, but as she boarded the bus to Winnipeg, and then the flight to Chase, Reiffenstein suffered wrenching doubts about whether she was doing the right thing.

She was sitting next to Goddard, and found herself speaking frankly. "I shouldn't have been sharing so much with a junior officer," she says. "But I was worried, you know, was I doing irreparable harm to my kids?"

Goddard told her about her own unorthodox, itinerant, and independent upbringing. "Don't worry about it," she told her major. "My parents left us all the time. I didn't even notice it until I was in my early teens."

Reiffenstein thought, "My God, this fantastic kid, this bright, compassionate kid, was trying to reassure me." And she did. "I thought if my kids turn out half as good, I'll be happy."

—

THE LAST TIME Sally and Tim Goddard saw their oldest daughter was on January 15, 2006, Sally's fifty-third birthday.

Nichola and Jay had come to Calgary for the weekend, after a side trip to Wainwright, Alberta, where they suspected she might be posted after the Afghanistan mission. The night before, they'd had a typical Goddard dinner, full of conversation, collegial argument, laughter, and lots of wine. Nich and Jay were leaving the next morning at the crack of dawn for Shilo.

Nichola didn't want her parents coming to see her off. "She said, 'You're not coming to the Crying Room,'" Sally says. "'I've seen enough people off on these missions. I'm not even going to let Jay come. I can't let my men see me like that.'" So they hugged her goodbye, "and she said, 'Don't worry about me,' as they do." Jay dropped her off at the building where the other families were gathering to watch the bus leave. "We both preferred it that way," he says, "instead of having a long public goodbye."

Only afterwards, when Sally discovered that Nich hadn't stripped her bed and thrown the sheets in the washer—unusual for her—did she realize how hard leaving had been for her daughter. "She was always incredibly organized," Sally says, "and she just wasn't [then]. I found stuff all over the place. So it was very difficult for her to leave. I think she was upset it would be a while before we'd see her."

The Goddards soon joined that nervous society of parents and spouses across the country who started watching television and surfing the Web with an edgy keenness and who fell asleep with an ear for the phone. Her parents got a portable one for the bedroom, so that when Nichola called, whatever time it was, they wouldn't sleep through it.

"The first two months," Sally said, "it was okay. We could handle this. Then as things became more tense, we became more tense. You're watching the news, saying, 'Thank God it's not my child, she made it through another one.' And then you feel guilty for feeling that and you watch [the repatriation ceremonies] sort of with respect but with this feeling at the back of your head: 'Thank God it's not mine.'"

Part of the reason Nichola chose RMC, Sally says, was born in her fierce independence: "She didn't want Tim and I to pay for her education." It was her parents "who threw RMC into the mix," and on the Saturday after Nich graduated from grade 12 at J.H. Gillis High School in Antigonish, Nova Scotia, where the family was then living, they drove their oldest daughter to Sydney, where she caught the plane to Kingston.

The army wasn't something Nichola always dreamed of, her sister Victoria says, but it appealed to many sides of her—the academic, the athletic, and the community service. Nich also applied to Trent University, where their mother had gone, but "as it turned out, she liked the army," and liked it immediately.

"She went away to summer basic training camp," says Victoria. "She complained a lot, but she really liked it too. You'd have to sit in a corner for four hours if you came out of a room in the wrong direction," Victoria says, "but she really understood the point—this is teaching me things."

Nichola was a little afraid of heights. She didn't like insects, and was worried about squealing like a little girl if she saw one of Afghanistan's infamous camel spiders, which, seeking the shade, follow your shadow as you walk, like an eight-legged stalker. But, Victoria says, "I don't think Nichola has ever been afraid for herself."

The Goddard children are the bold and adventurous products of bold and adventurous parents. Sally met Tim when they briefly taught at the same school in Papua New Guinea. Her contract with CUSO (Canadian University Services Overseas) expired six months after Tim arrived, and she returned to Trent University in Peterborough, Ontario. Tim wrote, and phoned that Christmas, and soon sent her a one-way plane ticket to join him.

Because she didn't have a job this time, the only way she could re-enter Papua New Guinea was if Tim agreed to marry her, or send her back within three months. Sally's father paid for the return portion of the ticket—"He didn't want me to make a decision based on a plane ticket," she says—and she went back. The couple was married in Alotau in July 1977 and stayed until 1984, spending two years on Trobriand Island, living without electricity or running water, with Nichola as their entertainment, as Sally puts it.

The little girl spent her days barefoot and dirty, and Sally would take her down to the river for a bath. She remembers Nich "holding on to my braids and sucking her thumb," and later, watching her daughter as she stared intently at her first flush toilet. "She had never worn shoes," Sally says, "never even seen shoes."

The family, which now included Victoria, returned to Canada when Nichola was four, first to Sault Ste. Marie, then a stint each in

Black Lake and Dundurn, Saskatchewan, the province where their youngest daughter, Kate, was born. They then packed up and moved to Pangnirtung on Baffin Island in what is now Nunavut. They stayed there almost a year before heading back to Saskatchewan, then Edmonton, then Antigonish, and finally to Calgary in 1999. There, Tim is an associate dean in the faculty of education at the University of Calgary. Sally has had a couple of temporary jobs with the Calgary board of education and still works at Onion Lake First Nations, north of Lloydminster, Alberta.

So it was an exotic childhood and adolescence, with parents who were curious, engaged in the world, and had strong and informed opinions. Despite the crapshoot that parenting is in the end, it is no surprise that the Goddard girls grew to have an appetite for travel, a thirst for knowledge, and a love of adventure tempered by a wide streak of responsibility.

Kate, just sixteen when her sister was killed, was then studying in France on an exchange program; Victoria was twenty-three, had just spent three months in Europe studying French and Italian, and had popped over to Wales to visit her grandmother.

When Sally says of Nichola, "I think, in a sense, we created that [spirit]," she means it of all their kids. "They've never been afraid to try anything." What she finds most difficult, she says, "is that there's no one to be mad at. And there isn't. People ask, 'Are you angry?' I'm upset because she's no longer here, but she wasn't deliberately targeted. I mean, they prepare them as well as they can. She was well trained, you know . . . maybe evil was stronger than good, I don't know."

Tim and Sally are convinced, she says, that Nichola "would much rather that she die" than lose one of her men. "Those World War One stories . . . those guys, they had to believe in what they were doing, and how many feet did they move in a day? Ten?" At another point, she says, "In many ways it's like the Charge of the Light Brigade—they go forward because that's what they do. And I don't think she did it blindly."

Victoria says her sister "found the military not without creativity, found that being a leader made her think and feel in different ways." While she believes Nich was already firm-minded, "being in the military really strengthened her. She thought about what she was doing. [The military] gives you a way to make meaning out of life. People have always found it glorious and terrifying . . . I see the modern experience in those terms. We're trying so hard to be inclusive sometimes, we can't make a stand."

Now studying at the University of Toronto for her Ph.D. in medieval studies, with two degrees (a master's in medieval studies and a Bachelor of Humanities) already under her belt, Victoria isn't sure she feels fully informed about the conflict in Afghanistan. "But I know Nich did," she says. "I didn't think we should go," she says, "but once we go, I support them. This particular mission, I don't have the answers for it. I don't know however else to go about it. Quite frequently, that's how it happens; you make things messier before you can get back to putting them together. That's a noble thing. It's a very complicated issue. I hope the people in charge are considering the thing that for me . . . it's extremely important to consider the motives and ideals behind it."

In the end, Victoria says, the Afghanistan mission may come down to what she calls "that great philosophical question: Do the ends justify the means? I'm not fully decided. The means can degrade the end, if you're not careful. But does it dishonour those who died, by leaving?"

Where Victoria is on sure and familiar ground, through her reading and her studies, is in the value of principles that are so dearly held they infuse a person's life and even reveal a path. "I've studied the classics," she says. "I'm a medievalist. Most of great literature is about the nobility of the warrior. We need people who will fight to the death for things. It's important. I can put Nichola up with people like the Spartans. She belongs in that class. I'd rather it didn't go to waste."

Literature, she says, "is part of what makes a civilization worth fighting for. . . . Being a medievalist, I know people were fighting against incredible odds to keep literature alive, to keep thinking alive."

Rather than fighting for civilization, she hopes to create one. Victoria is writing a book, a fantasy. "I'm trying to address big things," she says. "There's good and evil, and you can fight it. . . . I find I read old literature, classics from the Middle Ages—people are not different. . . . It gives you insight into what's going on: 'I believe in this; I will fight for it'—and I think the military helps people do that. Nobody likes to take a stand.

"I'm going to take a stand [in the book]," she says. "It makes me feel richer. Real philosophical conviction shows how wishy-washy and dull life is without that. It makes life really more meaningful. Once you get pushed and decide to take a stand, it changes you."

—

SOMETIME IN LATE APRIL or early May 2006, Nichola received a message confirming that she was to be posted to Wainwright at the end of the tour. The day before her death, Beam began the process of getting pre-approved for a mortgage so they could buy a house.

On the morning of May 17, he was at his computer, going through some of the mortgage paperwork. "I heard the screen door open," he says, "but didn't hear a knock or doorbell. I thought it was someone dropping off some flyers or something, so I went down to the front door to check."

Standing there was Liam McGarry, the acting CO of 1RCHA, and a padre. "At this point, I had realized what had happened," Beam says. He asked for a minute, let the dogs out, then let the men in. McGarry broke the news bluntly, as soldiers are trained to do. "Liam then left me with the padre, and I called Nich's parents."

Sally was at the library, doing research; Tim was home, but on the phone. Beam left a message, and in a few minutes Tim called back. "You talk about tough jobs you have to do in your life," Sally says. "That must have been right up there, to tell somebody that their daughter's been killed."

Sergeant Dave Redford, Goddard's FOO Tech in Kandahar, was in Canada on leave, Beam had the presence of mind to remember. He had the padre call him.

Then Tim Haveman arrived.

For almost a year in 2005, Tim and his wife, Lisa, both artillery officers, lived right across the street from Jay and Nichola. Haveman himself was slated to deploy with Goddard, but after years of being mysteriously ill and malnourished, he was belatedly diagnosed with celiac disease, a chronic condition in which the enzymes needed to digest food are blocked. Despite trying every diet he could find, he wasn't able to declare himself operationally fit because he couldn't eat the rations, and if he couldn't eat the rations, he, like Beam, didn't meet the "universality of service" requirement. He too will be given a medical release.

Because he and Goddard were in the same unit, he knew her better than he knew Jay. Once, when she couldn't get a new beret to shape properly, "she walked across the street to my house to ask me to help her." He ended up giving her his spare one. "She looked great in it," Haveman says, "and I was proud that my beret was now hers. A soldier's headdress is perhaps the most important part of his or her uniform."

More tellingly, on that awful day in the fall of 2005, when Haveman had to face the fact that he wasn't going to be able to deploy, Goddard had helped.

"If I wasn't sure that I could function at my prime, in the worst of situations, then I was not going to potentially put the lives of others in danger, or do further harm to my already damaged body." He had to tell Steve Gallagher, the battery commander. "I could see the disappointment in his eyes," Haveman says, "and that made it hard."

Afterwards, he was sitting in his office, crushed, when Goddard came to see him. "I remember her sitting across my desk and me telling her how broken-hearted I was about the whole situation, and the fact that I wouldn't be able to do the job that I was trained for. I felt like I was letting everyone down. I remember tears welling up in my eyes. Nichola was listening to my every word, and I could see in her face that she understood. She had tears in her eyes."

Gallagher quickly named Haveman as the "home front officer" for the regiment, and he got to work. He had a real understanding of the families back home, because for a time he was one of them:

Lisa deployed to Afghanistan in July 2005. He was the only man at the first meeting of the Military Wives Sisterhood. He also learned about the assisting officer job, hoping he would never be called upon to open his big binder. On May 17 he was, and found himself at Jay Beam's house on The Packway, his old street in Shilo.

There they were, two young men of twenty-six, both with military wives, both with two dogs, both betrayed by their bodies such that one was already an ex-soldier and the other about to become one. But for all that, they barely knew one another. "I knew he was a nice person," Haveman says, "loyal to his wife, good with computers, was very intelligent and had a quiet, keen sense of humour."

When he walked in, Beam was on the couch, obviously upset, tears in his eyes, but he gave Haveman a smile. "I gave him a hug and said, 'I'm sorry, Jay.'" Beam asked for a little time alone, to think and make some calls. He phoned his own family, sent out a group email to some friends, had a shower, and then turned on CBC and began recording their broadcast, a tape he still hasn't watched.

Within a couple of hours, reporters started phoning. Haveman kept track, and says more than thirty called, only one of whom offered condolences. "But I think that Jay felt he had a duty to talk to the media so he could share information with the many people who cared about Nichola's death. Jay was by far the strongest and most selfless person involved in the event. He never focused only on himself, and always thought about others."

It wasn't until the next morning, Beam says, that the impact really hit him. "I was expecting a fax to arrive first thing—more mortgage stuff. I was in bed when the fax machine started ringing. I jumped out of bed so I could watch the machine print off the pages. I went over to my computer to see if I had an email from Nich— they would often arrive overnight due to the difference in time zones. I opened my inbox and saw it was flooded with messages of condolence. It was at this point I realized it wasn't just a bad dream, and I collapsed to the floor in tears."

Major Reiffenstein had been on email with Goddard on May 16, talking about "just stuff that I would get." Goddard had reached the point in the tour, as everyone does at some stage, where the novelty has worn off and the enforced intimacy of living with her crew in one another's pockets was not wholly enchanting.

As Reiffenstein remembers of her own years as a FOO: "You spend an awful lot of time together, you know what buddy's wife makes as a tattoo artist, you know about their lives with their wives, you end up knowing intimate details. And they have the same level of intimate detail about my life. It's an interesting dynamic. And while everyone pitches in, you're still the boss . . . it isn't all sunshine and roses."

So they had talked about that sort of thing.

When Dave Poss phoned from Shilo and delivered the bad news straight out—"as there is no other way," Reiffenstein says—she told him there was a mistake because "I'd just been on email with her the day before." It was as if a member of her family had died, she says. "I had the shock, numbness, and just an overwhelming feeling of grief strike me. I wept and wept. Normally, hormones aside, I'm not much of a weeper."

She went right away to tell Captain Sonny Hatton, another officer who was in A Battery with Goddard. Many months later, Hatton told her he was in the grocery store, and bought Brussels sprouts because they reminded him of Nich. "He hates them," Reiffenstein says. "And his wife hates them. But Nichola loved them and would serve them every time she and Jay had Sonny and Chantal over for dinner in Shilo."

Reiffenstein remembers how, instantly, the press played up the "first woman" angle: Goddard was the first Canadian woman to die in combat since Korea; the first female FOO to be killed in action. She understood it, but was so "overwhelmed with the need to ensure that people understood that Nich was so much more than just some poor girl who managed to be the first one to die" that she responded to the reporters who called her.

It was graduation time at RMC, a busy time, and Reiffenstein was struggling through work when she got an email from an officer cadet who had been issued Goddard's pillbox hat. "It had Nichola's last name and service number in it," she says, "and she offered it to me instead of returning it to the RMC stores where college tradition sees the hats reissued." The young woman thought Reiffenstein would know what to do with it.

But she wasn't sure, really, until her husband said it would be a good thing to offer to the family at the repatriation ceremony in Trenton. She checked with the escort officer, and ended up giving it to Kate. "Her family's response was amazing," she says. "They welcomed me into their circle of grieving, as they welcomed everyone, and which in my mind gave me the right to grieve for the loss of their wife and daughter." She went to as many ceremonies as she could—including the funeral in Calgary and the interment in Ottawa—and has returned to that headstone since, "wishing desperately she wasn't there."

Before Reiffenstein left Shilo in 2005, Goddard gave her a letter and a gift, which she warned was "fairly touchy-feely and that I should know she meant it. I read it and teared up—damn it, I did not want to leave her and the others in my battery behind, but I sucked it up and did a polite 'take care' to all and left it at that, to my everlasting shame. No touchy-feely shit for me."

The gift was a copy of *Anne of Green Gables*, the classic novel by Lucy Maud Montgomery, and this is what Nichola Goddard wrote:

> Ma'am,
> As one can never have too many books, I wanted to share Anne Shirley's story with you.
> Anne Shirley is an orphan who spends the majority of her life being moved between foster homes and generally trying to fit in. She is constantly accused of "not being a boy!" Anne makes no apologies about her behaviour and mixes tomboy stunts with purely feminine concerns about her hair (red!) and nose (long!). Throughout the whole story, Anne only once regrets that she was not a boy. At that time, Matthew says, "I'd

rather have you than a dozen boys" (page 282).
Anne has earned her place and proven her worth to
all she has met.

I wanted to give you this story to thank you for
all the guidance and professional development
that you have given me. Most of all, I want to
thank you for showing me that there is nothing to
regret about being female and being a combat
arms officer. You have allowed me to develop my
leadership abilities while being proud of my gen-
der. You have caused me to view being a woman
as an asset—not a detriment to the team or to my
profession.

I can only hope to inspire other women to perse-
vere and take pride in their accomplishments as
much as you have for me. Thank you.

Nichola

"I think," Reiffenstein says, "that sums it up nicely. Mix in the
boy stuff, keep some girl stuff [including a few neuroses], and then
forget about all of it and get the job done."

In the fall of 2006, A Battery of 1RCHA held a memorial for their
fallen friend. In her memory, with Jay Beam and Sally and Tim
Goddard present, her comrades dedicated a trig marker to her.

A trig (for trigonometry) marker is used as a survey point, and is
thus a permanent fixture of the landscape. Like Goddard herself,
the marker is both practical and reflective—useful in orientation
and navigation, but also designed to act as a point on the soldiers'
moral compass, meant "to help us keep doing what is right and
good," as the description in the unit's official press release reads.

"The important thing to remember is the story," Reiffenstein says.
She mentions a soldier who died in 1991, then says, "Every year, a
friend in the mess rings the bell on the date of his death. So ten,

fifteen years after, kids who weren't even in high school, before they could imagine life as a soldier, raise a glass in his memory."

At the memorial for Goddard the guns fired five rounds of "fire for effect" in the artillery's traditional salute. Goddard's FOO party from Kandahar actually called in the mission.

Nichola Goddard left an in-the-event-of-my-death note, her mother says. "She had often held these notes for other soldiers. In it, she said how much she loved Jay, us, Victoria, and Kate." She also said to tell Sergeant Redford, who was on leave, "I didn't mean to leave the charge, but sometimes it happens. Strength and Honour. Nich."

It's a funny thing, that "strength and honour" business. Her parents had heard Nichola say it often enough that it now adorns a plaque they had laid in their daughter's memory in the churchyard on Remembrance Day, 2006. Sally assumed it was a military motto, or from RMC. But it isn't, and neither is it a motto of any unit in the Canadian Forces.

Jay found it only on a T-shirt he received after Nichola's death, in a package of gifts she'd bought for friends at the American PX (Post Exchange or general store) on KAF. It was a U.S. unit's shirt, he says, but can't remember which one.

The only intact reference I could find is in the Bible, Proverbs 31:25, in a section that can loosely be characterized as instructions on being a good wife and woman. The quote in its entirety (and it changes depending on the version of the Bible, with "honour" sometimes replaced by "dignity") reads, "Strength and honour are her clothing, and she laughs at the time to come."

The mystery was solved finally by Ian Hope, in whose company Goddard spent so much time. "It was indeed my mantra to TF Orion," he says. "I used to sum up my little preaching sessions with 'strength and honour,' so Nich would have heard it a few times from me." Familiar to many from the 2000 Academy Award-winning war movie *Gladiator*, in which the words were spoken by the fictional Roman general Maximus played by Russell Crowe, Hope says, "The writers of that script borrowed it from a Roman motto of a fighting legion long ago since lost in history." The phrase appears on the reverse of the Orion coin: *Robustus et fortus.*

So that's where it came from, though I still like the idea of Nichola Goddard laughing at the time to come.

Pte. Robert Costall

29 March 2006

—

"Okay, roll up the picture fast. Private Bob Costall, 1st Battalion, Charlie, Princess Pats Canadian Light Infantry and—oh boy, this is tough—we think of Chrissy, his wife, and his mom, Bonnie, and ah, I got one coming up. When you think of these guys here, you think, well, they're soldiers and that. . . . Watch this beautiful kid, that's Collin. I mean, he doesn't have a daddy now. Boy, these guys are the greatest guys in the world."

—DON CHERRY ON PTE. ROBERT COSTALL,
COACH'S CORNER, SATURDAY, APRIL 1, 2006

THE FIRST INDICATION for Canadian reporters working at Kandahar Air Field that something may be up is that the Internet becomes abruptly unavailable. That doesn't necessarily mean there are casualties, because the system sometimes crashes for the usual, more prosaic reasons, but the possibility is always there. When soldiers are killed or injured, reporters are forbidden by the rules of the embedding program from passing on the news until the families in Canada have been notified. Therefore, on the better-safe-than-sorry principle, the Net is shut down.

So it was in the early hours of Wednesday, March 29, 2006.

The uncertainty was short-lived. By 8 a.m., the flag at the small memorial for Canada's fallen near the press work tents was at half-mast.

Back at CFB Edmonton, flags would soon be half-masted, too, as they often were during Roto 1—so often that the sight became not jarring but normal. "It looks strange to see them at full mast now," Captain John Weingardt, an army captain and then the editor of the base newspaper, the *Western Sentinel*, told me once in an email written shortly after the last of the Patricias had arrived home.

Before nine on that March morning, Brigadier-General Dave Fraser, the Canadian commander of the multinational brigade, was standing before the press with his usual awkwardness, formally announcing the death of Private Robbie Costall. Just twenty-two, the young man who was born in the rugged rock-and-lake-scape of Thunder Bay, Ontario, and raised in the small seashore towns of British Columbia's Sunshine Coast died on a desolate piece of near-desert called FOB Robinson.

In the middle of the wild west country of Helmand Province, about 110 kilometres north of Kandahar, FOB Robinson wasn't even officially part of the Canadian patch, but rather under the then nominal control of British forces. It wasn't much of a base, either. Less than two months old, home to about 120 soldiers of the Afghan National Army, their American trainers, and some U.S. Special Forces operating in the area, it had nothing to recommend it—one rudimentary building, no tents, and a makeshift plywood toilet. It was nothing but a wide-open expanse of powdery sand ringed by a single row of Hesco Bastions, the supermodels of the sandbag world, and an outer cordon of concertina wire.

The only hint of why the area is held so dear by the Taliban was the improbably lush poppy fields here and there, then blossoming with pink-and-white flowers. The only clue to how hard they would fight to protect that ground came in the base's very name. Originally called FOB Wolf, it had been renamed FOB Robinson after the thirty-six-year-old U.S. soldier, Staff-Sergeant Christopher Robinson, who had been killed in action there just four days before.

The FOB sits in the Sangin River Valley, right in the middle of a well-known transit corridor for the Taliban as well as local warlords and assorted narco-criminals. In fact, as the plain-spoken British Colonel Chris Vernon, then his country's senior officer at brigade headquarters, said at the time, those very characters, with their disparate but intertwining interests, often are the Taliban, or what the military and the press for convenience sake's slap with that single label.

Vernon is a strikingly good-looking man and has an English accent, which never hurts. But what most endeared him to reporters was that he was sort of the anti-Fraser. He could think on his feet, answer questions (or deflect them) with humour and intelligence, and was confident enough to run his own show, regardless of what the handler assigned to him might try to do. In contrast, Fraser rarely met reporters without his press guy, Major Scott Lundy, hovering close by, and pretty much anything the Canadian general said sounded as if he were reading from a tendering document written for him in the bowels of National Defence headquarters back in Ottawa.

Several times when Canadians were killed, I remember asking Fraser if it wasn't a more difficult day for him because some of his own countrymen had died. He always responded that every soldier's death, whatever the nationality, was hard. I understood, of course, that he was commander of the multinational brigade, and that he took seriously his responsibility to all member countries, but it was still striking to me that he unfailingly remembered to make this point.

Costall was a member of Charlie Company's 7 Platoon. At the end of February, its thirty-eight young men had moved out of Charlie's Big Ass Tent on KAF and set up near the flight line, the better to throw on their kit and scramble to the choppers in the event they were needed somewhere in volatile southern Afghanistan. The troops were taking a turn as the base's rotating Quick Reaction Force, the air mobile group on standby 24–7 to respond to emergencies for all of Combined Joint Task Force 76, then the operational headquarters for southern and eastern Afghanistan. The soldiers would fall asleep to the deafening roar of aircraft—fighter jets, bombers, drones, cargo craft, and choppers of all kinds—that fly in and out at night.

Because of its godforsaken location, FOB Robinson was in constant need of resupply, with convoys regularly travelling out to neighbouring towns and back again. The call for 7 Platoon had its roots in what had happened the day before, on the Tuesday, when one of those convoys was ambushed by Taliban forces, with eight ANA soldiers killed. The first responders dispatched were two British Harrier fighter bombers, the second two U.S. Apache attack helicopters. The soldiers were able to fight off the initial attack, but as night fell, an IED exploded ahead of their convoy, destroying the road and stranding them about ten kilometres from the FOB.

Around 10 p.m., while the beleaguered ANA worked frantically to repair the route, the third element of support—7 Platoon—was mustered. The soldiers were flown to the FOB by U.S. helicopters. (Canada has no troop-carrying choppers, those having been sold off years earlier and, cruelly, still in use in southern Afghanistan by their

Dutch purchasers.) The platoon arrived shortly before the convoy finally made its way back. Costall's fire team partner, Chris Fernandez-Ledon, remembers that as they landed at the FOB they could see the fighting going on with the convoy, explosions and tracers in the air.

The troops had been on the ground for several hours when the Taliban, with more sophisticated organization than coalition soldiers had yet encountered, launched an all-out assault. Despite earlier descriptions to the contrary, the battle proper raged for less than an hour, though with air strikes and the like there was secondary action that went on well into the next day.

The enemy assault came from three sides. From a ruined mud compound to the north, from a large hill—or what soldiers insist on calling a "high feature"—to the west, and from the rolling poppy fields to the south, the Taliban attacked with AK-47 automatic rifles, RPGs, the occasional mortar, and what Vernon, with his usual frankness, later acknowledged was their usual fearlessness.

Costall was armed with the C9 machine gun, a weapon with a higher rate of fire (about sixteen bullets a second) and greater range than the standard Canadian issue C7 assault rifle. What he and the other C9 gunner held in their hands represented 50 percent of the section's firepower.

Firing from the prone position under a small berm—they were all on their bellies—Costall was acting as the firebase laying down protective cover for his platoon mates as they tried to move beyond the Hesco Bastion into the area ringed by the concertina wire, where they could better repel the attackers. All they had for protection was the Hesco, and those containers were not yet filled with sand.

Under a moonless black sky, at about 2:45 a.m., Rob Costall was hit twice—once in the head, the bullet entering from behind and tearing out through his mouth, and once at mid-chest, the bullet moving from left to right and exiting about armpit level. The incoming fire was so intense—there were mortars, RPGs, machine-gun fire, and an A10 strafing overhead—Fernandez-Ledon says that "you can hardly even lift your head." He was so close to Costall that he could have reached out and nudged him with an elbow, but it wasn't until the A10 came in and began its strafing runs and the enemy fire died down that he was able to look for Rob and saw him slumped over his C9.

Platoon Warrant Officer Ray Brodeur, shot in the leg and love handle, and two other Canadian soldiers were also injured in the fight. A U.S. Army medic, Sergeant 1st Class John Thomas Stone of the Vermont National Guard, who was in a different spot from the Canadians, was also killed.

Stone and Costall were respectively the 361st and 362nd coalition soldiers to die on Afghanistan soil since 2001, the vast majority of whom were Americans (the first U.S. soldier died in Afghanistan on October 10, 2001, less than a month after the 9/11 terrorist attacks). But each of their deaths was also the first of a kind. Though twenty-one soldiers with ties to Vermont had at that point been killed in Iraq, Stone was the first Vermonter to be killed in Afghanistan. And while Costall was the eleventh Canadian soldier to die in five years in Afghanistan—the twelfth fatality if diplomat Glyn Berry's death in a suicide attack is included—he was the first to perish while engaged in combat.

The reactions in the soldiers' home countries couldn't have been more different. Costall's death was enormous news in Canada, while in the U.S., where the war on terrorism raged on two fronts and where troops had been dying in significant numbers for years, only modest attention was paid to the loss of yet another soldier.

Stone was the baby brother of Dana Stone, a combat photographer who with Sean Flynn, the son of actor Errol Flynn, disappeared in Cambodia in April 1970. After years of being listed as missing in action, the two were presumed captured and dead.

Dana figures prominently in the best war book I've ever read: *Dispatches*, Michael Herr's 1977 memoir of his years as a Vietnam War correspondent. He, Flynn, and Stone—whom Herr described as "a lapsed logger from Vermont . . . twenty-five years old with sixty-year-old eyes set in deep behind wire-rimmed glasses"—were among a group of remarkable young journalists who spent years on the ground with American soldiers in Vietnam.

Tom Stone was a sixteen-year-old high school student when his brother disappeared, and the event appears to have shaped his life. Childhood friends interviewed by Associated Press reporter Wilson Ring, who wrote a poignant story about Tom's death, said that he joined the U.S. Army in 1971 partly out of a need to learn what had happened to Dana. Over the ensuing years, Tom Stone served in the regular army, the reserves, and the Vermont National Guard and was trained as a medic, expertise he used on his first two tours in Afghanistan when he set up a clinic for locals in a shipping container and which, on this last one, he was passing on to the soldiers of the ANA as a trainer.

Jared Smith, like Stone a part-time soldier, is also an instructor at the U.S. Army Mountain Warfare School in Jericho, Vermont, where Stone—or Stoney, as he was called—"was a perennial presence as an instructor and medic." Smith says Stone's "sense of the world as a big place, with room for all, was matched by the size of his heart." He calls him "a quiet American, and a great man."

Back in Canada, anchors on the all-news cable networks were donning shocked expressions, while editors rounded up various military experts to pronounce on the meaning of the country's first combat casualty. But at the BATs that day, Costall's peers were variously sombre, angry, and weepy, if hardly reeling with surprise.

On my way over to the BATs, I ran into a guy I knew a little, a military police sergeant named Pete Maltais. We'd met at the Gumbad Patrol House, where I'd spent about a week earlier that month, when each of us was sneaked in to visit the two sniffer dogs working with Alpha Company.

"It's God's lottery," Maltais said when I asked about Costall's death. He meant that it was a little like losing "someone in the family who's been very sick for a long time—death is expected, only you just don't know who" will die, who will lose the lottery. "It's like a punch in the face, and if you don't have your gloves up. . . . I've been preparing my guys for this for three months."

Because 7 Platoon was still up at the FOB, Charlie's 9 Platoon, under Sergeant Pat Tower, would provide the pallbearers for Costall's ramp ceremony that night. From the red-eyed group smoking outside the big tent, one of them, Private Jerry Conlon, emerged to speak to us.

Conlon knew Costall from basic training three and a half years earlier, but his most vivid memory was of the day, about a year earlier, when Costall came running up to him at the Edmonton garrison, shouting, "I got married! I got married!"

"He was extremely excited," Conlon remembered. "He knew his wife was The One, and expressed that openly." As Conlon spoke, his hands shook. Echoing Maltais's words, Conlon said they had been prepared for losing soldiers, but added, "I never thought it would be Cost."

Herr wrote in *Dispatches* that for all the violence and death a soldier (or reporter) sees in war, it is only when a friend is killed that it becomes real, in part because it feels as though your own odds have changed. Conlon seemed to be feeling some of that. "Whenever we go out again," he said, "I just hope it's safe."

Costall was not only a new husband, to Chrissy, but also a new father, to Collin. His platoon commander, Hugh Atwell, who had taught the basic infantry qualification course when Costall took it, says he'd developed from a young man with a typical young man's organization skills into "a really outstanding soldier and an outstanding family man . . . he'd grown a lot in the [previous] three years."

Perhaps it was these new responsibilities, Costall's OC said, that had made the young man unusually mature for his age. While reserved, "at least around his major," Bill Fletcher said with a wry smile, Costall "was carefully considered; you knew you should listen. He had real leadership potential." Fletcher knew him only as a very good soldier; "I know the bad apples more than the good ones," he said.

Fletcher had broken the news to the rest of the troops that morning. "I could have kicked them in the guts, it would have hurt less," he said. "It was the toughest thing I've done [to that point] in my career."

Costall's ramp ceremony was at 8 p.m. that night. It was a warm spring evening. Songbirds, confused by the bright lights of the big hangar optimistically called Taliban's Last Stand, made more noise than the thousands of soldiers marching onto the tarmac.

Rob Costall's body arrived in a LAV so scrubbed and shiny it didn't even resemble the vehicles in the field. The young pallbearers arrived in another. The ramps dropped, and the soldiers hoisted the casket on their shoulders and began moving between the two lines of troops, fourteen rows deep—Brits, Americans, Dutch, Danes, Estonians, French, Romanians, and Canadians. The casket was carried into the belly of the waiting Hercules C-130. A piper played the lament. A padre said a prayer, then came the goodbye: "Task Force Afghanistan, to your fallen comrade salute!" It was moving, dignified, lovely; it was also unspeakably sad. This part I wrote about for my newspaper.

I didn't mention the command that immediately followed the salute: "Carry on!" I didn't write that the ceremony was over too bloody fast and seemed not nearly enough. I didn't know what to make of it, so I didn't know how to write about it. I had cried throughout but at the end all I felt was empty. I was beginning to understand how it is that soldiers are so pragmatic, why they are so constrained in their grieving: If they weren't, they couldn't possibly carry on, and carrying on is what they must do.

This was in part why Hope deliberately left 7 Platoon at the FOB for a couple of days, "to keep their heads in the game," as he says.

Atwell concurs: "It probably actually did us good to be stuck out there, carrying on ops for the next few days. That way, the guys could be with the guys who understand best." In the familiarity of routine, Atwell says, was psychological comfort.

However, the CO was furious that a morning or two after the fight, a chopper arrived at Robinson with an American colonel and a chaplain to hold a service for Tom Stone. "I was unaware of this flight and not invited to go see the troops," Hope says now. "Nor was a Canadian chaplain invited to administer religious service to 7 Platoon, who had just lost their brother Costall, their platoon warrant, and two other soldiers. I was pissed, and so were most of 7 Platoon."

Also on that chopper were a Canadian military policeman and a Canadian legal officer, there to begin investigating the possibility that only the soldiers at the FOB and a very few others then knew about—that Costall and Stone might have been killed, and the others wounded, by friendly fire. Canada had managed to get cops and lawyers to the scene, which was clearly correct procedure, but no one had thought to tend to the emotional welfare of the troops, which was just as clearly the moral thing to do.

Four days later, I was in Pat Tower's LAV, part of an enormous convoy heading to FOB Robinson in Operation Ketara, the Pashtu word for "dagger." With 7 Platoon back at KAF now—as Fletcher said at the time, they arrived "a little lighter than normal . . . and they certainly fucking earned their keep"—the rest of Charlie Company was part of a major push into Helmand Province designed to secure the FOB, interrupt the Taliban, settle things down enough so the ANA with British support could start in on poppy eradication, and support the "kill-capture" mission of special forces in the area.

I'd sat in on two major briefings by then—Vernon's, given to reporters on the day Costall died, and Fletcher's, given before we left to his NCOs and junior officers—and knew enough to be apprehensive. The scariest things Fletcher had mentioned were how quickly this particular group of insurgents was able to activate pre-planted IEDs (on less than ten minutes' notice) and that there was intelligence that five or six suicide bombers were driving about Kandahar city looking for a good reason to blow themselves up. My notes show that when someone asked how long they'd be away, Fletcher replied "not less than twenty-four hours and no more than thirty-six days," but I've no record of how long we expected the trip to take.

We left KAF at 9:10 a.m., Tower firing up the MP3 player with Johnny Cash's "Sea of Heartbreak" and Toby Keith's "The Taliban." Our first unscheduled stop occurred about ninety minutes later, when a vehicle in the packet ahead of us took a wrong turn and broke down, and another hit a donkey. We were stuck on the side of a road smack in the middle of the teeming city, and among the sights so strange was an ice cream truck, playing the same kind of hand-cranked music you hear at home.

I was shooting the breeze with a couple of the kids, Privates Daniel Mahlo and Dawson Bayliss. Bayliss is a distant cousin of Toronto Police Constable Todd Bayliss, whose murder on a hot summer night in 1996 I'd covered while working for the *Toronto Sun*. I got to know Todd Bayliss's parents and brother Cory well, and covered the trial of his killer, Clinton Junior Gayle. Mahlo and I had a funny little connection too: He'd entered grade 8 at Lord Lansdowne Public School the same fall I'd bought and moved into the house where I still live, right across the street from the school. He credited the army with helping him turn his life around: He was married now, with a little girl.

We'd been rolling again for only about an hour, Bayliss and Mahlo back in the open rear hatches as air sentries, when suddenly there was a huge *crack!* and Mahlo came tumbling into the LAV, his face covered in blood. I didn't know what the hell had happened—had he been shot? RPGed?—but Tower and the other soldiers were calm and in control. Within seconds, someone pulled Bayliss inside to safety too, the convoy stopped, and the troops were out the ramp, guns at the ready.

It turned out that the cannon atop the LAV had been accidentally clipped by a passing truck that came too close. As the cannon spun around, it smacked the two privates hard in the face and head. Both were barely conscious and, while in no real danger, were hurt seriously enough that they had to be evacuated.

I remember that Mahlo's moustache was soaked with blood, and that when Bayliss briefly came to, he cried only, "Mahlo? Mahlo?" The medics and other soldiers stayed with them, someone was touching them both always, until the choppers came. I remember how gingerly Louie Palu, the *Globe* photographer with me, and I tip-toed around, feeling ghoulish, him not sure if he could, or should, shoot, and me trying to write notes and get everyone's names quietly. It was a sobering episode, but what was really sobering was how quickly you adjusted to what had just happened.

For these two young guys—Mahlo was twenty-three, Bayliss twenty-two—their adventure in Afghanistan was over, their war was over. Yet once the chopper carrying them back to the hospital at

KAF was out of sight, it was almost as though they had never existed except in the minds of their mates. There was a little more room in the back of the LAV and nobody played any music for the rest of the trip, but that was it.

The series of mishaps continued. A suicide bomber was still trying to make his way to the convoy, and on the radio I heard someone say, "He can see us, he just can't get to us." I remember thinking that if the bomber did find a clear route through, we might be able to watch on the thermal imaging screen as he approached. Theoretically, you could watch the car that was going to try to kill you seconds before it veered toward your vehicle and blew you up.

Next, a gun truck had engine problems, and for almost an hour we parked at the side of the road, right by an uncleared minefield. Lying in the sun in my body armour, land mines all around us, I felt safer than I had the whole trip.

Darkness fell.

We were going off-road now, trying to avoid IEDs, and more vehicles got lost or stuck. Ian Hope was on the radio a lot; the CO was busying himself with the lowliest jobs, recovering vehicles and making himself useful while staying out of Fletcher's hair. I heard Nichola Goddard's voice often, too, though I didn't know then who she was or what she did. We would all stop and wait as vehicles were recovered or redirected.

During the last of these stops, just before dawn, still chewing a wad of Nicorette gum, I bummed a cigarette. I had it to my lips when Louie snatched it from my mouth and broke it. I'd been off smokes for more than a decade at that point, I think, but the combination of nerves and boredom almost did me in. "You'll thank me for this tomorrow," Louie said. I didn't feel particularly grateful. I remember wanting to punch him out.

We got to FOB Robinson sometime in the morning. It had taken almost twenty-four hours to travel 110 kilometres.

—

AFTER A COUPLE OF HOURS' SLEEP in the heat of the spring sun, the four of us embedded with Charlie on this trip—Louie and me, my friend Rosie DiManno from the *Toronto Star*, and freelance film-maker Richard Fitoussi—were shaken awake by Sergeant Major Shawn Stevens and told we were going to be choppered out of the FOB. The party line was that General Fraser had decided the base was too sketchy, too dangerous, for reporters.

We bitched and complained, but got nowhere. We barely had time to see where Rob Costall had died—the north "gate," at the time nothing more than a break in the concertina wire, was now named after him, and would soon bear a plaque—before the heli-copter came to fetch us. We were bewildered, not sure what had changed, or why we were being given the boot, but we were back at KAF within a couple of hours.

Two days later, when Fraser and U.S. Brigadier-General Anthony Tata called a briefing, the light bulb over my head at last went on. The generals announced that Costall and Stone might have been killed by friendly fire, and that some of the two Afghans and three Canadians who had been injured might have been wounded in the same manner. After an initial probe, they said, further investigations were warranted, and each country would conduct its own.

These probes were formally announced on April 4, though Canada's, in the form of the military police and legal officers on the ground at the FOB, had actually started before then.

On April 2, in Toronto, an autopsy had been conducted on Costall's body (the bodies of all Canadian casualties are autopsied). It had revealed nothing of use. Military officials had been hoping for a bullet, or fragment of bullet, that could be positively identified as ammunition used exclusively by Taliban forces, thus putting to rest their worst fears. But Costall's body had two exit wounds, and not a trace of the projectiles that had done all the damage.

It was only in July of 2007, more than a year later, that the Americans were first to formally announce what the soldiers already knew—Costall and Stone had been killed by friendly fire. It's not that these investigations are as complex as the one conducted after the assassination of U.S. President John F. Kennedy, though they took longer. The Warren Commission completed its work and reported back within ten months. In Canada, the National Investigation Service, a branch of the Canadian Forces Provost Marshall, stalled in releasing its findings, despite repeated requests by reporters.

But Sergeant Smith, Stone's friend and fellow instructor at the U.S. Army Mountain Warfare School, says that while he was not on the ground at the FOB on the day in question, "this concerned my friends, and of course we talk, so that we may understand. . . . Yes, it was absolutely friendly fire, for both of them." Smith also said in an email he sent me from Afghanistan in the spring of 2007, "I'm not sure if Stoney knew from where the bullets were coming, but that clearly did not matter to him."

It shouldn't matter to anyone, in the sense that the two men died, as they say in the army, "going forward." They were doing their jobs, in a harrowing place that was being attacked on three sides, and were in a chaotic battle practically tailor-made for mistakes. Whose bullets stopped them—whether the enemy's or those of their own side—doesn't diminish a whit their deaths or the nature of their sacrifice. Soldiers understand this better, and are more appreciative of how easily it can happen, than any other group of people on Earth.

"Believe me when I say that when a soldier dies in a battle," Ian Hope says, "there is always more blame to go around than will be accounted for, from those who sent him to those who pulled triggers to those who hesitated under fire to help, etc., etc. When you fight, these kinds of investigations mean nothing. Costall died advancing into the darkness into very intense enemy fire, moving to the aid of Canadians in trouble."

This is what counts most to soldiers.

In late December 2006, the Canadian Press reported that the four of us embedded at FOB Robinson that day were removed because of complaints from allies. The suggestion was that Canada was just too damn aggressive in getting reporters out in the field and it made the soldiers of other nations uncomfortable. The story was based on documents obtained under the federal Access to Information Act and, reading between the lines, the inference was that we may have been turfed because the Patricias were operating with U.S. Special Forces at the FOB.

But *all* Special Forces soldiers, including Canada's, are the stealth counter-intelligence experts of their armies. They work, kill, and sometimes are killed in utter anonymity. Having a bunch of journalists cheek by jowl probably is their idea of a nightmare.

I suspect it wasn't just that, or even the much ballyhooed angst purportedly felt by coalition nations about the progressive nature of the Canadian embedding program, that saw Fraser usher us out of there. The possibility that Costall and Stone had been killed by friendly fire was already in the air like a bad smell by the time we left KAF for the FOB. By the time we arrived, on April 3, the military would have received the results of the post-mortem on Costall's body and realized that a more thorough investigation was unavoidable. My hunch is that the last thing they wanted was four reporters poking about the scene.

Moreover, since April 18, 2002, when American pilots mistakenly bombed Canadians conducting a live-fire exercise at Tarnak Farm near KAF, killing four soldiers and seriously injuring several others, the Canadian public is sensitive to the alleged trigger-happy nature of Americans in war. My suspicion, then and now, is that we were removed to avoid inflaming that sentiment and fuelling doubts about the Afghanistan mission. The lid went on—and stayed on tight. The military doesn't have confidence that we in the press understand, and can put into context, what a friendly-fire death does and does not mean. Keeping the thing secret only feeds the sense that there is something to hide.

—

AS HONOURABLE AND IMPORTANT as the rear party is to soldiers and their families, no one seeks out the job. It's like Groucho Marx and that club you won't join because it accepts you as a member. Rich Raymond's first thought when Ian Hope told him he wouldn't be deploying but instead would be the guy in charge back home was: "He thinks I'm incompetent." Raymond was the only Officer Commanding in the battalion with children, and Hope wanted the soldier who would be breaking the worst news to be a family man with a visceral feel for the devastation his few words would unleash.

At the time, Raymond was new to the 1st Battalion—he'd always been a 2nd Battalion Patricia based in Shilo before that—and as the OC of combat support, he was fully expecting to go to Afghanistan. "I was the only major with a wife and kids," he says. "No one wants to be the OC rear party." But he sucked up his disappointment, took his new job diligently, and brought to it the same seriousness he brings to everything.

Before the troops were deployed, Raymond and his sergeant-major, Don Reid, met with the soldiers and their families to introduce themselves and exchange contact information. "We had to get our message across to the families," Raymond says, "so they know who or who not to contact. It's not good enough to say, 'I can get by if I ever get hurt.' You have to know how to get hold of people. If it's going to work, it's by staying informed."

Raymond and Reid gave out fridge magnets with their phone numbers, showed the families slides, and set up a website. They told the wives, "You have to know his service number. If you know nothing else, know this. You have to know about your finances, insurance, vehicle information, mortgage. It's your responsibility. . . . If the furnace goes on the fritz, and he's in Afghanistan, we need to get that information to him and you have to know what to do."

They took a death notification course in Edmonton, put on by Mothers Against Drunk Driving and the local police victim services unit. They learned the value and mercy of bluntness. "At the course, they told us you have to use words like 'kill,' 'die,' and 'dead,'" Raymond says. "There can't be any misunderstanding."

The first two soldiers to die on Roto 1, Tim Wilson and Paul Davis, were from 2nd Battalion. Raymond's turn didn't come until March 29.

Chrissy and Rob lived in the permanent married quarters on the base. Raymond had to get it right the first time, otherwise in the close confines of base housing someone would notice the young major and the padre knocking on a door, and fear would spread like wildfire.

Raymond did a reconnaissance first, hoping he'd be able to tell whether someone was there, then summoned his nerve and knocked on the door. "I was scared as hell," he says. "She came to the door, holding Collin, and I said, 'Rob was killed in a firefight today.' She collapsed, and I caught Collin."

Chrissy, then just twenty, wasn't up to calling Costall's parents in Gibsons, British Columbia, so Raymond had to do it. He got Costall's mother, Bonnie, and told her the bad news. "I remember hearing his father in the background, it was incredible, they didn't believe it. 'Are you certain it's my son?'" He could hear Bonnie say, "Robert's dead," and then the sound of Greg Costall sobbing.

Raymond had to line up an assisting officer for the family. Within a few days, Chris Lindsay, a Patricia then assigned to the Canadian Scottish Regiment in British Columbia, was trying to think of how he could bring some relief to the terrible circle of grief into which he suddenly had been thrust. Realizing that it was Saturday night, that *Hockey Night in Canada* would be on the tube, Lindsay said he bet that Don Cherry would say something about Robert. "And he did," Raymond says.

Choked up, as he so often is when he speaks about soldiers, Cherry mentioned Costall, Chrissy, Bonnie, and Collin as pictures of the dead soldier and his thirteen-month-old son rolled.

It's curious how few people are content to let a soldier's death just be. It isn't only the press, though God knows many of us are guilty of this, who like our heroes and villains clear-cut and who paint the world of the dead in far starker colours than usually exist in imperfect living human beings. Just as Tony Boneca, the young man killed in action on July 9, came to be seen as a victim of the very army he had joined of his own free will, so did Robbie Costall and Tom Stone come to be viewed as uncomplicated men who were brave beyond all bearing.

After he was killed, Boneca's prospective father-in-law had repeated publicly what his young daughter, Boneca's fiancée, had told him in her distress—that the young man had been suffering in the field, was afraid, and felt unprepared. Sadly, that became Boneca's undeserved epitaph—he was that poor kid who died doing what he didn't want to be doing. In truth, whatever his feelings, and of course they were complex, Tony Boneca's actions spoke loudest: He was going forward, doing his job with his mates and friends when he was felled by a bullet in the neck.

In the same way, Stone's army friends have come to believe that the fifty-two-year-old medic died while racing to administer first aid to at least one of the Canadian wounded and that he threw himself upon Robbie Costall, trying to shield and save him. As one of them told me, "Tom's a medic, the soldiers are down and exposed, he goes to get them."

In fact, Chris Fernandez-Ledon says Stone *was* racing to a soldier's aid, an ETT officer who was on a rooftop, when he was killed. "Stone was going up the ladder to go and help him," Fernandez-Ledon says, "and that's when he got shot through the neck." That occurred in a different part of the FOB, not where Fernandez-Ledon and Costall were.

"The way the battle unfolded," Hugh Atwell says, "Sergeant Stone was not in a position to help our wounded before he was killed. Obviously, this does not diminish his character. By all accounts, he was an excellent person."

In much the same way, Costall is known to the public only through the prism of his brave soldier's death, as a terrific young private who had found a sense of direction in the military and died doing his job in a mission in which he believed so deeply. What Justin Kellehar, a military truck driver who was a friend of Costall's and stationed with him in Kandahar, has to say about Costall doesn't entirely square with that simplified portrait, but it sure is consistent with the normal feelings we all have roiling around inside.

I ran into Kellehar in July 2006, at Camp Souter in Kabul. He was there for a bit of a break, replacing another soldier who had needed one and now was ready to go back. "He was a gung-ho guy too," Kellehar said of his predecessor. "His view has changed. He knows how important it is to go home, that we're not playing a game now, we're not digging a trench in minus fifty–degree weather and sitting in it until 4 a.m."

Kellehar was tired, and he was particularly tired of being always afraid. Like most of the truck drivers working for the National Service Element, he'd been out on dozens of convoys—at that point, more than forty, if you count each round trip as a single mission—and he was frankly a little spooked.

"I was quite terrified," he said that day. "Every convoy, I was going in scared. My goal until my HLTA was to stay alive so I could see my kids."

His younger stepbrother, Nick Fenton, was on 7 Platoon with Costall, and Kellehar watched him change before his eyes. "He was all gung-ho, he'd never been in a firefight, but 7 Platoon has been ambushed, they've been in firefights more times than he can count. It's like the platoon is cursed."

Fenton had helped load Costall's body onto the truck. "[Nick] was just out of it," Kellehar said. "He saw these special gloves [black and white, they were thicker so Costall could hold his C9 more comfortably] Rob wore but he didn't connect that it was Rob. Rob was face down." Fenton called their mother that night from a satellite phone. "He's the youngest," Kellehar said. "She calls him her baby boy. He just broke down."

Kellehar was also shaken by how suddenly frightening his own trade had become. While none of the convoys he'd been on were hit by IEDs or ambushed, Kellehar was part of the grisly recovery effort on April 22, when Bill Turner and three members of Dave Fraser's personal protection team were blown up and killed.

"That was the worst thing I had to do," he said, "was recover that G-Wagon. The big bits were picked up by then, but there were still bits of human flesh on everything. . . . It was worse for the A Company guys. These were their friends, to see them like that."

Kellehar and Costall met through their wives—April and Chrissy walked the Edmonton base for exercise together and soon roped their husbands into joining them—and became very close quickly.

"Rob was sitting beside me when I found out we were pregnant," Kellehar said. In fact, Suzann Cromwell, Kellehar's and Fenton's mother, remembers that "Rob and Chrissy brought the pregnancy test over there" that day for April to use. The result of that pregnancy, Justin and April's third child and first little girl, was born July 27, 2006. She's named Robin, after Costall.

Kellehar and Costall had a cigarette at Canada House shortly before 7 Platoon was called out to what Kellehar refers to as "the dark side." "I told him he looked like a raccoon," he said. "He always wore those sunglasses and he was all white under the eyes. We were just sitting around. He was drinking coffee in forty-degree heat."

Costall, he said, "was here only so he could buy a house afterwards. He wanted to get out of the infantry, he just didn't enjoy it. But he wanted the benefits for his family. He would have received his corporal's, which means four years, after the tour."

Chrissy and Rob had thought of going to England when Rob got leave—he was due to go in May—but decided to save the money toward their house, Kellehar said. He admired his friend as "a really good, caring, loving father" and said that baby Collin was still asking for him. "Collin never spoke before Rob left," he said, "but while he was away, Chrissy taught him to say 'dada.'"

April was worried that he would come back colder, but Kellehar said he thought his experience in Afghanistan "has bettered me. I see how important my family is. Family was always important, but more now." While there were things he wouldn't miss—going out on convoys, and the feeling "you get when they tell you you're going out, your heart just drops, you lose your secureness, you know nothing is within your control anymore"—there was much he would. "The togetherness of my comrades, good times with my brother." Here, he grew a little teary: "I wouldn't be as well off if it wasn't for my brother. He sort of holds it down, helps me. He gives me something to look forward to."

Fenton had his platoon mates for company. If one of the guys ever needed to talk, Suzann says, they'd call an impromptu meeting and conduct ceremonial remembrances that helped exorcise the grief of Costall's loss. But Kellehar, who was part of a unit composed of soldiers from various platoons, was essentially left to manage on his own.

On Remembrance Day, 2006, there was a special service in Gibsons for Costall, and Kellehar was desperate to go. He wanted to be with Costall's family, Nick, and other members of 7 Platoon. His own folks, who live in Victoria, were coming to the mainland for the service. The Patricias, recognizing that this quiet young man was Costall's best friend and that he needed to go, offered to pick up the tab for Kellehar's flight, Suzann says. It was his own unit, 1st Service Battalion, that put the brakes to the plan. Kellehar spent November 11 at a ceremony near Edmonton that was utterly meaningless to him.

In the spring of 2006, Justin Kellehar was twenty-nine; Rob Costall, twenty-two; and Chrissy Costall just twenty. Products of their generation, they all had MSN screen names for instant messaging. Chrissy's was "pleaseprayforrobssafereturn." After Rob was killed, she changed it to "Icanseeyourfatherinyoureyes."

Kellehar's was simple: "Justininkabul." It revealed nothing about his fears, the guts it took to wrestle them down to manageable size so he could get on another convoy, the days when that was harder or easier, or the whole complicated ball of wax that is the ordinary human being.

Rob Costall's was just as plain: "Kandaharairfield."

Justin Kellehar hasn't yet been able to bring himself to erase Rob Costall from his MSN list. "I can't delete him," he said. "I just can't do it."

Lt.-Col. John Conrad

22 July 2006

—

Brigadier-General Dave Fraser, to Lieutenant-Colonel Ian Hope, in radio orders given at 11:30 p.m. on July 17: "You need to recapture Nawa and Garmser by 1600 hours."
Hope to Fraser: "Roger that. Recapture Nawa and Garmser by 1600 hours."
Fraser: "Any questions?"
Hope: "Just one: Where are Nawa and Garmser?"

ON THE NIGHT of July 17, 2006, the Patricias believed, hoped, and were all but praying that they were done with Helmand Province.

They'd been going hard for most of the month.

Except for the soldiers of Bravo Company, who were holding the fort in the treacherous Panjwaii area, Task Force Orion, the Canadian battle group, had already been in the British AO for almost two weeks. They were there at the specific request of then Helmand governor Mohammed Daoud, who had pressed Dave Fraser, commander of the multinational coalition, to get troops into Sangin to bring some order to this lawless part of his province.

The town and environs are a hotspot for opium thugs and tribal warlords, with "the Taliban just stirring the pot," Fraser says. "So we put together this brigade attack."

With Ian Hope at the helm and two U.S. companies attached— one from the 2nd Battalion, 4th Infantry Regiment, known as Task Force Warrior; the other from the 2nd Battalion of the 87th Infantry Regiment—it was the first time in anyone's memory that American infantry had been under the operational control of a Canadian. The soldiers were supporting the British in clearing parts of Sangin, containing enemy in the mountain passes of Ghorak, and operating east of the Helmand River, all the while sleeping rough, living on rats, and in the fight more often than not.

So they were tired. More critically, they were almost out of smokes.

"I can tell you," says Willy MacDonald of recce platoon, "when we did not leave for KAF when we were supposed to, it was a collective groan, as we were desperately short of cigarettes."

That night, the platoon was in a leaguer in the basic guns-pointing-out defensive square, with Kirk Gallinger and A Company in another nearby. The Canadians were spread out just east of Highway 611, the main north–south route in Helmand. They planned to leave the next morning for KAF, and pull into leaguers all the way back, just as they'd been leaguering themselves silly throughout the province.

"If you'd told me in training two or three years ago that on an operation we'd be doing a leaguer, I'd say, 'You're fucking crazy. It ain't gonna happen. You're Cold War; you think you're in Germany.' But we did it," Gallinger says, "and it actually worked."

Leaguers had been used extensively during the Canadian army's forty-two years under NATO in the former West Germany: It was an easy way to control the tanks. But with the collapse of the former Soviet Union and the Canadian pullout from Germany in the mid-1990s, the leaguer had fallen out of favour. In recent years it was taught to new soldiers only as an administrative measure, not as a defensive position.

"But in the desert," as Hope says, "it's pretty bloody good," especially if the vehicles are parked on the highest point: With the views stretching out forever, no one can approach unseen.

One night, on the way into Helmand, the Canadians turned that principle on its ear and parked 150 vehicles in a depression on the desert floor. From a kilometre out, the entire convoy was invisible.

Hope and the rest of his headquarters group, including operations officer Mason Stalker, arrived at the A Company leaguer late on July 17 in what Gallinger calls a "classic jugfuck"—vehicles moving through this sketchy area, pulling up in the pitch black, everyone grumbling and beat and desperate for sleep.

For Hope and Niner's Tac, it had been a particularly harrowing day. He'd gone out near Hyderabad, intending merely to say goodbye to Captain Steve Wallace and his Delta (or Devil) Company from Task Force Warrior, which was based in Zabul Province. The Americans were to be cut from them the next day, and Hope wanted to "coin" Wallace, give him as a thank you one of the gorgeous multicoloured Orion souvenir coins.

But when they arrived, the Yanks were smack in the middle of a battle, and as Hope and his two LAVs unleashed the welcome boom-boom-boom of their cannons, a great cheer went up from the Americans. "After only several minutes of fire," Hope says, "the enemy began to withdraw, giving us brief glimpses of dark-turbaned forms running between compound walls and into the green belt."

Wallace and Hope knew from previous experience that once the enemy got to the safety of The Green—lush orchards and fields with a maze of interconnected compounds replete with narrow paths, high walls, and irrigation canals—they were as good as gone. A platoon of U.S. soldiers dismounted and began the chase, with Hope and his LAV guns walking them in, covering their movement with fire, until they hit the first compound.

The LAVs put fifteen or twenty rounds into the thick wall, to no effect. Randy Northrup, Hope's RSM, even dismounted and tried to punch a hole in the thing with an M72 anti-armour weapon. Still nothing. Finally, Hope's driver, Stitch Hayward, rolled his LAV slowly forward and bumped the wall. It collapsed, leaving a seven-foot gap for the Americans to go through.

With the LAVs giving what's called intimate support, the soldiers began clearing compounds and orchards of enemy fighting positions, finding blood trails and body parts severed off by the 25 millimetre cannon fire as they went.

"I jockeyed Niner's Tac from firing position to firing position on the right flank of the U.S. infantry," Hope says—until, trying to take a tight corner between a compound and a house, they were hit by RPG fire. "The first round passed between the cannon and the driver's hatch and struck the wall beside me."

His language is low key, but this was a very, very close call. No one was injured but the fire disabled the comms on Hope's vehicle.

With a U.S. sergeant and dismounted soldiers just behind his LAV, asking for directions, and Hope unable to make himself heard over the firing to tell the Americans where the enemy was, the CO grabbed his C7, jumped out of the turret, and told the Americans to follow him. In a long single file, the then forty-three-year-old Hope in the lead, they worked their way around a compound, entered an open rice field, and were suddenly under heavy small-arms fire.

The American soldiers, many veterans of both Afghanistan and Iraq, responded instantly. "They quickly won the firefight," Hope says. "I reflected later upon this, and realized that at some point in the past decade we have had a fundamental shift in the culture of the Canadian infantry, making us identify most easily with American, and not British, infantry. Devil Company was easy to work with, reliable and very professional. They wanted to fight, and when the firing began, their leaders demonstrated decisiveness and tenacity, and their soldiers performed battle drills quickly and with great effect."

A young U.S. platoon commander then arrived and took charge, and Hope began making his way back to his LAV under "sporadic but quite scary fire." No one was happier to see him return intact than Randy Northrup. "I couldn't believe it," the RSM says. "I aged that day." He calls July 17 the day Hope "jumped out to be a platoon commander again."

As night was falling, Hope finally gave Wallace the Orion coin and they began the slow move back, lights out and off road, to the A Company leaguer.

"I was exhausted," Hope says, in the throes of what he calls "the post-combat adrenalin slide" and a brush with death. He checked with Stalker to make sure they were ready to begin heading back to KAF the next morning, and was assured they were good to go.

The boys were already snoring as Hope took his spot on the bench in the rear of the LAV, a scrunched-up raincoat as a pillow and a Ranger blanket to ward off the chill. He'd just loosened the laces on his boots, "was on the brink of instantaneous sleep," when a duty officer climbed in to tell him Fraser would be giving him radio orders in five minutes.

Getting orders on the radio was rare, so Hope knew something was up, and that they could forget about getting back to KAF for a shower. What he didn't know was that for a couple of days now, Fraser had been fending off Governor Daoud, who in the middle of the attack on Sangin, the very one he'd requested, had decided the coalition must now go to Garmser.

The first time Daoud asked, Fraser replied with a variation of the same question Hope asked that night: "What the hell is Garmser?" Fraser held the governor at bay for a while, but then the district centres in Nawa and Garmser—pro-government towns—fell to the Taliban and Daoud did what he often did when he wanted action. He picked up the phone and called President Hamid Karzai.

"This had now got to the point where it's not just this governor, who can't prioritize and everything's a priority to him," Fraser says, "but the president finally said, 'I need this thing done because it's strategically important to me, at this level.' When Karzai calls, I haul. It's as simple as that.

"So I look around and the only unit that has the potential of doing it, and more importantly when I look at all my units—the British, the Dutch, the Canadians, and the Americans—[is] the best equipped for firepower protection and mobility, [is] the Canadians. I don't say that because I'm a Canadian," Fraser says. "I say that as the brigade commander: The best unit I had there were the Canadians."

As he puts it, "I gotta use Ian, and Ian's tired."

His staff briefed him, and Fraser went into his operations room, told them to get Hope on the radio and tell him, "I'm gonna give him orders. On the radio. I will talk to Ian, no one else."

Soon enough, he was doing just that—giving brigade orders to a battle group at the tail end of a brigade operation. "So I went through the entire orders with him and Ian being Ian just clicked his heels and went, 'Yup. Got it,' and then he asked the infamous question: 'Where are these places?'"

Hope remembers Fraser saying, "They're in southern Helmand."
"Roger," he replied. "But we have no maps."

"We will get maps to you as soon as possible," Fraser said.

There was obvious tension, Hope says, after the radio orders, "as everyone knew we were staying out in the heat and the dust and danger for another week. It had already been eleven days. The sentiment was, 'Isn't there anyone else they can task to do their hard work? We're tired of rescuing everyone.'" Hope's resilient group was momentarily feeling victimized, so he gathered together a few key leaders and told them to "get over it." Then he told Stalker to relay the warning order to the company commanders by radio and arrange for a resupply and an area where everyone could meet—they were now spread out over about seventy kilometres—for orders the next day.

Gallinger was sleeping on the ground by his LAV when someone "came over and kicked me and said, 'The colonel wants to see you in the command post.'" It was well after midnight when he walked into the command post "and I can remember Colonel Hope smoking on a cigar. He had just got his radio orders to retake these two district centres, and he tells the story, you know, 'Any questions?' 'Yeah, where's Nawa and Garmser?' Because literally we had no maps, we had no idea where they were."

Not far away, in recce's leaguer, Jon Hamilton's signaller, Corporal Kelly Smith, was soon on the coms telling him, "'Sir, there's a warning order in like ten minutes,' and I'm like, what the fuck?"

Hamilton loves Smitty, and he loves talking about Smitty. They call themselves the Windtalkers, after the Navajo who in the 2002 John Woo–directed movie enlisted as Marines and became code talkers, using their ancient language to defeat the Japanese code breakers. Hamilton and Smith, a Metis born in northern British Columbia, talked in a code all their own—both are stutterers.

Hamilton has a smidgeon of a stutter, almost unnoticeable. He tends to repeat letters or syllables. But Smith, a gifted signaller, has the sort of stutter where despite magnificent efforts, he can't get words out at all. He can't start a sentence unless he swears, most particularly unless he uses some variant of "fuck."

As Hamilton says, from the first moment Smitty got on the radio, "trying to say 'contact,' and he's trying: 'Ca . . . ca . . . con . . . ' He goes, 'Fucking contact!'" So he quickly became "the only guy in the army permitted to swear on the net because it's the only way he can get it out. When we'd get on the horn, sometimes you can't understand what we're saying because of the stutters, so we call ourselves the Windtalkers."

The warning order that Smitty announced in the very early morning of July 18 was that recce should get ready to move: They weren't going back to KAF.

Ian Hope went back to his bench in the LAV and fell into a deep sleep. Kirk Gallinger quickly briefed his second-in-command, Damon Tedford, leaving him with more questions than answers, then collapsed back on the ground and grabbed a few hours' rest. That was all most of the troops knew for the moment—not that they were about to turn south 180 degrees, travel another 160 kilometres deeper into Helmand Province, and retake two towns now in Taliban control, all while in a full-fledged cigarette crisis.

—

HOPE WOKE with first light—on those long summer days, it arrived at the unholy hour of 4 a.m.—grabbed a coffee, and Gallinger, and they waited for the bird that was going to take them on an air reconnaissance.

They jumped aboard and asked the pilots if they had the maps. Negative. They had only aerial ones, though blessedly they knew at least that Nawa and Garmser were south of Lashkar Gah, the provincial capital, on the Helmand River. Further complicating matters was the fact that the headsets weren't working, so Hope was the only one who could talk to the pilots. Gallinger was basically a passenger, but what he saw impressed the hell out of him. They flew first to pick up Wallace, the American commander, who'd been ordered to stick around, and then proceeded south.

"Without a map and with no real knowledge of where Nawa and

Garmser were," Hope says, "I took out pencil and paper and began to sketch our routes. I told the pilots I needed two routes traversable to LAVs and heavy vehicles."

From the air, the CO watched the roads and prominent tracks, tried to memorize details of various intersections—that corner marked by an ANP station and a flag; that turn there by a little bridge—and then quickly drew them.

"Flying in a helicopter," Gallinger says, "and trying to highlight a route where to me most routes look the same, it was just an example of his capacity, his fairly unbelievable capacity, and you know, just very very switched on. And it worked. It was a route we needed to take and it got us there. Without getting blown up, which is always a big plus."

From the air, Nawa looked to Gallinger "like what I remember in Croatia and Bosnia. . . . It looked like it had been torched, and it looked like it had been ethnically cleansed, so we knew, uh oh, this is not good, because if there's no civilians around, obviously the enemy is probably hiding, and in my mind I'm thinking this is going to be pretty ugly."

Then they flew over Garmser, and it, sadly, was on the east side of the Helmand, with only one bridge over the river south of Lashkar Gah. "A fairly large bridge," Gallinger says, "and again in my mind, I'm oooooh, this just sucks."

They flew back, linked up with the troops, and made a road move to a tactical assembly area. There Hope issued a quick set of orders. As he spoke, copies of his crude hand-drawn map—the route highlighted—were being distributed.

"I remember the orders," Hamilton says. "I didn't go to staff college in Toronto to be a CO, but I know that he probably would have failed for those orders, but he had nothin' to go on. I'm just looking at Kirk, 'Okay, let's go, fuck!'"

Hope puts it rather more delicately: "It was something very much less than I expected in modern warfare in 2006." Still, with no maps, only sparse intelligence, a grainy air photo of each district centre and his sketch of the routes, "I was confident," he says.

So was Gallinger. "It was very clear what we had to do," he says. "We had a good plan. We were gonna go in two large company groups to take these two district centres, and [Hope] was going to roll with our gun line with Steve Gallagher."

Heading for Nawa were Wallace's Devils and Kevin Schamuhn's 1 Platoon for added firepower. Because the Yanks were in Humvees and 1 Platoon was in G-Wagons, they were accompanied by an American route clearance package to scope the roads for IEDs. Gallinger had his own 2 and 3 Platoons, recce, and some Afghan National Army, and was destined for Garmser. Bill Fletcher and C Company would stay in Lashkar Gah to protect the British PRT and the town itself, and to do escort duty for the resupply convoys.

The minute the orders were done, "The CO [said], 'Kirk, how fast can you be outta here?' And I think I said, 'Well, sir, I think I can probably be rolling in about an hour.' And that was the state that we as a battle group had got ourselves to—we could, on the turn of a dime, look at a problem, zip zip, okay, this is what we're gonna do and all right, let's roll. If you'd thrown that problem at us back in Wainwright, or something like it, we'd have just hemmed and hawed, but we were completely different personalities and mindsets at that point. We were just so goddamned tired, and just so, I guess, fed up—let's just go and get this over with."

Willy MacDonald, down to his last pack "of sweet, sweet Canadian cigs," dispatched the interpreter to buy some local smokes. The fellow returned with a couple of cartons of Seven Stars, a Japanese import, which, MacDonald says cheerfully, "We gratefully smoked until our fingers turned yellow."

With Gallinger in the lead, they tore out of the leaguer around noon and made great time into Lashkar Gah. They made it through the city without being attacked and headed for the district centre to meet a British liaison officer and some ANP. Neither showed, so they kept rolling.

Within about four hours, Schamuhn and Devil Company took Nawa over only mild objections. Gallinger's aerial assessment of the torched landscape had been on the money; the local school was still smouldering, the children's books and desks in ruins, as Schamuhn's platoon got there.

At the same time, A Company had travelled about 160 kilometres and was on the west bank of the Helmand, across from Garmser, in position to assault the bridge that would lead them to the district centre. They would have gone charging right across, but the big guns of the artillery were still out of range and they had a problem with a vehicle.

By 6:30 p.m., the vehicle was fixed and the guns were in range, so Gallinger thought perhaps they could do "a bounce crossing"—basically cross their fingers, run up to the bridge "and maybe you get across to the other side . . . either the enemy has it open or the enemy has closed it by explosives or barriers or stuff like that, so it's always hit or miss whether you're going to get across." This was a narrow, five hundred–metre bridge, fifty to seventy-five metres above the river, "so we had no other option to get across unless we were ducks," Gallinger says.

They started toward it, and 3 Platoon spotted some movement to the left and called it in. "I said, 'Yup, roger that. We've been observed; big surprise.' They probably knew we were coming the entire way down, the way their network of watchers works. And I said, 'Okay, roger that, let's carry on. Let's see what happens.'"

They rolled in closer to the bridge, staged themselves to scope it out. "And just after suppertime, all hell broke loose," Gallinger says. They hadn't committed to crossing the bridge. "I'm always deliberately cautious in our operations, make sure we don't get sucked into anything, and in my mind this was, could have been, a huge trap," he says. As they began to take RPGs and small-arms fire from the length of the village, they proceeded to "get into a huge gunfight. And we were fortunate, we were at the effective range of our weapons, and they were not very accurate with theirs, although they threw everything they had at us—everything, and the kitchen sink. And we sat and shot it out at each other until the sun went down."

They had the LAVs firing. The snipers were able to get out of their vehicles and set up on a little mound. Master Corporal Chuck

Prodnick got the 60 millimetre mortar going. Stephane Pelletier, the acting LAV captain, had the ANA shooting. Gallinger's FOO, Bob Meade, and Willy MacDonald, a Forward Air Controller, were respectively calling in artillery fire missions and two 500-pound GPS-guided bombs on enemy positions, in MacDonald's case on an enemy vehicle with three or four men firing RPGs at them.

"I could not in all of my experience and everything I've seen," Gallinger says, "could not have created a better range for us to employ our weapons systems."

Even Jon Hamilton and recce, deployed to the flanks doing perimeter security because they were stuck in their vulnerable G-Wagons, were taking a few shots. "I'm telling ya," Hamilton says, "I wish I had a dollar for every RPG that was fired over the top of my head and missed, because I'd have $100 at least, enough to drink for the night."

He had Jeff Schnurr on top of his G-Wagon with binoculars, looking at the town where the firing was coming from and trying to pick the shooters up. "And we have the snipers up there and they're having a look, hopefully taking guys out, RPGs are flying over, we're looking at them," Hamilton says. "Boom. Boom. Jeff's up on the G-Wagon, I'm standing here, I'm looking with [binoculars], all of a sudden: *Clink. Clink.* Off the top of Jeff's car, the hood of his car, where Jeff is, it bounces off, it lands right about there and I'm staring at this fucking thing and it's an RPG and it's a dud, it doesn't go off."

Hamilton describes Schnurr as typically expressionless, whether he's happy, angry, or sad. But he looked at Hamilton and asked, "Did you fucking see that?" And when Hamilton responded, "'Jeff, I fucking missed it. It landed right there,' even Jeff finally cracked up."

And then night fell.

They had shot the hell out of the enemy—"I don't want to call it a turkey shoot," Gallinger says, "but it was pretty much a turkey shoot"—and everyone was "chomping at the bit to go do what we naturally get paid to do and I was caught up in the moment and then the sun went down, and I was, 'Ah shit, what do I do next?'" Should they try for the bridge or wait until morning?

Gallinger knew his men were looking to him for a decision. He felt the loneliness of command. "You know, in your mind, you're trying to work through options for your next step. And it had been a thoroughly exhausting day. I was bone tired by this point." He was not keen to cross the bridge. "Especially now, at night time," he says. "To go into a fight across the water, basically do an assault crossing if we needed to do an assault crossing, and then get ourselves sucked into an urban area, at night, without necessarily all the support I thought I would need."

On every course he'd ever taken—a graduate of RMC, he'd been a Patricia for seven years at this point—Gallinger had been taught, "If you want to hurt an enemy, blow up the bridge or ambush him on the bridge." He could not shake the fear that one of these tactics would be used against them if they tried to cross, and had a terrible picture in his mind: a LAV full of soldiers moving across while attacked or while under them the bridge is blown up. "You lose ten boys into the water," he says. "Trying to rescue them under fire, you know, is a bad, bad thing to do."

He decided to stay put: They would leave 2 Platoon in a compound, with all-round protection, to keep eyes on the bridge, and pull everyone else back to a patrol base at a location Damon Tedford and Warrant Officer Todd D'Andrade had scouted.

Tedford and Gallinger formulated a plan for crossing the bridge in the morning. Before Gallinger crashed, he got on the radio to the CO, told him what they'd done, and, with some trepidation, what he'd decided not to do. "And he said, 'Okay. Excellent. I'll give you everything you need.' And you know, that was such a relief not to be second-guessed, or to be prodded into doing something that I was wary to do. . . . There's times when you need to give people a kick in the ass, and there's times when you need to listen to them, and hats off to [my CO] for being supportive and for trusting the guy on the ground. Like I said, we have as an army come so far, where we can do that when there's lives at risk. That for me was really gratifying to see."

At dawn on July 19, with 2 Platoon in a supporting role, the engineers went forward for a close look at the bridge, to see if it was rigged. "And then we pushed the troops across and we went through in a leapfrog technique," Gallinger says, always careful not to get caught "with our ass hanging out."

As Hope puts it: "By first light, Kirk's company and recce were advancing into Garmser. A Company skirmished all the way through Garmser, forcing the Taliban out block by block. Kirk maintained a very deliberate and balanced approach, never extending his soldiers so that small groups could be isolated, ambushed, and cut off. Instead, he always presented a powerful front to the enemy, so that they could not hope to ambush anyone and survive. Because of this, A Company suffered no casualties, inflicted dozens, and broke the enemy's resolve to defend Garmser. By 8:30 a.m., A Company owned Garmser."

Hope arrived not long after, with forty ANP, the Helmand police chief, and the deputy governor. "Kirk met them and I gave them [an Afghan] flag to hoist above the district centre. This they did, I think to the satisfaction of A Company and recce platoon soldiers, who knew they had achieved something special."

As the soldiers swept through the area, they found enemy small-arms and machine-gun ammunition, many RPGs, mortar ammunition, and a remote-controlled IED—in a mosque.

"We saw the damage that we did," Hamilton says. "In the part of the town we had to exploit, I found a roomful of about forty RPG rounds, lots of small arms," and a dead man who "basically, he was splattered against the wall pretty much, lying there."

Hope departed Garmser a little later, leaving the ANP behind. They, as was often the case, were a handful. "We had a hard time keeping them, as best [we could] within our powers of influence, from looting," Gallinger says. "They got to a lot of looting in the bazaar area."

Hamilton was so infuriated he told his interpreter, "'If I see one more guy steal a case of Coke out of a store, I'm gonna shoot him myself,' and they stopped doing it." He knows he was a little heavy-handed. "Willy was telling me, 'Settle down, settle down.' But some things I can't stand—these guys are the police, and they're stealing from the civilians? I don't care what your culture is, you don't do that. Willy looks after me, doesn't want me getting all worked up—rightly so. He's looking after my best interests. Once again."

Over the next three days, A Company stayed put at the end of this astonishing, unprecedented supply chain 264 kilometres from the main base at KAF.

"This required a daily drop-off of ammo, water, and fuel," Hope says. Thanks to John Conrad and the unsung troops of his NSE, the CO says, "Never did we want for any of these commodities. They performed yeoman service for days on end, without sleep, to keep our forces fighting, and endured bad weather, worse roads, and several terrible Taliban ambushes in order to keep us supplied."

One night, Hope remembers, the infantry officer escorting one of those resupply convoys complained about the NSE's sloppy driving on the way in. Hope went over to the NSE sergeant in charge and asked how long they'd been on the road. "He answered, 'Four days.' I was gobsmacked. I realized just to what extent John [Conrad] was driving his people to keep us supplied."

Hope ordered the sergeant and his troops to sleep by their trucks "until I personally woke them—not before 7:30 a.m. the next day." When he roused them, he gathered them for a pep talk. "I needn't have," he says, "because I could see that their understanding of the seriousness of the situation sustained them."

Throughout this time, Gallinger was being eaten up with frustration. Every time the soldiers pushed the bubble outward from the district centre itself and stuck a foot into the green space that ringed the canals, they found themselves in a fight.

"We didn't have to go far," Gallinger says. "Basically, anywhere we drove we could get in a fight."

The Canadians didn't own Garmser. They owned the district centre. Period.

"This is the stuff I think about at night," Gallinger says. "The issue of whether or not, if we'd been bolder, and if I hadn't been reluctant and we'd carried on and charged that night across the bridge, or if we'd just rolled across . . ."

He knows the district centre was deemed "the big prize," but he frets that because he was loath to move that first night they gave the enemy not nearly enough of a decisive defeat. The area was still so rife with Taliban it could suck up the battle group's resources for a long time, and it wasn't even in the Canadian AO. "It was just a really ugly area," Gallinger says, "reminiscent of what you would see in fighting on the Scheldt [River] in northwest Europe, just canal after canal after canal, just bocage [mixed woods and pasture] and bad terrain."

It was yet another instance where fighting a modern insurgency in 2006 was more like traditional warfare of earlier eras than anyone would have predicted.

At last, the Patricias were told they would be handing over to the British.

"This poor British Pathfinder Platoon and their armoured Land Rovers with exposed soldiers came rolling into the village and met us at the district centre," Gallinger says. "And I started giving my big brief on the area: 'Here's what's happened the last forty-eight hours, here's all the fights we've done, here's what I think the enemy is doing.'"

At some point, the young British platoon commander piped up and said, "Well, sir, my commanding officer's made it quite clear we're not to get decisively engaged in Garmser. So as soon as you withdraw, we're going to follow you out."

Gallinger was dumbfounded: What the hell had his men been busting their balls for, then, if not to secure the district centre so that the Brits, whose turf this was, could move in?

"They were given orders not to go into the town itself, but to stay five kilometres [out] in a buffer zone," Hamilton says. "I don't know where that came from, I'm not pointing any fingers at anybody. But somebody fucking should have looked at it and shook their fucking head and had an idea what we went through there. What the fuck have we done here the past three days?"

Gallinger got on the horn to Hope, and they decided they would stay overnight at least. The Brits were happy to stay then, too.

Soldier to soldier, Gallinger says, the British are excellent troops, but they didn't have the firepower and the equipment. "They were such a light force. I can understand their CO not wanting to get his soldiers decisively engaged. Nobody else in Afghanistan had that wherewithal and had that ability, that operational tactical ability to manoeuvre, like we did. And quite honestly, no one else was willing to take those types of risks to be able to support the Afghan government like we were."

In the end, after getting more and more ANP into the area, Gallinger broke it to the ANP's American trainer that he and the Afghan troops would be staying while everyone else buggered off. "He took some convincing," Gallinger says. "He knew it was a bad situation, and I wouldn't want to be in his shoes."

Early on the morning of July 22, as the Patricias were about to pull up stakes, an ANP commander started an operation to clear the area south of the district centre. "No word of a lie, within ten minutes," Gallinger says, "they were in a gunfight. We were trying to help them, without getting decisively engaged, and [the ANP commander] was very much trying to get us decisively engaged, get us sucked into staying there longer."

Their coalition partners were in a fight; to leave felt very much like abandonment. But the Canadians had other missions to do, they weren't the force in charge. Besides, Hope was on the radio telling Gallinger, "Kirk, you will be out of that village, you will be on the other side, on the west side of the Helmand River, by noon."

Gallinger says, "I knew if I was not on the other side of that river by noon, I knew that I would be removed, because it was so significant we not be drawn into a prolonged fight." In his estimation, the point Hope was trying to make was that the Canadians had done what was asked of them, and were not going to be the coalition patsies every time the going got tough.

"But to top it all off," Gallinger says, "as the clock was ticking down, and we're in there with my company tactical headquarters and 2 Platoon—I had everybody else on the other side of the river, everything had been smoothed over, everything was all right—the ANP started bringing in seriously wounded soldiers."

The platoon medic and troops immediately swung into action; it was a reflex. Warrant Mark Pickford and Sergeant Dwayne Thir were pulling the wounded ANP from the back of their pickup truck, ripping off their clothes while medic John Gute plugged in IVs and Chuck Prodnick put on bandages.

"They were doing a fantastic job," Gallinger says, "getting these soldiers squared away, and I realized very quickly we're going to have to get these guys evacuated by helicopter." There were at least three seriously injured men, "to the point where they needed to get out of there or we were going to lose them."

By this time, Gallinger had completed his handover to the British officer, so he asked him, since it was now nominally a British show, to get on the radio and call in a bird for the Afghans. "And he was like, 'No, sorry,' and he gave me some long song and dance that it wasn't their policy to do that type of evacuation and stuff like that. And I know, if I could have choked him out, I should have. He was definitely sidestepping his responsibility, maybe for good reason or bad, but I just couldn't believe it and for that nanosecond I said [to myself], 'All right, is this our problem?' But our boys were working like gangbusters to save these guys, and I couldn't say, 'All right, boys, wrap it up, we're outta here.' It just would not be the right thing to do."

They got the wounded men to the other side of the river—late for the noon deadline by only a few minutes—and then called the Brits themselves to come in a helicopter.

"They came in a big Chinook and took them off, much to their credit," Gallinger says. "Basically, we just had to ask, and they came."

He was standing around, wondering "Jesus Christ, what else can happen here?" when the ANP announced that they too were going to evacuate the district centre. "I was, in the back of my head, thinking, 'All for naught, all for naught,'" Gallinger says.

But he got on the radio with Hope, who passed on the message that the ANA, ANP, and their embedded trainers had been directed by their chain of command to stay there. Reluctantly, the ANA and ANP relented, but said they had no batteries, food, or water. The

Patricias began handing over batteries and extra ammunition, started stripping the LAVs of rations and bottled water. "We would have given them the shirts off our back," Gallinger says—anything to get out of there.

Even so, as they left Garmser, it was hardly over. They now had to travel almost three hundred klicks back to KAF. "We'd telegraphed where we were, there was only one route out, and the whole route back," Gallinger says, "everyone's on pins and needles, because you're just expecting that IED . . ." Moreover, they all had the nagging suspicion that they shouldn't be going, that they were leaving an unfinished job behind. As Hamilton says, "We left and we did our job, yeah—but Jesus, it's not a good feeling. I know we did them some damage and put a scare into the Taliban and then we took the town back, but I didn't have a good feeling leaving."

They made it to a big leaguer in Helmand, where Hope had gathered everyone he could: A Company, elements of Charlie Company, the artillery, and the NSE. They refuelled, and thanks to Hope, recharged.

"He gave us a big speech," Gallinger says, summarized what they'd accomplished, and "had everybody pumped up."

They got on the asphalt of Highway 1. They were in the home stretch.

—

JOHN CONRAD WAS PRESENT for Hope's speech at the leaguer in Helmand. As the NSE commanding officer, there was absolutely no need for him to go out on convoys, but he made a point of doing so at least once a week. "It wasn't about the technical things that I brought to it," he says. "To me it was about the moral plane: These guys need to see that I am here with them, I trust them, and that my life [has] exactly the same value as yours, we're in this together."

Like his friend Hope, Conrad knows that as the boss, "You can't show you're afraid—and I was, every time I went out on a convoy, I was damned afraid."

The resupply convoy, Conrad aboard, left KAF at about 3 a.m. on July 22. They were bringing diesel, rations, water, a low bed truck for vehicle recovery (it was already full by the time they got to the leaguer; a Coyote had broken down), and a wrecker for towing. "It's just a package of capability," Conrad says, "like dragging a Canadian Tire store somewhere to where you're working."

He and Hope had a cigar together. "It was a very long day," Conrad says. "It's a helluva long drive from KAF to where we needed to be in Helmand, but a great day. Ian's guys were coming back, they'd done battle, everyone was triumphant."

As the troops were running, buoyant, to get into their trucks, Conrad pulled Hope aside, told him he had a Coyote down, and asked for a LAV, "just so I could have two big cannons. And he said, 'Yep, no problem. Just stay with us. Just stay with us at the back of the convoy.'" But it didn't work out as they planned, because one of Conrad's cargo trucks broke down. They had to stop and put it on the wrecker, and suddenly, they were behind the tail end of Hope's convoy.

"Then we cross the Arghendab River," Conrad says, "and generally when we crossed that river, I usually think, 'Okay, I'm out of the bad place.'" But they had to stop again: The brakes on the broken-down truck were grabbing, and the mechanics needed another ten minutes to back them off. "And that just widened the gap between Ian and me."

Conrad had gone out in a G-Wagon, but for the trip back had switched places with the crew of a ten-tonne diesel truck because its air conditioner was on the fritz and he wanted to give the poor guys a break. Directly in front of him was a Bison armoured vehicle.

"So we're coming into that urban sprawl that kind of gives way to Kandahar," Conrad says, "and there's a terraced village over there, like high ground, and on this side there's off in the distance three mountains, but it's kind of like an open field. And we're just moving along, a little bit slower because we've got a couple of vehicle casualties," he says, when he noticed a small cab-over truck. A Toyota Hiace, he thinks, approaching.

They were then about five kilometres west of the city.

"Right up to the time the thing detonated, you're looking at a car that's white, harmless looking, right? Yeah, it's kind of winking its way on the left-hand side, but that's because we're taking up the entire road. . . . We actually saw him in one instant—it's a little truck," Conrad says, "and the next instant it's BOOM!"

Twenty-five feet in front of him, the Bison was hit, parts of it flying into the cab of Conrad's truck, smoke rising everywhere. The driver, forty-four-year-old Frank Gomez, who was in the Canadian Airborne Regiment with Ian Hope, was killed instantly by shrapnel to his head. As the Bison was blown off the road, embedding itself in a culvert, the young air sentry, twenty-nine-year-old Jason Patrick Warren of The Black Watch (Royal Highland Regiment) of Montreal, was killed too. There were wounded soldiers inside the vehicle—ten altogether.

"You open the back, it's just a bloody mess," Conrad says. "The doors were awash in blood. Tony Ross, one of the captains, was vomiting; he had shrapnel in his ear. It was just complete hell gothic."

It was only Ross's second time out; Conrad had offered him a chance to "go out and see the results of your staff work," and now he was puking his guts out.

Conrad saw Warren lying on the ground, with "a huge trauma to his shoulder, and quite obviously dead." The soldiers were enormously upset. "One of the guys says to me, he says, 'Do you smoke?' I said, 'No, but I really would love a cigarette right now.' I have no idea who he is, just some young guy."

Conrad, for a time, believed Warren was Travis Boudreau, one of his own corporals. The two men looked a lot alike. Later, he found out it wasn't Boudreau. "Boudreau is standing there in the flesh, and this is a guy I've known, my soldier, I've known him a long time and he's alive. . . . In the first nanosecond, 'I'm so happy to see you, I'm so relieved,' and then immense guilt: My God, how could I feel that way?"

He helped extricate Gomez from the driver's seat, out the back and into a body bag. It was the first time in his twenty-four-year career John Conrad had done that, and "all I could do was give him a pat on the shoulder as they zippered the thing up."

The next two hours were nightmarish, the ANP trying to keep civilians back, Black Hawks circling in the air, the Immediate Reaction Force (IRF) arriving from the Canadian PRT office not far away.

"We fumbled our way through it," Conrad says, "as best we could as soldiers, as human beings."

Then, taking with them the dead and minor casualties not in need of air evacuation, the IRF pulled out. That's when a man wearing a suicide vest walked into the crowd of civilians and blew himself up.

"There were children," Conrad says, "and you know, seeing an Afghan father picking up his child, just wrapping up a dead child as if it's part of his everyday life. It's just the ANP, throwing bodies into the back of a pickup truck, and blood pouring down the tailgate. And they just accept it, you know? It's not the way things should be."

Some Afghans approached him, asking for help, and he had to say, "'I'm sorry, I can't help you, I can't even help myself right now.' I felt really helpless. I felt I couldn't even get my own soldiers out of there, and I felt guilty afterwards, because, you know, to me it just seemed like the Taliban, they're totally playing with us. It doesn't matter how many books you read, or how you read all about Napoleon, it doesn't matter how smart you are, they're kicking our ass."

Conrad was furious at the claims, afterwards, that Canadian soldiers had been firing into the crowd. Steve Chao for CTV reported the allegation that night, and also that Canadian authorities denied it. The network's "fixer"—a local who can speak the languages and go places Westerners can't or won't—had arrived at the scene quickly, and interviewed purported witnesses, one of whom said on camera that the Canadians had fired at everyone, "including women and children."

As soon as Conrad arrived at the PRT, "two glorious Apache gunships" in the air above them, he called the Deputy Task Force Commander, Colonel Tom Putt, and said, "Tom, I give you my word:

We didn't fire on that crowd. It was ball bearings, it was the metal that the guy was wearing."

He was also furious at General Fraser, who a day or so later described the aftermath and the extractions as "textbook." "Do you want to hear about it, sir?" Conrad thought. "Do you really want to hear about it? Of course not. I've always told General Fraser the truth, when he's bothered to ask me. I've always told him the truth. Sometimes, the truth is not that great."

All Conrad, a father of two girls and two boys, could think of on the drive to the PRT, and for much longer, was his oldest son, Aidan, now eleven. "He's kind of a nerd," Conrad says, "plaid shirts, a bit socially inept. He's a normal child, but who's gonna put up with him like his dad? Or my second one, Morgan, the other boy, who's very, very quiet. You really need to dig to get him to do things, and who's gonna take the time to do that like I will? All I could think of was, I almost checked out there, and it made me very, very sad to think that my son, with his bolo ties—no one wears those anymore—he's just gonna get even more weird without me to give him some balance."

When he phoned his wife, Martha, that night, he burst into tears, and is not embarrassed about it. "We're spending human capital there," he says, "the very best that this country has to offer, and there's no harm in pausing for reflection and grief when this is being spent. The cause is just. The Afghan people are deserving, but more important, the Canadian people are deserving of national security, and the cause is, I believe, just. But as we're spending these diamonds, it's okay to be human. In fact, it's fucking necessary."

Ian Hope knew nothing of what had happened until he was pulling into KAF and got the first radio message about the bombing. He'd been mulling over what his soldiers had accomplished, planning to get the press out to interview the returning troops so they could get some public recognition. Instead, he spent the night in the hospital, writing letters to soldiers' families and thinking, as he says, that "this indeed was 'the long war.'"

I was one of a couple of reporters who had walked down to the tactical operations centre to see the convoy come back. I love watching them return from the field, the troops filthy and exhausted but always indomitable.

Hope was the first one I saw. I had some small idea of all that they'd done, and was expecting him to be excited and proud. He was quiet, so subdued. He looked miserable. Only hours later did I learn why.

All that Task Force Orion accomplished—running with those sudden, insane orders to go; defeating the logistics of that unforgiving place; kicking the snot out of the enemy; riding out all the twists and turns and complications; the protracted and painful leave-taking—had come to the same bloodied end so common in that country. "It was," as Kirk Gallinger says, "a very Afghan day."

On July 23, John Conrad was back at KAF. The last thing he felt like doing was joking, but he knew he had to show his soldiers what he was made of. "By God," he says, "they've taken their hits. . . . That was the first time I had a suicide bomber detonate right in front of me, so I wanted to show that, yeah, I'm good to go."

He walked into his orderly room on the ground floor, where the task force's administration was. He knew people would be sneaking peeks at him, wondering how he was. The hellos that met him were tentative.

James Brooks was there, and "I said in a very loud voice to Corporal Brooks, 'I need a general allowance claim, right?' We have these forms—like when you have a claim against the Crown, like you had to make a phone call or whatever—we have this watershed claim to reimburse soldiers. So I said, 'Brooksie, I need a CF-152, general allowance claim.' Brooks calls it up on his computer, starts typing in the claim: Service number, name, and says, 'Right, sir. What is it for?'"

Conrad replied, "One hugely soiled pair of underwear."

Pte. William Jonathan James Cushley

3 September 2006

—

"When you watched them all go off on that bus, you'd have sworn to God they were going on a school trip."

—ELAINE CUSHLEY, ON WATCHING HER SON WILL AND HIS CHARLES COMPANY MATES LEAVE FOR THEIR FLIGHT TO AFGHANISTAN

WHEN THEY LEARNED their strong young son was deploying to Kandahar in August 2006, Errol and Elaine Cushley knew they would go mad if they simply sat in their house in the village of Port Lambton, Ontario, on the St. Clair River just south of Sarnia. For months, they planned that during part of Will's tour, they would travel the famous Pilgrim's Walk, the Camino de Santiago, from the French side of the Pyrenees, over the mountains, to Santiago, Spain.

Errol is a sturdy retired ironworker in his late fifties, Elaine a wiry smoker about eight years younger, and this walk, at about 750 kilometres, is no piece of cake. So the Cushleys started training for it, and by the fall of 2006 were walking as many as twenty-eight klicks a day, carrying heavy backpacks to load themselves down.

It made them feel close to Will, too. They were testing themselves physically and suffering a little, just as infantrymen always do.

They were to fly to France on September 8. On Sunday, September 3, Errol got up and, as usual, checked the Internet to be sure that nothing significant was happening in Afghanistan.

"Another day we're worry-free," he thought.

Elaine didn't feel like going out, so Errol put on his shorts, a pair of boots, and a singlet, and off he went. "I was going to do about 14 to 15 K."

He walked about eight kilometres, and had just turned for home when he heard a vehicle coming up behind him. "I just started walking to the side of the road, pulled over to the left. And it starts slowing down and I'm going, 'Come on, buddy,' and it's going slower and slower, and it's my neighbour, and he's crying, and I looked at Tom and I thought, 'Boy, this ain't good.'"

Tom Atkins rolled down the window and said, "Get in." Errol asked what was wrong and Tom said, "The army's here."

"'Don't tell me that, Tom.' I said, 'I don't want to fucking hear that.'"

Tom was one of the many folks in town who had actively sought out Will Cushley's company; Will was that kind of young man: easy to be with, even charismatic. Tom's house is on Broadway Street, directly across the road from the Cushleys' place. From his window, he had seen the army officers knocking on their door.

From her window, Elaine saw them too, and heard them ring the doorbell, and she thought, "I'm not letting you in, because I remember what Will told me [that officers are dispatched only for deaths]. So I go back to bed . . . your brain I think just zones out. Eventually, I did get up, because they were there quite a while, walking around the neighbourhood, walking around the house, trying to [rouse someone]." When she did finally open the door, she found herself smacking the young officer who told her Will was dead, and crying, "Liar! Liar!"

Tom, weeping, was halfway across the road by then. He saw the door open and heard Elaine's scream. He knew he had to go to find Errol.

"In a way, I'm kind of glad it was a friend who told me," Errol said. "Not that it makes any difference, it was a blur, a total blur."

I first met Errol almost ten weeks after his only son, just turned twenty-one and only two years out of Wallaceburg District High School, had been killed. Errol is a new friend of Dave Needham, a Toronto police officer I've known for probably fifteen years and have come to like and admire. Dave's son, another strapping young man also named Will, was a member of the same unit as Will Cushley. Will Needham was in 8 Platoon, Will Cushley in 7 Platoon.

The Wills were together in The Royal Canadian Regiment, 1st Battalion, Charles Company—and for the record, it *is* Charles, not Charlie, the curious formality born as legend has it when the RCR was serving in Korea and a snooty British officer, remarking upon the Canadians' shiny kit, sneered, "They probably polish their razor wire and call themselves Charles Company too."

Errol was in Toronto for a soldiers' memorial service at the Ontario Legislature, over which Premier Dalton McGuinty would preside. Errol felt a responsibility to attend.

We met the night before the service, and ended up with quite a crowd at our table. The four of us—Dave and Errol; Amanda, one of Errol's daughters from his first marriage; and me—were soon joined by others. Pat Tower of the Princess Patricias, whom I knew from earlier trips to Kandahar, was en route to Ottawa for Remembrance Day ceremonies. He had just been awarded the Star of Military Valour, and was now enjoying his brief "rock star" phase, as he put it. His dad Bob came for a few drinks too. Later still, CTV's Lisa LaFlamme, who also knew Tower from Kandahar and had just interviewed him about his medal, joined us.

My tape recording of the night is loud and occasionally raucous, as we drank beer and ordered food and yelled over one another to be heard. The two dads, both British born, call their sons "my boy" or "my Will," and it was striking, listening to the tape later, how often someone was saying "my boy" or "my Will" throughout the evening.

Both Wills had had a devil of a time getting into the Canadian army. It took Will Needham two years to move from the reserves (The Lorne Scots Regiment) to the regular forces, and at one point he was so frustrated he emailed his dad's old regiment, the British Parachute Regiment, to see if they wanted him. Will Cushley, in the meantime, weary of the Canadian army's apparent lack of interest in him—someone in the recruiting office had told him to stop emailing—decided he was going to join the U.S. Army and, with a friend, took the ferry across to Marine City, Michigan. The immigration officer told them, essentially, "We don't need you pinheads—go join your own army." Errol noted wryly, "This was before Iraq."

Maj. Bill Fletcher addresses the troops following the death of Pte. Robert Costall.

Provincial Reconstruction Team memorial service at Camp Nathan Smith for CWO Robert Girouard and Cpl. Albert Storm, November 29, 2006.

Sgt. Sean Jamieson (standing, right), Cpl. Jeremy Barnes (kneeling and firing) and Cpl. Brad Sauffeldt (fingers in ears) fire a 60 mm mortar. Behind them is Capt. Jon Hamilton. They are engaging a Taliban observation post near the village of Chenartu.

After spending most of the day pursuing and engaging the Taliban through a maze of mud walls, compounds, and orchards in temperatures exceeding 45 degrees celsius, soldiers of C Company 1 PPCLI take a break while the Afghan National Army continues the fight, May 17, 2006.

Cpl. Andrew (Boomer) Eykelenboom and Cpl. Brett Hodgins. Boomer's platoon commander, Capt. David Ferris, sent Maureen Eykelenboom this photo with the assurance that "Where he [Boomer] may be holding a cigarette, he is holding it for me."

Ramp ceremony held for Pte. Robert Costall, Kandahar Airfield, March 29, 2006.

Lt.-Col. Ian Hope and Afghan elder, July 2006.

The reality of life in the field for Cpl. Eykelenboom and B Company 2 PPCLI, 6 platoon.

Will and Errol Cushley at CFB Petawawa. Mr. Cushley was shaken, after Will's death, to see that in this shot, he was in sunshine, while Will was in shadow.

Members of Charles Company, 1st Battalion, The Royal Canadian Regiment, prepare for their departure for Afghanistan from CFB Petawawa in August 2006. Pte. William Cushley (centre left by open bus door) was killed in action on September 3, 2006 and Pte. Mark Graham (third from right, with back to camera, shaking hands with Pte. Will Needham) was killed in a friendly fire strafing on September 4, 2006.

Sgt. Willy MacDonald moves in to clear a room of a compound near the former Gumbad Safe House, with Capt. Jon Hamilton backing him up.

Near the former Gumbad Safe House north of Kandahar, Capt. Jon Hamilton and a local Afghan boy under the watchful eye of a village elder.

Canadian soldiers evacuate injured personnel after their LAV was struck by an oncoming vehicle outside Kandahar City, March 31, 2006.

Dave Needham had phoned the Canadian recruiting sergeant three times, saying, "I'm talking to you as a father. I don't want my boy to [join], but what the hell is going on?" The man told him they'd lost Will's transfer documents twice and said this sometimes happens accidentally on purpose when a reserve regiment doesn't want to lose a good soldier. In the end, both Wills roused the Canadian army bureaucracy and were accepted.

The talk on that November night was of the Wills, Dave's tales from his days in the Parachute Regiment, and the unchanging nature of armies (intransigent) and soldiers (unfailingly honest, as though born without the bullshit gene).

Pat Tower spoke of how when he arrived at a fancy hotel in Calgary to receive his award, wearing jeans and a sweatshirt, he was directed by the bellhop to the delivery entrance. Dave remembered that when he got back to Swinging Sixties London from Aden in South Yemen and went looking for a suit at a tailor's, a clerk approached him and said, "I don't think you can afford to shop here." Dave whipped out a wad of bills and "told him to shove it up his ass."

Amid a discussion of army food, Tower gaily reminded Lisa of the first time she was in a LAV, when she ended up throwing up in a bag. The bag had to be passed by hand, soldier to soldier, until it finally got to one of the air sentries, who first thought someone had handed him a meal and then on closer inspection realized to his horror what it was and tossed it out. Dave remembered how the Brits used to put curry powder on their rations to make them palatable (it didn't work with the tinned bully beef). Grinning, he looked at Bob Tower, who spent part of his long Canadian army career as a cook, and said to Pat, "He probably killed more people than you and I together."

The fathers, who had met when Dave attended Will's funeral and memorial service, told stories about their boys who had been best friends. Will Needham used to joke with his dad and say, "If I lose a leg and an eye, Dad, I'm gonna get a parrot." He came rather too close: On the morning of September 4, he'd been talking to Mark

Graham by the garbage fire, said he had to go get his gear, and was but thirteen metres away when the company was mistakenly strafed by a U.S. A-10 aircraft in a friendly fire incident.

"Mark died exactly where Will left him by the firepit," said his dad. Will was one of thirty-eight soldiers who were injured that day—he took shrapnel to both feet—in the devastation that reduced Charles to "combat ineffective" status.

Errol told a story that Will Cushley's section commander had told him. The platoon was on exercise in Wainwright when, one night, the troops couldn't get back to base and had to crash in a small-town fire hall. Two months later, photographs started to emerge. The boys had posed in the buff, with only firemen's boots on, like calendar pin-ups. Will, ever mischievous, was the photographer.

Errol once asked his son why Canada was in Afghanistan. Errol was reading Romeo Dallaire's *Shake Hands with the Devil: The Failure of Humanity in Rwanda* at the time. The book describes how Dallaire's small United Nations force became a prisoner of its own rules of engagement and chronicles the failure of the UN, despite Dallaire's pleading, to send in reinforcements. In the end, the general had been left helpless in preventing the wholesale execution of Tutsis in Rwanda.

Will Cushley told his dad, "You're reading that book by Dallaire. Well, the upshot of that was, they asked for our help and we looked the other way. That's the truth. Now I'll tell you, in Bosnia, Canadians did pretty good, but it was too little too late; they asked for our help and we looked the other way too. Now these guys [Afghans] have asked for our help. How many times can we look the other way?"

The mission, Errol said, was never about "little girls going to school" for his son. "Will said you have to give them the chance to look after themselves. That's what we have to do. Will would say, 'I'm not fighting for that—those people can do that on their own.' He said, 'We got it good here. That's what they want the chance to have. If we can give it to them, I just want to make a difference.'"

Will Cushley had said that so often, to so many people in Port

Lambton, that after he was killed the townspeople made T-shirts with Will's picture on the front and "I just want to make a difference" on the back.

—

IN MID-JANUARY 2007, I went to Port Lambton to see Errol and meet Elaine. As I drove in on Broadway, I passed a small graveyard, and wondered whether it was there that Will was buried, never really thinking that it was. But it is, of course: His parents can see his grave from the front steps of their pretty house.

We sat around the kitchen table. They told me about the various scholarships they have set up or are planning in Will's name: one at Sacred Heart School, an art award because Will was a keen artist; one at Wallaceburg District High School, a bursary for students who want to enter the military; and another free-floating one, the first recipient of which is Dave Needham's daughter Heather, who will study folklore and ethnomusicology ("All I know is it involves east coast, Gaelic, and Canadian fiddle music," Dave said in an email) at the University of Cape Breton.

They talked about the good things that had come out of their boy's death. They now know all their neighbours, Elaine said; indeed, she couldn't have made it through those first days without them. There were so many people at the house, in a sort of protracted wake, that by the end there were twenty-seven empty cases of beer in the garage. At one point, their AO insisted they move to a hotel room for a few days, so they could get away from it all.

They spoke of what gave them solace: the fact that Will had an escort officer and was never alone; that his funeral in Port Lambton was enormous. ("A bit like a state funeral," Elaine said.) The road was closed all the way down to the 40 Highway, the bank and a few shops in the village shutting down out of respect. The fire service blocked off all the streets. The soldiers lined up and marched to the cemetery, and five or six hundred people walked behind.

They love what the local Port Lambton kids, childhood friends of Will's, have done. Eleven young men had Will's name tattooed on their arms, and three young women now have yellow ribbons tattooed on their ankles. Errol says he's also going to get a tattoo—"of St. Michael [once considered the patron saint of soldiers], for the boys."

They remembered the elderly veteran who approached them while Will was lying in the church just a block away from their house. "He's obviously in his eighties, and he's got his wife with him, and he came up and he's shaking my hand and he started crying," Errol said. "He reaches into his pocket, and there's a picture of a young lad and he pulls it out, he's trying to point at it but he's crying, and she said, 'That's his brother, that's his gravestone—he never came home. Be glad your boy came home.'" And they are.

They were touched by the number of visitors to their son's grave. A girl from a local school asked permission to put up a Christmas tree. Elaine thought it would be a little one, but it was a twelve-footer that ended up with more than 120 decorations on it. Other people brought candles and notes. One of Will's mates who was home on leave, Michael (Peaches) O'Rourke, left a T-shirt on the grave that reads, Life is Too Short to Date Ugly Girls. (Elaine put it in a plastic bag to protect it from the weather.) Errol and Elaine went to England for the holidays, to get away, but Tom Atkins told them that on most nights there was a crowd at the grave, people having a drink with Will. "He said that ground must be saturated with beer and Jack Daniels," Errol said.

They were able to save one voice message they got from Will, when he had landed safely in the Middle East and was just a flight away from Kandahar. There had been other ones, but they'd been erased, when no one imagined such things would matter so much. Elaine put the message on her phone. "I actually hear his voice," she said. "Thing is, what it is, is sometimes you forget what his voice sounds like," Errol said. "You need to listen to it."

They had been able to go through only one of the thirteen boxes of Will's things they received. "Two cotton earplugs," Elaine said. "That breaks my heart." A packet of unopened Trident gum. "I can't do it, I'm not ready. It's crazy, the little things [that set you off]." She has taken to wearing Will's clothes. "I'm wearing his pants right now," she said. "I wear his jockey shorts, his T-shirt. If it gives me a bit of comfort, I wear it. He's probably going nuts up there: 'For God's sake, Mum!'"

Elaine had all Will's shoes, knew no one else would ever wear them, but couldn't yet bring herself to throw them out. She missed Will physically, the physical touch of him. "He used to whack my ass when I was washing up the dishes," she said, smiling at the memory, "because he knew I hated it."

They spoke of how good the military had been for their son, how he had thrived, and how proud they were of him. "Before," Elaine said, "he was a mummy's boy. Even the day we put him on the train to go to boot camp, I'm like, 'If anybody touches him up there, bullies him, I'm taking the first train and I'm going to kick some ass.' He came back a man. He was serious. He actually enjoyed every bit of it. He said, 'I wouldn't give in, Mum.' He said he cried a couple of times, at night. 'I don't know if I can do it,' he said, 'but I did do it.' Because they are tough on you. He said, 'I understand now the reason they do it, to see how hard they can push you before you break, or if you're going to break.' Because there are guys who couldn't handle it, who were coming home. He said it takes a special kind of person to be able to do that."

They talked about how terrific Will's mates on 7 Platoon have been at keeping in touch by email. And how they, Errol and Elaine, still mail parcels to the soldiers, one with thirty-six miniature shots of booze, others with fresh beef and venison jerky, dried fruit, Pringles. "A couple of dirty magazines," Elaine said with a grin, "because they tend to like it."

"I know Will Needham said as soon as they opened them up and saw what it was," Errol said, "they raced to the bathrooms."

They asked, since I'd been to Kandahar and out with the soldiers, if these were the right things to send, and I assured them they were. All that, I told them, plus Pop Tarts and the instant soups and noodles in a cup.

Errol said that before Will deployed, he told his dad he was frightened. "And I said, 'Will, I don't know how to answer that. I've never had anybody shoot at me.' He said, 'Oh, that don't bother me.' He said, 'I'm not frightened of that.' He said, 'I've got a gun to defend myself and I'm pretty good.' He said, 'What I'm frightened of is that when the shit hits the fan, I won't be able to do anything, I'll let my friends down and somebody will get hurt or killed. I'm frightened I won't react or I'll run away.'"

By then, they pretty much had the story of Will's death, how it had happened, and knew that Will hadn't let anyone down. The short version is that exactly a month to the day after Pat Tower of the Patricias earned his Star of Military Valour for the courage he displayed under enemy fire, exactly a month after four of the Patricias, including Tower's best friend, were killed at a place called the White School in the Pashmul area west of Kandahar, the Royals saw four of their own cut down there.

By January 2007, when I met with the Cushleys, Errol and Elaine had been contacted by Brigadier-General Dave Fraser. For all of the Patricias' Roto 1 and part of the Royals' Roto 2, Fraser was both the Canadian and the multinational brigade commander. He offered to visit the Cushleys and answer any questions they had. The meeting was tentatively set, but the Cushleys cancelled because, as things ended up, they wanted to get away, to be alone and away from people looking at them with pity. They hadn't made any effort since to arrange another meeting, and were still a bit torn about whether they wanted to see Fraser.

As Errol put it that night in the bar, "Command's an awful thing. You talk to Sergeant Tower about the decisions you make in the field: If you're right, you're a hero; if you're wrong, you're a goat. But a general is in a field all of his own, because he has what he calls acceptable casualties. William would have been an acceptable casualty. I can't blame [Fraser]. My wife doesn't want him in the house. I said you can't do that. . . . If every general was hated for every operation where someone died, there'd be no army."

The question Errol would have asked, he said, is this: "After [the Patricias] ran into a hornet's nest and basically had their ass handed to them only one month before, whatever made [Fraser] think that day there was nobody there? What made you think there was no one in there?"

—

THE AREA OF THE WHITE SCHOOL was a well-known kill zone by the time the Royals, under Omer Lavoie, completed their handover from the Patricias in mid-August.

. The Panjwaii-Pashmul region—Pashmul, within Zhari district, is north of the Arghendab River; Panjwaii is on the south side— had been on Task Force Orion's radar since late May, when, Ian Hope says, after a stretch of particularly hard fighting they began to realize that the Afghans who'd been warning them for weeks that the Taliban were massing there were correct. In June, with the help of the ANP, Hope enlisted some former mujahideen fighters to walk the ground with them, to point out old ambush sites and the like.

Hope now believes that from June to July, at least seven hundred Taliban fighters were pushed into the Kandahar area, and that in July, when most of the battle group was diverted to Helmand Province with only Nick Grimshaw's B Company left to watch over Panjwaii, as many as seven hundred more may have slipped in. God knows there were enough rusting tanks dotted throughout the area to suggest that this was much-loved fighting turf for Afghans, particularly during the former Soviet Union's near-decade-long occupation of the country in the 1980s. Then, as now, some of the most lethal areas in the country are the green zones along the Arghendab River.

As retired U.S. lieutenant-colonel Lester Grau writes in *The Bear Went Over the Mountain: Soviet Combat Tactics in Afghanistan*, a study of select battles fought during the nine years of Soviet occupation, Afghanistan "is not all mountains and desert. It has forests and tangled green zones—irrigated areas thick with trees, crops, irrigation ditches and tangled vegetation." It was this study—the vignettes written by Soviet commanders who had been in the field, first collected in a book at the Frunze Academy, the staff college for Russian combat arms officers, and then translated into English and edited by Grau—that Dave Fraser, sensing something familiar, dug out of his barrack box in July.

"Panjwaii and Pashmul are in there several times," Fraser says. "I went and checked on the chapters. I said, 'My God, they've just pulled a page from one of their old tactics books, when the mujahideen were fighting the Soviets.' They beat the Soviets in that area. So I said, that's all they're doing: It ain't broken, they just want to do it to us again."

But if that recognition was months in the making, August 3, when the Patricias lost four men at the White School, was the day when all came clear. It was no longer possible to deny that, as Fraser puts it, Panjwaii was going to be the Taliban's "major fight for the summer" and perhaps of the entire campaign. "The third of August," he says, "that was the defining day that we knew exactly what we were facing, and what the enemy wanted to do, the enemy's intent."

What the Taliban wanted to do, Fraser says, was isolate the city of Kandahar, demonstrate President Hamid Karzai's inability to protect it, and perhaps set in motion something bigger. Fraser's thinking was, "[If] the city fell, the government would have fallen. And if the government had fallen, then NATO [which had just taken over from the Americans the running of the International Security Assistance Force] would have been in crisis because it did not prevent the defeat of the major city in the south. And then the Afghan psyche—well, as you know, what happens in Kandahar affects the entire south."

Thus, in the early part of August, Operation Medusa was born. No one person wrote it: As Hope says, "The germ came from the Afghans; we just concluded they were right."

Fraser briefed the plan to NATO headquarters and General David Richards, the British commander then in charge of the alliance's entire force in Afghanistan. "I said this is a fight we can't lose. This is the main main fight."

Because of the ground—which Fraser describes as "World War I plus-plus-plus: They don't have to dig trenches, they're already there"—he was reluctant to engage the enemy in a battle of attrition. "If we fought the way the Taliban wanted me to fight, I would have incurred casualties that would have been unacceptable by any nation in the world."

The first step was to make an approach to the three main local leaders from Zhari-Panjwaii-Arghendab to try to enlist their help. Fraser bluntly told Steve Williams, the American national contingent commander he dispatched precisely because he knew Afghans have confidence in U.S. military might and would be reassured by the presence of an American officer, "Whatever it costs—you start renting and buying them [locals]." This building of alliances, however achieved, is a classic function of one of the oldest military doctrines in the world. Shaping the enemy, it's called, its goal to make an enemy do what you want him to do, even if it means making friends of his allies.

They tried that for several weeks, Fraser says, "just to try to prevent combat ops." At the same time they gathered intelligence on which, and how many, Taliban were in the area.

During this phase, Fraser and team went on a long-planned leave: They were on a nine-month rotation, as opposed to the six-month tour of the battle group. "I said, 'Okay, keep up the key leadership engagements.' I was not gonna get into any combat operations when I went on leave. I had planned, when I got back, we would have shaped the enemy up to the point where we could then go into combat operations," Fraser says. "But I said, 'Okay, if the enemy does A, B, or C, you call me and I come back because that means [the enemy's] not doing what I want him to do and we're gonna have to move up the plan and go into combat operations sooner.'"

Fraser left Kandahar in late August, flew to Ottawa to brief Chief of Defence Staff (CDS) Rick Hillier and Prime Minister Stephen

Harper, then flew out with Hillier to Edmonton for Ian Hope's change-of-command ceremony (Hope was turning over the reins of the 1st Battalion to Dave Anderson) and his own (Fraser was handing over 1 Canadian Mechanized Brigade Group to Colonel Jon Vance), both held on August 30.

Fraser's first official day of leave was August 31, and he was on the fourth or fifth hole at Northern Bear Golf Club when Hillier's cellphone rang. It was General Michel Gauthier, the commander of the Canadian Expeditionary Force (the operational command charged with all overseas deployments), who was phoning from theatre. Hillier talked to Gauthier for a minute or two, then said, "Dave, it's for you," Fraser remembers.

"And Gauthier tells me what's going on, and it's A, B, and C, and by the seventh hole, I look at the CDS and I say, 'I have to go back.'" When he left theatre, Fraser says, the Taliban were doing what he wanted them to do. When Gauthier phoned, it was to say that the Taliban had begun reinforcing their positions in Panjwaii and had started to fight back. "We were actually trying to sit outside of where [the enemy] could reach out and touch us," Fraser says, "and we kept reaching in and touching him and cutting off the heads as we saw them, so to speak." It was from the Greek mythical character Medusa, who when beheaded grew two offspring heads, that the operation took its name.

Fraser phoned his wife, Poppie Veenstra, from the seventh hole and told her he had to go back, but not that he'd be leaving that afternoon. She picked him up after he played out nine holes. Hillier walked to the car with him, carrying Fraser's bag, and said, "See you at four o'clock today," whereupon Poppie, who'd been teary on the phone, realized her husband was returning that very afternoon and burst out crying. Fraser then had to call his two teenaged sons, Andrew and Daniel, with whom he'd been planning a white-water trip in Jasper, to tell them that the holiday was off.

He left Edmonton the same day, hitching a ride to Ottawa with Hillier on the government Challenger, grabbing a military flight to Manchester, then flying Air Emirates to Dubai, and finally catching a ride on a Hercules to Kandahar. There, on September 1, with a half-day of leave under his belt, he got a quick briefing and was soon on a chopper to Panjwaii.

I was in Afghanistan over the Christmas–New Year period of 2006 and 2007, and talked about September 3 with the soldiers of Charles Company. They were unanimous in one thing—that their original orders, given late in August and on which they'd been briefed to a level of detail dependent on their rank, had called for air strikes on various kinds of enemy nodes and three days of bombing that would precede their entry into Pashmul.

Jeremy Hiltz, a junior officer in charge of Charles' 8 Platoon, remembers those orders like this. "Originally," he told me in December 2006, "it was supposed to be eighteen command-and-control nodes that were known to be engaged simultaneously, then three days of artillery and air. Then, five minutes to the hour when it was supposed to [happen], it got diverted or called off, and basically decisions were made at a higher level that they weren't seeing [any enemy] and there was no requirement for the air campaign."

Omer Lavoie, the CO of the RCR battle group, says that Charles Company originally wasn't slated to move into Pashmul until September 5, after seventy-two hours of artillery and air bombing. It had always been a "conditions-based" plan, meaning it could be bumped up or delayed, and sure enough, at 10 p.m. on September 2, with the troops on the south side of the river in Panjwaii pounding Pashmul, Lavoie got word that the brigade wanted them to move across at 1 a.m.

On the brigade net radio Lavoie pushed back, as he puts it, arguing it was folly to do a night assault water crossing. Though he mostly spoke to his operations officer, Lavoie says at one point he did talk to Fraser directly on the net, eventually persuading him it was wiser to wait until first light on September 3.

Lavoie was never given a reason for the change, but suspects that because they'd seized Panjwaii so smoothly, "higher-level intelligence may have indicated to higher headquarters [the new NATO headquarters] . . . there was an opportunity to exploit." When Charles Company had moved into Panjwaii on the morning of September 2, he says, everyone was expecting a real fight, but it never materialized. "We rolled through, whether we caught them off guard or not, we rolled through the village unopposed, seized the high features [Masum Ghar and Ma'ar Ghar], isolated the village, and then started pounding the enemy on the other side."

Thus, instead of four days of bombing, there was only one—all day and all night of September 2, enough ordnance that Lavoie remembers not being able to sleep for more than a minute or two because of the constant explosions. "I'm not sure three more days of bombardment—yeah, it may have worn them down, it may have inflicted more damage on them," he says, "but in the end it probably wouldn't have changed the concept. . . . And there's no doubt, because of the fortifications they had, there still would have been a considerable number of enemy there that would have survived the bombardment."

Fraser doesn't dispute any of this, except the haste with which it seemed to the on-the-ground soldiers the orders changed. "I don't make decisions that fast," he says, adding wryly, "and nothing happens at the brigade that we would make a decision that fast." But he says that given "the intelligence and the way the enemy was shaping up," bombing and artillery might "have made us feel good, but we would not have achieved anything more than what we were facing that day we decided to go in."

He also says that "you don't fight [according to the dictates of] a plan, because if you fight a plan, you've ignored the enemy." Even within the Canadian army, Fraser says, there is a reluctance to depart from good plans. However, in his view it is critical to remember that "the plan is a guideline, and what are you going to do to adjust to the realities on the ground, because the plan is already two or three weeks old. It's almost a history lesson."

The Charles Company Combat Team, as they called themselves, were leaguered up on the piece of ground—smack in the middle of gorgeous hills—at Masum Ghar, hammering the hell out of the other side. On the night of September 2, Fraser says, "I talked to Omer, and you know . . . the first step is always the hardest, and the first step is, you gotta cross that river. And bear in mind, [for] everyone who had crossed the river before, going back to the third of August when Ian Hope got hit in that same area, it had been a pretty painful step every time we crossed that river. It was going to be painful, and we just had to take the pain and move on."

Then forty-nine, Fraser was operating under extraordinary, often competing, pressures unique to his position. He had the Afghans, who wanted the operation done and who, after decades of fighting and death, are inured to casualties in a way that Westerners are not. He had NATO headquarters, where the desire was the same— get the job done—but where people were acutely sensitive to the possibility of casualties, particularly civilian casualties, and particularly during this immediate post-handover period. Lavoie confirms that: Before moving on September 2, he went on numerous overflights of the area by chopper, doing what's called "civilian pattern-of-life analysis," making sure no civilians remained.

Fraser also had the eight individual coalition countries involved in the south, with their various national caveats or restrictions on how their troops could or could not be deployed. And most remarkably, he also had two Canadian military lawyers—Randy Smith, who advised him on Canadian law and national policy, and Bruce Wakeham, who advised him on the international laws of armed conflict—hovering at his shoulder at all times, even in mid-battle.

As Fraser says, "Oh fuck, oh yes, absolutely. Military lawyers. All they do is, whatever we're doing, they know the law and they won't say you can't do it, they say, 'Here's the law, here's where you stand vis-à-vis the law.' . . . And I had two of them arguing with each other, because I had two hats on my head, the multinational hat and a national hat."

Charles Company crossed the Arghendab in their LAVs and G-Wagons at first light on September 3. The engineers dismounted first, using their armoured bulldozer, a Zettelmeyer, to open up a couple of breaches and check the way ahead for visible IEDs. Other soldiers were grabbing the leaflets that had been dropped from the air, warning civilians to leave and the Taliban to give up or prepare to die. The Canadians were in pot fields taller than their vehicles, and some of Jeremy Hiltz's troops were taking pictures.

"It's still quiet," Hiltz remembers, "and there's no indication that anything's wrong, except for guys are looking at each other, there's that feeling. But I think at that point, we're still pretty young and I think a lot of guys didn't recognize it [for what it was]." He remembers watching Shane Stachnik, a sergeant with 2 Combat Engineer Regiment, walking through the first breach with his men. He remembers seeing Warrant Officer Rick Nolan driving through the same breach in his G-Wagon, looking out of the window. "Like he can't roll down the window," Hiltz says, "and he was kind of like a mime, going like this, smiling and giving me the thumbs-up. And I remember giving him the thumbs-up back, and everything was great."

Then all hell broke loose—small-arms fire and RPGs—and in a matter of a few seconds, Stachnik and Nolan were dead. The Taliban, dug into their irrigation ditches–cum-trenches and hiding in the thick marijuana fields, were firing from everywhere, even the trees.

But so were the Royals: Hiltz remembers hearing the OC on the radio, "saying he was watching trenches collapse and thirty guys get mowed down. We were definitely putting a hurt on them, but the most difficult and frustrating thing was not being able to see them."

The battle raged for hours. As OC Matthew Sprague says, "This wasn't some one-hour big firefight we were in, we were fucking fighting for our lives, for seven hours."

At some point, the order came to withdraw, but two soldiers, Will Needham and Travis Rawls, couldn't oblige. They were too far from their LAV to get back to it, and were effectively pinned down by heavy fire in a ditch near the small buildings of the White School. Hiltz and Captain Derek Wessan—armed only with his pistol, his rifle having been scooped up with the casualties—finally found them and provided covering fire so they could return to their vehicle.

"Here [Wessan] is with a pistol, chasing me around with an eighty-pound pack [Hiltz had the radio] and we're running around this open field and one of my master corporals said it was the funniest sight ever, because he looked back—one guy with a pistol, two young officers running around like idiots," Hiltz says.

Will Cushley, in the meantime, was in another LAV with Warrant Nolan's body and some of the injured. There were ten or eleven men crammed into the back of a vehicle that can carry four or five comfortably, soldiers forced to sit on their beloved warrant's body, when the LAV, in that forest of pot fields, missed the breach and crashed into a ditch.

It was stuck there, half-suspended, wheels spinning in the air.

Sean Niefer was in the turret. Their 25 millimetre cannon was jammed, they were out of ammo for the pintle-mounted machine gun, and the enemy was in the ditch with them.

The LAV was hit by at least two RPGs, Niefer says. One of them tore through the front right; Drew Berthiaume, a powerful, tattooed thirty-year-old from Windsor, Ontario, could feel the concussion go through his body.

Berthiaume is one of the many who considered Will Cushley his best friend. "I remember the last thing I ever said to Cush was—and we all had the same look on our faces, it was chaos, I didn't think I'd see my wife again—was, 'It's gonna be okay. We're gonna get through this.'" It took everything Berthiaume had to reassure Will, he says. "I didn't believe it myself for a minute. I would have said something different if I'd known it was the last thing I'd ever say to him."

Niefer, as crew commander, issued the "abandon boat" order. The troops were trying to lower the ramp—it was stuck, and would go down only a little—when a round came tearing in and hit it. The soldiers in the back had to squeeze out, one by one, through the small emergency door. Once out, they had to run a hundred metres under fire to a position of marginal safety. As each man landed in the ditch, he provided covering fire for the next one out the small door.

They couldn't take Warrant Nolan with them. It was the only smart, rational option. The alternative would have been suicide.

"It fucking ate me up," Berthiaume says. "I hated leaving the warrant behind. It took a long time for me to forgive myself for that. Everyone told me I had no choice, and I knew I had no choice, but it ate me up."

He and Niefer were the last to leave the LAV. They all ran to what they hoped was shelter. It turned out to be just a stack of wheat or hay, Berthiaume says, so they had to run again—another sixty metres—to the back of the Zettelmeyer, the engineers' bulldozer now being used as a casualty collection point.

They were there when Frank Mellish came running up: He'd heard about Nolan, his fellow warrant, and was on his way to retrieve the body. He stopped long enough to ask Will Cushley to go with him, and that's when a round from an 82 recoilless rifle, a massive weapon designed to take out a tank, came roaring into the Zettelmeyer.

Will Cushley was on one side of Sean Niefer, Frank Mellish on the other. Sergeant-Major John Barnes and Drew Berthiaume were close by. Niefer, who was awarded the Medal of Military Valour for his conduct during the battle, was unhurt. Barnes was knocked out. Mellish and Cushley were killed.

When the dust cleared, Drew Berthiaume saw Cush on the ground. "The docs were working on him," he says, "but he was gone."

—

SEPTEMBER 3 WAS NOT the first time Will Cushley had been in a fight.

Alpha Company, Charles's contingent borrowed from the 2nd Battalion of the Patricias under Major Mike Wright, celebrated Afghanistan's Independence Day on August 19 with a ferocious fight in which, with the help of some particularly tenacious ANA, they managed to hold on to the Panjwaii district centre. Wright was later awarded the Medal of Military Valour for the "outstanding courage and exceptional leadership" he displayed under intense small-arms and RPG fire that night.

7 Platoon, Errol has been told, was outside the wire for eight days—involved in what became a protracted battle to keep that district centre secure, a fight that saw seventy-two Taliban killed and garnered some headlines. The platoon returned to KAF for a nine-hour turnaround, and then went out again for the leaguering and posturing that preceded the Medusa combat operations. Will's section commander, Brent Crellin, told Errol that during that eight-day fight, Will was on the LAV cannon: "Will was calm, talked all the way through. He said he was very steady under fire. He said the day they were there, it was like a routine—triple tap, triple tap, fire back-back-back, cover, as they fought their way back. He said he was just so steady."

Errol is comforted by knowing that Will would have known this of himself, that despite his earlier fears he was able to keep his head, do his job, and not, in army speak, shit the bed.

"As a mum," Elaine said, "after he got back from those eight days, as a mum, I said to Errol, 'There's something not quite right about his voice.' His voice was not the same, I mean, obviously, what he'd seen . . ." During that phone call, Will told his dad, "You fire, and they're running behind walls and when the LAVs start hitting them, it takes the wall and everything. When you see this crap going up in the air. I can't tell you where I was but I'm sure you saw it on the news."

It was during that quick turnaround, the Cushleys believe, that Will sat down and wrote the letters.

When the soldiers retrieved Warrant Nolan's body from the LAV, in the gutted interior they found Will's valise without a mark on it, and in the valise were the letters: one each to the three girlfriends (two local girls and one in Petawawa) Will had had in his whole life, and one each for his mum and dad.

When I met with them in January 2007, they showed me the letters and let me copy them. Handwritten on lined schoolbook-style paper, undated, they are brief but complete. The one to Elaine reads:

> Mother,
> If you are reading this, I'm sorry, but I will not be coming back home. Thank you for everything you have ever done for me. I really do appreciate it.
> You were always there for me, even when I didn't want you to be. I have one last favour to ask of you. In this envelope is [sic] two more letters, one for Tasha, one for Brandy. If you could please deliver them to them I would really appreciate it.
> I just want you to know that I love you and that I fought bravely and did everything I could to come home.
> Do not weep too much. I will always be with you in heart and spirit.
>
> Love always and forever, Will.
> P.S. You can keep the $50 LOL.

The postscript is a reference to the bet they made, the last time the three of them had dinner. Will warned his mum not to cry when he left and she bet him she wouldn't. She did, of course. "But that's my Will," she said. "He has to have the last laugh, it's his sense of humour, you know what I mean?"

The letter to Errol reads:

> Father,
> Well, what can I say dad. Things just didn't work out the way we wanted. All I wanted you to know is that I fought bravely and with honor.
> Thank you for everything you have ever did

[sic], you were always my idol and I always tried to
have your attitude towards everything I approached.
You raised me into the man I always hoped to be
and I am forever thankful.

You take care of yourself and Mother too, try 'n
keep her off the wine LOL at least for a little
while. I will always be with you in heart and spirit.

Love always and forever, William.

Errol disappeared for a few minutes then, to get some pictures of
Will. Many were from his twenty-first birthday/leaving bash, held at
home in Port Lambton on July 28.

Will was then on pre-deployment leave—Drew Berthiaume, grinning, told me that Will had taken out a $4000 loan and spent half on
beer that summer, and half on new tattoos—and the pictures show
a huge, handsome young man. He was 208 pounds, six-foot-four, his
dad said. His newest tattoos were the black flames on his upper
arms and the classic, a sexy girl, on his calf.

But many of the pictures were from the last day the Cushleys saw
their son, at Petawawa, as he and his platoon mates waited for the
bus that would take them to the airport. Will Needham is in many of
these; as a member of 8 Platoon, he was leaving a day later, and
came in street clothes to see his former roommate and best friend
off. Mark Graham, the former Olympian who was killed in the
September 4 friendly fire strafing, was there too.

Elaine said they looked like a group of overgrown schoolboys.
She's right.

"The bus left half an hour early," she said, because they were all
packed up, and some of the boys were pissed off. "I said, 'Well, you
guys are ready to go.' Now that he got killed, I'm thinking 'God, I
wish I had that extra half an hour.'"

In one of the shots of Errol and Will together, Errol is in sunshine, Will in shadow. "That made me shiver when I saw it," Errol
said.

Will took his seat toward the back of the bus, then made his way up front again and—unusually, because as his dad said, "He's not that kind of guy to do that"—came out to ask his mum for another kiss.

"One last time, Mum," he said.

"Maybe he had a feeling," Elaine said.

That day, as the boys were joking around, Errol Cushley told Will Needham, "'You need to look after each other's backs over there. It's very dangerous.' And Will just kind of laughed and he said, 'Mr. Cushley, I'll promise you, I'll bring him home.'" Josh Klukie came over and grabbed Will Cushley and said, "'I'm sticking with the big guy.' He says, 'My only chance to get home alive is sticking with him.'"

The last picture from that day shows the bus pulling away.

"Elaine said, 'Well, what do you think?' And I said, 'You know what? The PPCLI has taken hits, and just the law of averages said three guys on that bus, of the forty, ain't coming home.'"

Mark Graham and Will Cushley, who were on that bus, didn't come home. Josh Klukie, who left the next day with Will Needham, was killed on September 29 when he stepped on a buried IED while on foot patrol.

"I said to Errol," Elaine said, "he knew, there's no doubt in my mind he knew we both loved him. On that level, I don't have no worries and I think I find some comfort and I can cope a bit better."

About two weeks after Will's death, the battle group finally took Pashmul, Lavoie ensuring it was Charles Company that actually seized Masum Ghar. "I needed to have those same soldiers take the piece of ground where they lost their comrades," he says, "so they knew it wasn't in vain."

The troops actually recovered Will Cushley's flak vest, buried it where he'd fallen, and erected a little memorial. It wasn't far from the ravine where on the afternoon of September 3, after he'd taken care of the casualties and come up with a new plan, away from his soldiers and all alone, Omer Lavoie sat down and sobbed.

Lt.-Col. Omer H. Lavoie (second from the right) and CWO Robert Girouard (third from the right)

27 November 2006

—

"I think, literally, if you did the math, I probably slept with him in that last year and a bit leading up to 27 November, I probably slept with him more than my own wife. We were always together."

—Omer Lavoie, on the loss of 1 Royal Canadian Regiment RSM, and his friend, Robert Michael Girouard, Sr.

IT NEVER OCCURRED to Jackie Girouard to really worry about her husband. For one thing, before 1 Royal Canadian Regiment (1RCR) actually deployed to Kandahar, the family's concern was focused upon Robert, Jackie and Bob's oldest child. Then twenty-two, Robert Girouard had just arrived at the battalion in Petawawa and was slated to be part of the battle group heading to Afghanistan. "He's a young fellow," his mom says. "He wanted to go." But Commanding Officer Omer Lavoie and his RSM, Robert's dad, decided Robert would have to stay behind: His safety would have been too much of a distraction for his father, who had to put first the welfare of all the troops. "If he'd been there," Jackie says, "then his father's mind would have been elsewhere sometimes."

Lavoie and Girouard factored something else into their hard-nosed calculation: If Robert went, and something happened to him, the regiment wouldn't be down just one soldier but also their spiritual leader. Robert was frustrated, Jackie says, but understood: "Because he didn't want to put his father in danger, he didn't give his father a hard time about it, said, 'Whatever helps keep you safe.' We never thought anything would happen to Bob. . . . When was the last time an RSM got killed, if ever? So I guess it just never entered our minds."

Regimental Sergeant Major is not a rank but an appointment, rich in military lore and best understood in the old saying that if a regiment is commanded by the lieutenant-colonel, it nonetheless belongs to the RSM. Tradition decrees that while soldiers may address him as RSM, officers must refer to him as Mister.

Equal parts stern father figure and mother hen, the RSM is considered the soul of a regiment, the keeper of its institutional memory and guardian of its dearest rituals. Long before the corporate world discovered the value of mentoring, the military had refined it. To the civilian eye, the RSM is most easily recognizable from war movies, where he's usually portrayed, as Lieutenant-Colonel (Retired) Ron Bragdon says, as "the guy standing up and walking as the bullets are flying, walking through fire."

The CO–RSM pairing is the culmination of the relationship between officer and senior non-commissioned officer (NCO), which begins when the former, as a lieutenant, is linked with a platoon warrant officer. The officer is young and stupid, the warrant experienced, usually in his thirties, and wise. "He's like the uncle," Bragdon says. "He doesn't want to see you make a mistake; he feels he's let you down."

By the time the officer comes back to a unit as a company commander, a major, his new NCO is a sergeant-major: The two are probably closer in age, and while the officer is the boss, the NCO is now more of a confidante. Ideally, the two will complement one another, as Bill Fletcher, the Patricias' Charlie Company commander in Kandahar, and his sergeant-major, Shawn Stevens, did. "I'm not a details guy," Fletcher says. "I'm not all that smart, but I talk pretty well. He's brilliant. He doesn't stand up and thump his chest, but he's brilliant. Between the two of us, we probably made one whole person."

But the higher up the officer moves, the fewer people he can talk to as peers, and the more palpable becomes the loneliness of command. As Bragdon says, a young officer at first has company: "There's a hockey sock full: There's a few captains; majors have a peer group; between the DCO and the OCs, there's five majors." But, "There's one CO. Frigging one. He [the RSM] is your everything." By the time a CO and RSM are paired, the men are more of an age and more equal, but the RSM continues to watch the CO's back, or as it's called, his six o'clock.

Though RSM Girouard was at forty-six of a new breed, he came from "a long distinguished line of RSMs in the RCR who have normally evolved in a manner that allows them to keep one foot in both the CO's tent and the sergeants' mess, and their heads on straight," says Lieutenant-Colonel Geordie Elms, the Canadian defence attaché in Kabul. Many of these RSMs had nicknames (Busher, Buzz, Big Jim) that spoke to their larger-than-life characters, Elms says. But RSM Girouard's nickname was simply Bobby, earned when he was one of the best hockey players to don a Royals' jersey in an era when hockey was the only regimental sport that mattered.

"Then," Elms says, "Private Girouard was fast and skilful and used his ability, both mental and physical, to compensate for not being big. As an RSM, he didn't tower over anybody but he never had to. From the beginning, he was smart and hard working—on the ice, on the mortar line, or in any one of the jobs that prepared him to assume the appointment of RSM. He was one of those people you always knew would be an RSM in his regiment—and probably, down the road, of the army."

Elms' father, Bill, was an RSM, and Elms saw through his dad how enduring was the bond with the COs under whom he served. "That pair," he says, "will always find one another on common ground as friends who once served together."

Unusually, for the RCR is a small unit within a small army, Omer Lavoie and Bob Girouard didn't know one another before the summer of 2005. "We'd just never been in the same place at the same time, serving," Lavoie says, "and it was probably a concern [of mine], and probably a concern of his as well: 'Hey, I'm working with this guy I've never met before.'"

Girouard was never scheduled to be his RSM, Lavoie says, but because the previous RSM couldn't stay on, Girouard was appointed. They took over the battalion on the same day, June 24, 2005—another oddity, because usually appointments overlap to allow continuity in leadership. When Lavoie learned Girouard would be his RSM, he did some homework, asked around. "I heard nothing but praise for him," he says. And within thirty seconds of meeting him, and talking to him, "I knew I could work with this guy. And we'll work well together."

In the prolonged lead-up to Kandahar, they began every day with a ten-kilometre run. "That's where we discussed all the issues facing us as a battalion, and sorted those issues out, and we sorted out our day's issues and challenges. And then we did Wainwright together, and innumerable other exercises where we spent time together," Lavoie says. "So professionally, we became very close. And I think we had a very high degree of confidence in each other."

But something else happened along the way: The two clicked personally, and so did their families. Only six years apart in age, Lavoie is from the northern Ontario town of Marathon, Girouard from the small New Brunswick city of Bathurst. Well-and-long-married products of their unpretentious hometowns, they discovered they shared similar interests (Lavoie loves fishing, Girouard camping; Lavoie hunts a lot, Girouard a little). Soon Lavoie was taking his teenaged son Alex over to the Girouards' place on the Ottawa River for breakfast after ice fishing. To seal the deal, their wives, Jackie Girouard and Erica Reichl, also hit it off.

"I think, even in a peacetime paradigm, it's a bond—the CO–RSM bond—it's almost holy, in a sense, you're so close." Add to that combat, with its terrors and discoveries, and the bond is steel tempered by fire.

—

OMER LAVOIE HAS BEEN a soldier since 1983, when he joined the Marathon branch of the reserve regiment, the Lake Superior Scottish, or Lake Sups, transferring a couple of years later to the regular force.

Bob Girouard was going on twenty-nine years in the Canadian Forces.

Both had served in Bosnia, Lavoie also in Kosovo, but despite their collective half-century of service, neither had ever seen combat.

Despite their exalted positions, the two had exactly the same fear
that grips every untested soldier: How would they do when the shit
hit the fan?

"I think the deepest sense, the biggest fear of any soldier," Lavoie
says, "myself included, and [Girouard] and I discussed this, is that
you truly don't know what's to happen the first time the bullets fly.
And in his case and my case, both with twenty years' experience in
the army but never really involved in intensive combat other than
potshots being taken at us in Bosnia, we truly didn't know. And guys
can say they know, or think they know and that kind of stuff, but
until the bullets are flying on a two-way range, as opposed to a one-
way range, you truly don't know."

On August 15, four days before Lavoie formally took command,
they found out. They were on a recce with Ian Hope, at grimy Patrol
Base Wilson (PBW) for the very first time. "We'd just pulled in,"
Lavoie says, "and within seconds a mortar attack had been initiated
and I think it was the first round that came in detonated just to the
left of my vehicle."

Lavoie's machine gunner, Aaron Coxworth, was wounded in the
hand, and the gun—which sits in front of the crew commander's
face; in other words, right in front of Lavoie—was pretty much
destroyed. RSM Girouard, despite modern army doctrine that
minimizes the notion that on the battlefield the RSM looks after
resupplying ammunition and casualty management, swung into
action as smoothly and without hesitation as his famous predeces-
sors. "The first thing he did," Lavoie says, "was start taking care of
the casualties—and we took a few serious ones."

It was just the beginning of their almost non-stop tour of violence
and bloodshed, but on every occasion, Lavoie says, Girouard's
immediate concern was always keeping the boys supplied and getting the wounded to safety. "He spent his entire tour in Afghanistan
forward with the troops, and the troops respected him for that,"
Lavoie says. He and Girouard were forward, in the field, with all
their men who were killed in action.

On October 14, 2006, when a fortified position called Strong

Point Centre just south of PBW was attacked, the two were drawn into battle in an unusually active manner. They'd arrived at the base in mid-afternoon to see Ray Corby, a young lieutenant who had taken over Charles Company's 9 Platoon just three weeks before when the casualty toll—the battle group had already seen fifteen soldiers killed and eighty-five wounded—made a personnel shuffle necessary. Earlier that day, one of Corby's LAVs had hit an IED on a Canadian-built stretch of road called Route Summit, which links PBW to the north and the base at Masum Ghar to the south. While nobody was hurt, the vehicle was lost and the soldiers bewildered that someone had managed to plant a bomb on a road they thought they had complete "eyes" on.

Lavoie says he and Girouard visited troops in the field almost every day to "give them direction, bullshit with them, have a cigarette with them, that sort of stuff." They were also going to pick up Colonel Bernd Horn, a former 1RCR CO, now the Deputy Commander of the Special Forces Command and director of the CF's Leadership Institute (a centre of excellence), and the regimental historian.

Lavoie and Niner Tac (his tactical headquarters) were loading up to leave when a warning came over the radio that there was an imminent threat of attack. Within a minute, Strong Point Centre was under intense RPG and small-arms fire. As Horn later wrote, Niner Tac had "just started to roll when an RPG rocket swished to the rear and exploded in a ball of flame approximately eighty metres behind the convoy, where mere minutes prior, the CO, platoon commander, and others had been standing. The three LAVs and the RG-31 Nyala, which made up the tactical HQ, quickly swung around and immediately began to engage the enemy, adding an enormous amount of fire into the fields and buildings to the west where the enemy assault was originating."

It was too late. The Taliban always rely on surprise, and in the first thirty seconds of the attack, Private Blake Neil Williamson and Sergeant Darcy Tedford were killed and three others wounded when shrapnel from an explosion showered their LAV. The battle that followed was marked by countless examples of tenacity—most notably from the baby-faced Jess Larochelle, alone in an observation post, damn near out of ammunition but still composed and fighting. Only after Larochelle had helped carry Williamson's casket in the ramp ceremony did he even admit that he was injured. He had fractured vertebrae in his back and was sent home to heal. He was later awarded the Star of Military Valour for the courage he showed that day.

As Horn wrote, also of note was how intimately the CO and his headquarters were involved in the actual fight. After the battle, Horn said, they returned to PBW. "The CO, RSM, and a few others sat around exhausted. Little was said, yet the silence spoke volumes. Quietly, Warrant Officer Keith Olstad . . . walked up to the RSM, Chief Warrant Officer Bob Girouard, with a very sombre, painful look on his face and a clenched fist. He then took the RSM's hand in his own and placed two dog tag stubs into Girouard's palm. The RSM closed his hand immediately with a firm grasp."

During that battle of October 14, Girouard was in the Nyala, a purpose-built South African vehicle specifically designed to protect the crew inside from mines and bombs. Good as the vehicle is at doing that, it's lousy for casualty extraction and not terrific for ammunition resupply. Lavoie says Girouard was constantly pestering him and his operations officer, Major Jay Harvey, to get him a Bison instead. "In his mind," Lavoie says, "he could stuff that thing full of 762 and 25 millimetre ammo, and medical supplies, and his logic was, 'We get involved in these firefights ourselves all the time. If I had a Bison full of ammo, I could do sort of an emergency ammo dump, my resupply, right on the position.' And at the same time, with the Bison and my Tac, with a Bison and three LAVs, you got a lot of firepower, we could help in the casualty extraction, drop medical supplies off, and even throw casualties into the back of the Bison to get them to treatment, which you couldn't do with a Nyala."

Girouard was still pushing for the Bison when he and Lavoie went on leave in early November. Girouard, much against his will, actually returned to Canada a week before Lavoie. The merit boards, which decide promotions, were being held in Ottawa. "He didn't want to leave the battle group prematurely, but there's career stuff that has to happen for senior NCOs," Lavoie says, "so I ordered him to go back a week early so he could attend these merit boards, which normally we would attend together. But because I couldn't be there, I wanted him to be there."

Jackie travelled to Ottawa to stay with him, and then they went home to Petawawa. At one point, she says, they thought of going away, "but he always wanted to come home and see the kids." It was the same when he was twice in Bosnia: She could have gone overseas to meet him, and then taken a glamorous trip somewhere in Europe. But Girouard always wanted home and his three children, "even though they're all grown up," Jackie says.

Girouard was a career soldier, with overseas postings and exercises that took him away from home for months at a time, but also a committed family man. "Bob never tried to go on tours," Jackie says. "If they came up, he went. But he never tried to position himself to go. He really did like being home with the family. But he'd go on tours if he had to. . . . He was just who he was, and if you didn't like it, too bad."

Indeed, the importance of family was one of the things that endeared the Lavoies to Jackie. The military is redolent with careerists, ambitious soldiers (and their ambitious wives, notorious for using the royal "we," as in "We're a full colonel now") who seek tours and even service medals only to boost their chances of promotion, and to whom minute differences in rank matter exquisitely. "And Erica's so not like that," Jackie says. "Neither one of them is like that. We all just kind of clicked, because both families are a lot alike, so far as being down to earth and wanting for our kids, stuff like that." The RSM appointment, while pleasing, never defined Girouard, she says. "Bob was very low key. So I don't know, how can I explain that? He was just really good at just being who he was."

When Girouard was home, he was home. "He did the hockey, he did the coaching ringette, he did the ball, he did the soccer," Jackie says, weeping at the memory. When he was stationed at CFB

Meaford, the former tank range on the southern shore of Georgian Bay now used primarily as a reservists' training area, Jackie used to cut hair, and the young troops who came in would often ask her about how Girouard managed both roles. The good fathers, she says, "are able to, what I used to tell the young fellows, they're able to take that hat off, you know? The good ones are able to do their job at work but also be good at home. And the ones who aren't usually don't stay married. Because they are away a lot, and it's hard on the families. And that's what he used to tell the young fellows—be good to your wives, be good to your girlfriends or to your kids, because you know what, if you're not, they don't have to put up with it. It's a hard enough life without having him come home and not really be there."

It is precisely to remind himself of the two great loves of his life that Randy Northrup, Ian Hope's RSM in Kandahar, always wears two rings. On his left hand is his wedding ring; on his right is his PPCLI ring. "One reminds me of my responsibility to family, the other of my responsibility to the regiment, and why I joined. There's a time when one is heavier than the other," he says. "It took me a lot of years to figure it out." A set of train tracks lead out of Edmonton, on the way to his home, then in St. Albert. "That's my jettison point," Northrup says, "where I dump everything on this side of the tracks. Judy will say, 'What was the highlight of your day?' I say, 'Coming home.'"

In November 2006, it was too cold to camp, so the Girouards stayed put in Petawawa. Bob had time with each of the kids—Robert, then twenty-three; Jocelyn, twenty-one and engaged to be married; and the baby, twenty-year-old Michel (pronounced Michael), who is at the Royal Military College in Kingston and training to be a pilot. When Lavoie returned to Canada, the two couples went out for dinner a few times.

But mostly, true-blue Maritimers to the core, the Girouards spent time in the extra garage they call "the shed," away from the phone and the television, drinking hot chocolate and talking into the night by the wood stove, as they had done for their almost twenty-seven years of marriage. "People used to laugh at us," Jackie says, "because we've got a big home, and they'd come in and [say], 'You've got a big house and you guys are in the shed?'"

Jackie and Bob met at high school in Bathurst. She was fifteen and in grade 9; he was in grade 10. They married when she was eighteen, and grew up together. They brought to their family and their way of life an almost old-fashioned sensibility. Jackie thinks they were that way because of what they saw in their own quite different homes. "My family, we had major problems growing up, so I always said to myself I wouldn't be like that. I would take a different direction with my kids, and with a husband." And Girouard's parents, while "very good people," she says, were "very much hands off, like to tell your kids you love them, they're not comfortable with that. They're old school, where you don't show too much affection to a boy because it might make him weak."

The family that Jackie and Bob built together is tight, yet each of the members is self-reliant. "I can bring out my own garbage," Jackie says. "I can split wood. I can do all that stuff. I can take care of myself, because [the men are] not always around."

Cheerfully, like many military wives, she put her life on hold to be with her husband whenever she could. "I knew Bob was going away, so I actually didn't work when we came here [to Petawawa], because I knew he was going and we wanted to spend as much time as we could together." Neither did she work while he was in Afghanistan because she knew, when he came home on leave, she couldn't bear the thought of working all day.

Only when he headed back to Kandahar, on November 24, did she begin to work. She started driving a bus, and got a job as a cashier at the local Pharma Plus for the Christmas holidays. She started on Sunday, November 26.

She would put in only that single shift.

—

LAVOIE AND GIROUARD FLEW BACK to Kandahar together, arriving to find that Jay Harvey had at last procured a Bison for the RSM. On that Sunday when Jackie was working the drugstore cash for the first time, her husband and his driver, Corporal Albert Storm, were gleefully cramming every inch of their new vehicle with ammunition and medical supplies. "Corporal Storm couldn't have been any more proud than to be the RSM's driver," Lavoie remembers, "and they were just happier than pigs in shit."

On Monday morning, Lavoie's reconstituted Tac was to go forward again, back to Masum Ghar. Their four-vehicle packet—the order of march was Lavoie's LAV first, then the RSM in his Bison, then the other two LAVs—left KAF around 8 a.m. Shortly before nine, the convoy was still on the outskirts, about a kilometre or so east of the famous double arches that mark the entrance to the sprawling city.

Stretched along one side of Highway 4 is a series of car dealerships—most businesses in Kandahar are grouped together, with lumberyards all in one part of town, hardware stores in another, etc.—a sort of market area, and, set back off the road a little, in a dilapidated low building, the Shahid Abdul Ahad Karzai Orphanage. On the other side of the road, that morning, was gathered a group of Kuchi nomads and their camels.

Lavoie, in the lead, saw nothing unusual among the several hundred cars sitting in the dealership lots to his right. "I certainly didn't notice it at all," he says. He's not sure, now, whether the bomber ever drove the vehicle, or even moved it. "I think he just detonated it as [the Bison] passed," he says, "because the smoking wreck of the vehicle was sitting off by the side of the road quite a distance."

Lavoie could feel the heat of the blast and its concussion roll through his body. The explosion was sufficiently large that it killed about a dozen camels on the other side of the highway, shattered windows in the orphanage, and added another blackened hole to the many that mar city roads.

The LAVs stopped right away and, "a quick check over my shoulder, I'd seen his vehicle come to a rolling stop at the side of the road. I still don't know what the casualty situation is, I just know the vehicle's been hit," Lavoie says. "I guess where the training kicked in is that you have this overwhelming desire, because you know it's your best friend in the vehicle and you don't know whether he's alive or dead, but you also recognize there's steps you've got to take to make sure you don't take any other casualties."

He got on the net and told battalion headquarters to get a chopper in the air, gave orders to the other vehicles to establish a security cordon, and then took his LAV to the RSM's vehicle so they could cross-load casualties. "All that stuff took place in the first, oh, sixty seconds," Lavoie says.

He hopped out and ran to the Bison. At first glance, it appeared untouched, but that was on the left side. On the right, the side closest to the bomber, the Bison "was completely plastered with shrapnel," the tires flattened. Bobby Girouard and Albert Storm were dead, killed in the rain of hot metal.

"I remember going back to the vehicle and having to call in the situation report," Lavoie says, "and vital signs absent and then reading his and Corporal Storm's zap numbers from their dog tags, and confirming it. Because I sent it over the net, and realizing who it was, they asked me to confirm the numbers."

They waited until the Quick Reaction Force arrived to secure the site, and for the chopper to pick up the RSM and Corporal Storm. Then Niner Tac limped back to KAF.

After he called the rear party back in Petawawa, initiating the next-of-kin notification, Lavoie phoned his wife. "And just sobbed like a baby on the phone to her," he says. "Never in front of the troops." Much later, Erica told him that after that first week, "based on how I was on the phone to her, she didn't think I was going to be able to stay in theatre."

Lavoie and Girouard had shared quarters at KAF, their rooms directly across the hall from one another. "Just walking in there at nighttime, and seeing his now-empty room, was really hard to take, and being in bed and knowing across the hall his was empty."

For the ramp ceremony, Lavoie was able to bring all of the company commanders and sergeant majors into the base for the night. There, he called a war cabinet and made it clear that he didn't want soldiers trying to even the score. He told them that they couldn't see every vehicle that came within fifteen or twenty metres as a suicide bomber, that they couldn't shoot indiscriminately, drove home the message that "it's not time to even the score, we've got to bring the fight to the enemy the same way that we had" before.

Lavoie couldn't get out of KAF fast enough, and the day after the ramp ceremony he headed to Masum Ghar. "That was probably the most difficult thing I had to do—go forward, for the first time, without the RSM at my side," he says. "For both me and the troops, because any time they'd ever seen us—we did line tours on almost a daily basis—it was always him and me. And they'd always seen us together. And here's the first time that the CO's here and the RSM's not at his side. I was always looking over my shoulder, expecting to see him, and he wasn't there.

"I had a chance to talk to every soldier, I think, in the battle group, and they were very shaken up. And I talked to them, and let them have a chance to talk to me about the whole thing. Again, I think that helped a bit.

"There's no doubt in my mind . . . there's no impact greater than losing your Regimental Sergeant Major in a battle group. The CO's job is important, but to the soldiers, which is 90 percent of the battle group, they aspire to be like the RSM. They're not officers. They don't aspire to be like the CO. They aspire to be the RSM. They look up to him and want to be like him. And when you have an RSM of Mr. Girouard's calibre, it's even exponentially more apparent when something like that happens."

It was easier, he says, to be with the troops. They were frank, said their piece directly. Others, Lavoie found, "really didn't know how to react with me, how to interact with me. It's a new thing," he says. "It's the first time in fifty or sixty years that an RSM was killed in combat, and I could be wrong, but from my own regimental history of RCR, I can't remember reading, or recall, that an RSM was even killed in World War II. So it was a new thing, a different thing, and

I think people had real difficulty even being around me, not know-ing what to say or what to do, in a sense."

In Petawawa, Jackie Girouard opened the door of her big house to find six uniformed high-ranking officers there, including brigade commander Colonel Denis Thompson. "Bob's been in a lot of years," she says, and "I just think they couldn't figure out who to send." They offered to tell her kids, "and obviously I understand what their logic was, but there was no way I was having anybody else tell the kids."

She found Robert first: With his recent experience as part of the rear party—he'd driven for people who had lost sons or husbands, he'd been part of an honour guard at a funeral, he'd been to Trenton to help with the pickup of a body—he knew immediately. Jocelyn, less familiar with what the sight of all those high-ranking men means, "thought maybe Bob was hurt; it took her a little while."

Then, with a military driver, Jackie got in a car and headed for Kingston and RMC, three hours away and the longest drive of her life. In September, before Michel had his phone hooked up, Jackie had called him once at RMC and had him paged, inadvertently scar-ing the wits out of him. "Mum," he told her, "don't ever do that again. I thought you were coming to tell me something about Dad."

"And I said no, Michel, if something happens to your father, I'll come right to your door. I'll be the one to tell you." So he, too, knew as soon as he saw her.

She spent the next five nights in the shed. In the daytime, she could stand to be in the house, but when the sun set, "I'd go out there, walk the property, and have the fire going. People probably thought I was weird, but . . ." There, she was alone with memories of her wonderful husband and the three decades they'd had together. "Thirty years," she says, "and he never hurt me once."

They had started talking about what they would do in three or four years when he would qualify for an indexed pension and he could retire. He'd always wanted to drive truck, so there was talk of that. They owned a Fifth Wheel, a towable recreational vehicle, and thought maybe they'd just work at campsites, go from one campsite to the next, "do some fun stuff." My hunch is they wouldn't have gone too far, or stayed away too long: The pull of home, and their children, was too profound.

Jackie was comforted by one thing: Bob was buried at the National Military Cemetery, in the very heart of Beechwood Cemetery in Ottawa, and now Jackie and her children have also bought plots there. "We had no idea where we wanted to retire," she says. "We had no idea where we were going to end up. And now we know." For an itinerant family of the Canadian military, there is solace in that.

Just before Christmas, the new 1RCR RSM, Chief Warrant Officer Mark Miller, arrived in theatre. I saw him on the ground as the sun rose on December 21. In the middle of the Arghendab River plain near Howz-e-Madad, the Royals charged their glasses in their famous "Ortona Toast," a rum–brown sugar–warm water concoction, in celebration of the regiment's 123rd birthday. The toast had been served to officers and NCOs on December 21 in Ortona, Italy, sixty-three years earlier. This was the first time since then that the Royals had celebrated the toast in the field in the middle of combat operations.

A forty-six-year-old from Minto, New Brunswick, Miller had been the RCR's drill sergeant-major and was slated for promotion. Lavoie had called him to assure him "he wouldn't be getting the appointment if I didn't think he was able to do it and if I wasn't confident in him doing it. So I made sure he knew that. And then, like I told a lot of soldiers who had to be appointed when someone else was killed in action—it doesn't make you any less deserving of the position."

The first thing Miller did, Lavoie says, was to tell the troops: "'This isn't how I wanted to take over as the RSM, so I'm now the RSM but I'm not Mr. Girouard and I don't intend to be.' . . . I think that was the right way to do it, not to try to become who he wasn't."

In April 2007, Omer Lavoie was in Gagetown, where he had a chance to meet up with Warrant Frank Mellish's wife, Kendra. "I was telling her, I look at it now, back about a year ago I guess it was, almost a year from when it happened, CWO Girouard, Warrant Nolan, Warrant Mellish, and I did a rucksack march for a day. Marched thirty kilometres for a cancer charity drive that Warrants Mellish and Nolan had organized. I look back, a year later, and three of the guys that we did the march with are now dead."

In Petawawa, as the weeks turned into months, kind and well-intentioned people began telling Jackie Girouard, "Oh, you're young, you'll start over." She couldn't imagine it. "I got married to Bob, obviously," she says. "He was my first boyfriend, and my only boyfriend. I've never dated anybody else. I've never been with anybody else. I wouldn't even know how."

When we spoke in spring 2007, she was preparing for Jocelyn's marriage to Eric Ranger, a private with 1RCR and a young man, Jackie says, with a big heart. Jocelyn was stricken at the thought that her beloved father wasn't going to walk her down the aisle. Luckily, Jackie says, at Christmas of 2005, Jocelyn had attended one of the mess functions and had waltzed with her dad. "So she feels like she got to do that, and that it was meant to be."

In those days, whenever she saw her dad at work Jocelyn would also see Lavoie. She knew how much time the two men had spent together, and because she is a thoughtful young woman and suspected it would help Lavoie's heart heal, she asked him if he would walk her to the altar on August 18. Grateful and touched, he agreed.

As for Jackie Girouard, late in our interview she sprung a real surprise. She was talking about how she suspects her daughter, the child most like her dad, will end up in the military too. "I think I'm joining," she said casually.

Turns out, she already had. When her husband had been in Ottawa for those merit boards early in November 2006, Jackie walked into a Canadian Forces recruiting centre and signed up. She told him, of course, and "he was okay with it, he got a kick out of it." She was looking for a decent job. That's part of it: There's no money in cutting hair. But it was never just about money. ("Obviously," she said wryly, "I wasn't looking for a pension.") It was something she wanted to do, and after Bob was killed the desire grew even stronger.

She returned to the recruiting centre in March 2007, told them that her husband had been killed and that her daughter was getting married. "Call us when you're ready," they told her. "If I go, it'll probably be in September," she said.

In some measure, she says, she's doing it for her children, her two military sons and the daughter she believes will join up. "To let the kids know that it's still okay, to let them know I don't want them to change paths because of this. I want them to stay on the path, and I know that's what he would want." She's no martyr. She's doing it for herself, too. "It's that sense of family, that's what it is. And there's that special bond I don't think you get anywhere else, really."

Jackie turned forty-six in July 2007. For almost two-thirds of her life, from grade 9 on, she was with Bob Girouard of Bathurst, New Brunswick, who was so very good at being just who he was. She learned a thing or two.

Afghan school girls

14 July 2006

—

"There—that is the future of Afghanistan."

—IAN HOPE, DIRECTING A CAPTURED TALIB TO GAZE
UPON JANIE DUGUAY

IN THE EARLY HOURS of July 13, 2006, the Patricias slipped unde-tected into Helmand Province under cover of a sandstorm, their convoy of about 150 fighting vehicles making excellent time. It was here that at first light, near the village of Tal-e-Gawmishi along The Green of the Helmand River, Jon Hamilton's recce platoon moved out on what looked to be a simple task—set up a cordon around a suspected Taliban opium- and IED-making compound. That task turned into a Taliban ambush on a bridge and a battle so fierce that 2 Platoon of Alpha Company, with their big LAV cannons, joined recce's dozen soldiers in the fight. The formal battle damage assess-ment revealed five confirmed enemy dead; another ten suspected injured; and a huge seizure of opium paste, arms, and the jihad propaganda that specifically mentioned Canada.

That same morning, Bill Fletcher and Charlie Company left the battle group's desert leaguer and headed off to bring supplies—water and rations—to the beleaguered Brits further north in Sangin. As CO Ian Hope later said, "My heart ached to watch Bill and crew have to go, knowing they would be in the shit by morning of the fourteenth. Sure enough, they made contact bursting into Sangin, but Bill's big nuts and the LAV saw him safely into relief of the Brits."

The following morning, as the rest of the convoy was pulling out of the leaguer and heading toward what's called a "rolling replen"— a meeting with the resupply and refuelling trucks of the National Service Element—the Afghan National Army (ANA) contingent with the Patricias arrested a Talib. The man, who said he taught in the local madrassa, or Islamic religious school, was on a small motorbike and suspected of trying to report the convoy's position in their desert hide. The ANA took the man with them as they moved the five klicks to meet up with the resupply trucks. As the LAVs and other vehicles topped up and put away the fresh rations, there was a lull. Hope sat down with the Talib, showed him pictures of his two youngsters (a cartoon version of the Canadian notion of torture, I thought, when he told me about it: Really fuck with us and we get out the home movies), and told him through the interpreter that the next time he tried to blow up a convoy he would be leaving children like these without a father.

Around 10:30 a.m., a few of the ANA soldiers began to stunt-ride the Talib's bike. By this time, the man was sitting, blindfolded, in one of the ANA pickup trucks.

Hope watched as a young brunette, a twenty-one-year-old female gunner from A Battery, 1st Royal Canadian Horse Artillery, fired up the motorcycle and began riding the hell out of it. Soon, Hope's RSM Randy Northrup said, she pulled her long hair out of a pony-tail "and let it loose." Everyone was watching now. "I remember her riding the piss out of that bike," Steve Gallagher, the A Battery commander, wrote me in an email, "as the ANA looked on in amazement . . . a *woman* driving a motorbike."

Hope had the ANA bring the Talib over to him and untie his blindfold. Then he pointed at Janie Duguay, "with her hair flying out, in a T-shirt, free and tough, doing things on his bike that he couldn't do."

"That," Hope told the Talib, "is the future of Afghanistan."

After I'd spent months trying to track her down, Gunner Janie Duguay, from Gaspé, Quebec, phoned me in January 2007. I suspect it was at the strong urging of her battery commander.

She remembered the incident, but it had barely registered with her, certainly not as it had with Hope and Northrup and, much later, in the retelling, had resounded with me.

"It was just a big field," she said.

She listened in silence as I told her how Hope had made the Talib watch her, how the man had grown visibly angry, and what the CO had told him.

"This was just a small bike," she said, "a 250cc maybe."

Gunner Duguay, back in Shilo, Manitoba, drives a 600cc CBR. The lesson learned, as they say in the army: Beware of over-romanticizing a soldier or a soldierly moment.

Cpl. Andrew James (Boomer) Eykelenboom

11 August 2006

—

"Yesterday, from the lush countryside of Tuscany, I logged onto the Star website, breaking my promise to myself not to read my paper while on holidays. Immediately, I recognized the photo of Eykelenboom, taken apparently while on an R'n'R leave in Thailand, bottle of beer in hand, laughing.
"It was like a kick in the gut and I wept as I read the story of his death."

— *Toronto Star* COLUMNIST ROSIE DIMANNO, ON
BOOMER EYKELENBOOM, AUGUST 15, 2006

THE CANADIAN ARMY is so small. The troops say that a lot. On the bad days, when soldiers are dying, as George Petrolekas, a former Canadian liaison officer to NATO, once told me in an email, "It's like a shitty fiction book where all the characters are interconnected . . . the ripple of these deaths is felt throughout. Maybe only two degrees of separation, instead of six."

I understood this exactly on August 15, 2006.

I was back in Canada. My friend Rosie DiManno of the *Toronto Star* was in the middle of a summer-long vacation in her ancestral Italy with her recently widowed mom, her brother, and his two youngsters. Usually, Rosie and I are both incapable of staying out of our papers for more than a couple of weeks (it has to do with a gnawing fear of being forgotten, I'm afraid), but I knew on this trip, because of her family, she'd sworn she wouldn't work. She had astonished me: From the end of June, when the DiMannos left Canada, until August 15, she hadn't written once. But on that day she broke her self-imposed exile and filed a column. It was about Boomer Eykelenboom, the twenty-three-year-old medic who had been killed in a fiery suicide bombing a few days earlier.

She was writing about a young man she called sweetly goofy and with whom she had spent almost twenty-four hours in the cozy confines of a LAV about six months earlier on that endless trip to FOB Robinson. I was on that trip too, in another LAV, when a local truck accidentally sideswiped the 25 millimetre cannon on our vehicle and smacked it into the two rear air sentries. Boomer was one of the medics who swung smoothly into action, the first to tend to the injured troops, murmuring reassurances in their ears and holding their hands.

I was right there, inches away, and wrote about it, but my attention was on the two injured soldiers from my LAV. It wasn't until I read Rosie's column that I realized I also "knew" the young man whose body arrived at CFB Trenton on the night of August 15. Boomer may even have been the medic who calmly asked me to get the stretcher off the side of the LAV, a task that as a hapless civilian I barely managed.

Andrew James (Boomer) Eykelenboom was a medical technician, or med tech, but like all medics who have been embraced by the front-line soldiers with whom they travel, he was mostly called Doc, especially when the shit hit the fan. "There's no better feeling either," says Don Haley, a senior med tech with 1 Field Ambulance in Edmonton and who in Kandahar was in charge of the evacuation section, the six armoured ambulances that deployed with the infantry companies. "When you go out with a company in the military, when they don't know you, at first they tend to shy away from you and say Master Corporal or whatever," Haley says. "But when they start calling you Doc, you know that you're fitting right in."

It didn't take long for that alchemy to happen on Roto 1. Because the troops were under attack one way or another almost as soon as they hit the ground, the medics began travelling with them quickly. There's little so endearing as seeing a medic staunch the wound of a bleeding friend or tenderly hold him as he draws his last breaths.

Gord Hickling, another senior med tech, was on his way to the Gumbad Platoon House on March 10 when his Bison ambulance hit an IED. "It was just the most surprising day," he says. "It kind of woke me up to what the tour was going to be like." Hickling and his two-man crew were called back that same night to KAF. With their ambulance blown up, they had to return in a G-Wagon. "I'd felt pretty safe in my Bison," Hickling says, "so we had to go back in a G-Wagon, oh great."

As they drove through Kandahar, he was stunned by how they moved, slowly down the streets, the doors of the vehicle open with soldiers hanging out, rifles at the ready. "That was the big day of just waking up," he says. "Then we were coming down that highway there, the boys were firing off warning shots: It certainly wasn't like the first twenty-two years of my military service."

Shaun Kaye had a similar early-in-the-game experience. He was the medic on the convoy ferrying the board of inquiry members, who on March 3 were re-enacting the route that diplomat Glyn Berry's convoy had taken in February when Berry's G-Wagon was hit by a suicide bomber. Berry was killed that day, and three soldiers were seriously wounded, including Master Corporal Paul Franklin, Kaye's fellow medic. The board's re-enactment was a little too accurate: Ian Hope's LAV, that day minus the CO, who was in a conference with the new brigade commander, hit an IED. Kaye was one of the rear sentries.

"When the blast went off, we ducked inside the carrier and then shortly after, we stop at the side of the road, the place was covered with smoke. It was hard to see, hard to breathe," he says. "Everyone in the back was okay, we made sure, but as soon as I got out I heard them screaming for the medic and—oh God, here we go—I look up at the crew commander, that was Loewen. He was still in his hatch, his arm was just dangling. You could see the bone sticking out, blood everywhere. He had shrapnel all along his face, his face was just black. I couldn't get to him at the top of the vehicle, so I told him to come down to me, so he got down, the arm was just dangling, blood was just everywhere."

Kaye put combat tourniquets above Loewen's right elbow—combat medicine has done a complete 180 in recent years; where tourniquets were once deemed the course of last resort, now, in recognition of the fact that blood loss accounts for most battlefield deaths, they are the first—and a couple of field dressings on the wound itself. Then they loaded Loewen onto a regular troop-carrying Bison and began tearing back to KAF. Just outside the gates to the base, the Bison's engine caught fire and the vehicle lost all power, with the driver, Paul Jones, actually engulfed in flames for a minute. They transferred Loewen to the roof of a G-Wagon travelling with them. "I jumped on, and a few other guys jumped on," Kaye says. Like that, physically holding on to his patient, the driver leaning on the horn, they got Loewen to the base hospital—in time for his arm to be saved.

Kaye was then just twenty-two, and for him that was "a day that really changed my life." He realized that when someone was hurt, "I didn't have time to be scared, there was too much adrenalin. Besides, we're talking about the welfare of our Patricias here. Even when I was scared shitless, I never let it show to any casualties when I worked on them. It makes the soldier feel better and more confident when the medic looks calm and collected."

It was Kaye's first overseas tour, only the second time he'd gone outside the wire of the big base at KAF, and to that point his most critically injured patient. "It was a wake-up call for me," he says. "All of this training I did prior was becoming a reality."

Monitoring from home in Edmonton with a double-edged interest was Chris Kaye, Shaun's father and also the RSM for 1 Field Ambulance. "As soon as they went over," the RSM says, "within weeks it was, 'Holy mackerel, we're into this up to our elbows now.'"

The sixty-soldier-strong Health Services Support Company had four separate and distinct jobs in Afghanistan: to provide a regular medical clinic at both KAF and Camp Nathan Smith, the small base housing the Provincial Reconstruction Team; to staff the evacuation platoon with its Bison ambulances, each of which travelled with two med techs and a "Strat," a driver from Lord Strathcona's Horse (Royal Canadians); and for the dismounted section of medics who went into the field without an ambulance, to follow the troops wherever they went. Finally, the medics were to pitch in as extra hands whenever mass casualty situations threatened to overwhelm staff at the Canadian-led Role 3 hospital.

These were enormous and unremitting demands upon such a small contingent. Soon enough, especially once the cycle of scheduled leave kicked in and troops began rotating out of Afghanistan, the six-teen designated dismounted medics had to be supplemented by some of the mounted ones. The result by tour's end was that virtually all of the med techs had worked everywhere, spent weeks on end in the field, seen too much, and were close to spent.

While the combat troops rotating into KAF for a break were able to grab a day or two of rest, the medics were in such hot demand—the dangers of southern Afghanistan so pervasive that no convoy wanted to go out without at least one of them along—that they would often come in off one mission and go right back out on another.

"To ask young men and women to go out and perform constantly, on a daily basis, day after day, and sometimes in life-threatening sit-uations day after day," RSM Kaye says, "I think that just wears and tears at young people, at any age actually, to be constantly sub-jected to fear and combat stresses. That just emotionally wears people down."

As Marilynn Chenette, the Officer Commanding of HSS Company, says, "Most of them had been involved in tough situa-tions, and had dealt with many serious casualties and their peers dying in their hands. Some of them also had to 'fight the fight' first, before they could safely treat casualties."

The army's universality of service requirement ensures that sol-diers, whatever their specific trade, are soldiers first, and trained as such. During live-fire exercises, for example, the med techs were right in there. And while the infantry did their assaults, everyone practised patient evacuations from ground to air to hospital. But whereas on other, less violent overseas tours medics may have been able to imagine themselves simply as healers, there was no room for such luxury in Kandahar.

As Don Haley, who was in Bosnia on three tours says, "Psychologically, in Afghanistan, you're definitely a soldier first. Somewhere else, not so much. Out of all the tours I've been on, the rest of them were like a vacation is the best way to describe it, com-pared to this one, because you didn't know from one day to the next if you were going to come under small-arms [fire], or if you were going to have someone try to run into you and blow themselves up, or if you were going to get RPGed or missiled at the FOBs and stuff."

No one knows this better than Haley and the young medic, David Blythe, who was his sidekick on the battle group's major move into Pashmul on the weekend of July 8–9, 2006. As the convoy in the early hours of that first morning headed toward the infamous White School and the bridge over the Arghendab River, Blythe was the air sentry in the back of the ambulance. The Bison was with two other vehicles at the rear, a little behind the rest of the convoy, with most of the vehicles already over the bridge and moving toward the staging area.

"They were probably sixty or seventy metres ahead already," Haley says, "on a narrow road, and there's no way they can turn around." It was then, he says, that Blythe "noticed the RPG teams coming out from behind the wall, getting ready to lay down fire on us as we went by the White School and were crossing the bridge."

For the first and only time in Roto 1, mounted medics had to return fire, with Blythe on the C7 rifle and Haley on the spindle-mounted C6 atop the Bison. Certainly, they had help from the LAV just ahead of them, whose gunners swivelled and started firing, but Haley is certain that being able to get on the machine gun in those first minutes saved their lives.

Says Blythe, who'd just turned twenty-four days before, "It was weird to think that our job is to save people's lives. Even the bad guys, we're supposed to save their lives if we can. And it's just really weird to think that we probably took a few lives that day. It felt good, I'm sad to say, [because of the] so many people they've taken from us, you know?"

It was just the beginning of what Blythe calls "a very crazy" few days. "We just had RPGs flying over our heads, and mortars," he says. "It seemed normal. For that two- or three-day period, it did seem normal—you're just kind of always scared."

At least part of the Haley–Blythe historic double—it was the medics' first time firing in self-defence and also a first for the company since the Korean War—was caught on tape. CTV's Steve Chao and Tom Michalak were in the Bison with Blythe and Haley. Michalak continued to film, head and camera out the turret, until the ambulance actually came under contact. They were lucky they were travelling in one of only two ambulances with a permanent mount for the C6 on the vehicle roof. The other four had no such capability, and no machine guns.

The arming of ambulances had been the subject of much internal debate before deployment, with Marilynn Chenette and Ian Hope pushing hard for all Bisons to have mounted C6s for self-protection. Those arrangements—approval had been given and Chenette believed it was a done deal—mysteriously fell apart only after the troops landed in Afghanistan. Chenette and Hope both fought to have the other Bisons fitted up retroactively, to no avail.

Chenette succeeded in convincing the brass to do it only two weeks before 2 Field Ambulance set off with The Royal Canadian Regiment to start their tour in August 2006. "To know that my med techs and crew would be better protected and [that] Roto 2 would be well set up and not have to fight this battle," she says, "is a great feeling." The weapons system was never intended to form part of the overall company defence or offence, but rather to allow medics to protect themselves and, most of all, their vulnerable patients.

I interviewed some of the med techs in late July, when a handful of them, including Haley and Blythe, were enjoying a brief respite at KAF. By this time, they had all been in or on the edges of enough fire-fights that the subject of their gunless ambulances was a hot topic.

Until that month's Battle of Pashmul, Gord Creelman had been the only medic not directly involved in some sort of incident. That changed over July 8–9, when Creelman's ambulance, *sans* machine gun, was left in the rear during the fighting. But "the rear" doesn't mean what it once did. Logistics boss John Conrad describes the modern battlefield as "water droplets on a walnut table, with the droplets [being] the safe haven." Those droplets are few and far between, and often hard to locate. In a war without a fixed front line, there is no fixed rear echelon.

So Creelman's Bison sat there, with only one LAV as security. "We had no weapon to reach out and touch someone," he said.

"We're lucky no one was hurt." With rounds from RPGs and recoil-less rifles landing too close for comfort, he described the frustration and fear of knowing what to do—the three-man crew is made up of ex-combat arms—but being unable to do it.

Brian Sanders, the Strat driving Creelman's ambulance that day, shared this feeling. Lord Strathcona's Horse is an armoured regiment—they're the tankers—and as Sanders said, "Being a Strat, you're always a big gun, always a guy who knows what he's doing. . . . We were kind of exposed." As Sanders wrote in his *Soldier's Diary* for CBC online (where in the same dispatch he said of himself and his crew, "We don't have post-traumatic stress disorder—we're just car-riers now"), the first casualty his med techs treated over that week-end was an injured Taliban fighter, whose collapsed lung was reinflated and wounds were bandaged before the chopper arrived to take him to hospital.

At least their gunless ambulance wasn't also identified by the tra-ditional red cross. To show the cross or not was the subject of another heated, pre-deployment debate, Chenette says. "We didn't want to display the cross, to identify ourselves as a weak target. That's what they [the enemy] always go for, the one that appears the weakest. Why would we take that chance in a country that does not abide by, nor seems to want to abide by, the Geneva Conventions?"

The First Geneva Convention, the oldest of the four, is entitled "For the Amelioration of the Condition of the Wounded and Sick in Armed Forces in the Field." It allows medics to carry weapons purely for self-defence while travelling under the protection of the long-recognized red cross on a white background, the distinctive sign of the medical services of armed forces. Yet in Afghanistan, as in other corners of the planet, neither the red cross nor its Islamic equivalent, the red crescent, buys any more protection than that claimed by any other non-governmental organization working in the area. All are considered fair game for attack, ambush, bombing, or kidnapping.

Chenette successfully argued that there was good tactical reason not to display the cross on her vehicles in Kandahar. "Since we usu-ally only sent ambulances on larger combat missions and with larger company groups," she says, "the enemy could easily figure out what those missions were and where they were going as soon as they saw a 'marked' ambulance with the convoy. We didn't display the red cross at all during the entire mission." In fact, the only time it was ever shown was on the medics' armbands, or brassards, during Village Medical Outreaches (VMOs), when the situation was deemed tactically safer and under control.

In late July, when I met Don Haley and some of his colleagues over coffee at KAF, they were ready to go home. Every one of them had been shot at and in a firefight; every one had driven through an ongoing battle to pick up casualties; every one had been RPGed. And they were dog-tired, rarely grabbing more than a single day of rest between missions that routinely went on for weeks. Haley, for instance, was out in the field for as long as thirty-two days at a stretch and, not counting the first three weeks on the ground during the handover, was at KAF for only thirty-eight days out of six months.

"Right now," he said that day in his fine Newfoundland accent (he is from St. Lawrence, a coastal town on the Burin Peninsula), "we're so close to the end, we've had enough, and we still have a job to do. We'll go out for one more kick at the cat, and all come back safely."

—

ABOUT TWO WEEKS LATER, Haley was at the FOB at Spin Boldak, near the border with Pakistan, having lunch with Nic Lewis and Boomer Eykelenboom. Usually attached to Charlie Company's 8 Platoon, Lewis had been intimately involved in the Battle of Pashmul in July and in the fierce and lethal fighting on August 3 during which four men were killed. He'd been sent to Spin for a bit of a breather. Boomer had returned to KAF the night before after spending several weeks at Patrol Base Wilson, previously known as the Zhari District Centre until the creaky bureaucratic wheels turned at last and it was deemed officially okay to call it Wilson. The troops had been doing so for months regardless.

Named for Master Corporal Tim Wilson, who was killed in a traffic accident in early March 2006, the base is periodically subjected to RPG and mortar attacks that range from desultory to intense, and is frankly depressing. Even by the standards of Afghanistan's squalid bases, two weeks there feels like four anywhere else.

On the night he returned to KAF, Boomer popped into Marilynn Chenette's office, told her he was tired and needed a little time. She knew that; it was why she'd brought him back. The new Roto 2 crews would soon arrive from Canada, and she figured she'd be able to give Boomer a good stretch to recuperate from the recent weeks of battles and strain. In the meantime, the boys at Spin needed supplies.

The first convoy slated to arrive, Haley remembers, had mechanical difficulties with two vehicles, so it turned around. The second saw one of the new Nyalas roll over and never made it either. "We were stretched pretty thin because people had started to leave [for Cyprus and home] at this point," Haley says. David Blythe, for instance, who had to leave a little early for a course, was already back in Edmonton.

Haley thinks Boomer volunteered to go out on the third convoy. However, Chenette says that she was so short of people, she reluctantly had to ask his supervisor to send him out. It may be that because he was so damn mellow about everything, with that easy smile of his, it *seemed* to Haley as if he must have volunteered. Or, with typical Boomer goodwill, he may have told Haley he had volunteered, so Haley wouldn't fret on his behalf.

After all, the young man was the "max relax" kid, Haley says. "Nothing seemed to get him too upset, or bother him too much. He never ever had anything negative to say. If the military could be built with soldiers like him, it would be a great place to work."

Sean Marshall also saw Boomer at KAF that night. "We pretty much figured that was the end" of the hard going, Marshall says, and they joked around. As much as their leaders told them not to, everyone was counting down the days. And a trip to Spin was then considered a relative walk in the park. Spin, by comparison to Wilson, was a luxe spa, so going on the convoy would not have seemed a particularly onerous task.

As Chenette says, "Although it wasn't good news for him, he took it like a good soldier would, and prepared his kit to go out again. I saw him the next morning, just before he left for his task. He was leaving his room with all his kit, still with a smile on his face, as always. I told him I wished I didn't have to send him because I knew how tired he was, but I needed him to go. I said to him, 'It's a quick jaunt down to Spin Boldak, we'll see you tonight.' He smiled and said, 'Yes ma'am, I'll see you all in a few hours.'"

The resupply convoy arrived at Spin before noon and Haley and Lewis, delighted to see that Eykelenboom was the medic aboard, sat down with him for lunch and a bullshit session.

"We had about two weeks to go before we were flying out," Haley says. "[Boomer] was actually on the same decompression block as me, and we were talking about going to Cyprus, and he wanted to go diving, he wanted to play golf, and stuff like that. We sat around and had lunch, and shortly after lunch, they left to go back up [to KAF]."

About twenty minutes later, they got the call on the radio. "They told us they had one VSA [vital signs absent]," he says, "and then they sent the number, the zap number. And when I saw the zap number—because I had a copy of all our medics' zap numbers, just due to the position I was in there—I knew it looked familiar. So that was when I went back to the UMS [the medical station] to get the ambulance ready to go, and I grabbed my clipboard to go back for more info and I grabbed my sheet, and I knew then it was Boomer."

At KAF, Chenette got the call. "I have to say my heart came to a complete stop when I found out it was the convoy to Spin Boldak," she says. "I immediately thought of him and wished he was okay. I was then immediately informed that the casualty was the med tech. My feelings then, I can't even begin to describe."

Gord Hickling was at the PRT on the day Boomer got hit. He'd been there for a couple of weeks and, at forty-five, kept a fatherly eye on the young medics as they came rolling through, making sure they had everything they needed. "You got your leather gloves? Got your ballistic glasses?" The medics often went out on short notice, and the younger ones in particular were prone to just grabbing their gear and running. "They'd always be short of something," Hickling says. "Particularly Boomer. I remember asking, 'You got clean socks?' 'No, I don't have clean socks,' and I'd be giving him my clean socks."

Whenever someone was killed, they'd lower the flag to half-mast at the PRT, as they did at KAF. "It was around midday," Hickling says, "and then the flag went to half-mast, so we knew somebody got hit. And then there was a convoy coming in from Martello [one of the FOBs] and, you know, I would always go to greet the guys. I was smiling and happy and the other guys were just staring at me. So I jumped up on the Bison and it was Jeff Muir, he goes, 'You didn't hear?' I said, 'Hear what?' He still had the vehicle on, so there was loud engine noise, but I could just read his lips: 'Boomer.'"

Hickling later read in some of the coverage of Boomer's death a line that said he had arrived in Afghanistan a boy and become a man. "I would never agree with that," he says. "He was a grown man when he [got] there."

Back in Edmonton, the news came down through the chain of command, as always it does. The Commander of Land Force Western Area called Lieutenant-Colonel Chris Lennox, the CO of 1 Field Ambulance. Lennox called Chris Kaye, and the RSM's heart sank.

He calls Boomer Andrew, the name he preferred, though his mates rarely could manage such propriety with their laid-back friend. "Andrew was a physically rugged kind of young guy," Kaye says, "and a spiritually gentle fellow. As soon as you meet his parents and his brothers, you know exactly the family he came from. They're just a wonderful family."

At Spin Boldak, Don Haley prepared to go the scene. As soon as he knew who had been killed, he knew he couldn't take Lewis with him, though Lewis was the scheduled medic in the ambulance. The two were good friends—the same age, they'd spent months at a stretch on exercise together—and Haley knew too well what sort of grisly scene awaited them. Boomer had been riding in a G-Wagon when a suicide bomber exploded his vehicle. Though the other two soldiers with him were uninjured and managed to escape before the

G-Wagon burst into flames, Boomer had taken the brunt of the blast and was badly burned in the fire that raged afterwards. Haley didn't want that picture even to enter Lewis's head, so he grabbed Gord Creelman, older and more seasoned, instead.

Ian Hope, back at KAF, wanted to move to the scene himself, but knew that if the CO appeared, it would seem as if he didn't trust his men to properly recover Boomer's remains. Yet he didn't want the soldiers, Boomer's brothers-in-arms, to have to carry out this macabre task themselves. Hope ordered that the G-Wagon, Boomer still in it, be wrapped in a tarpaulin and moved that way on a low-bed trailer back to KAF. Hope waited there. With Randy Northrup solemnly standing watch, the CO himself gently and carefully extracted Boomer's remains from the vehicle.

Months later, in an email to me, Hope said, "It was hard, but when my mind wanders to it, I am steeled by the knowledge that he was recovered by caring hands."

—

FOR MANY YEARS, Maureen Eykelenboom worked in the volunteer sector: at Misericordia Community Hospital in Edmonton, when the family lived there, and with the Soroptimist International women's service club once the Eykelenbooms moved to Comox, on Vancouver Island. "I used to say that I worked with the cream of the crop of society," she says, "because I worked with people who were willing to volunteer their time. And especially hospice/palliative care volunteers."

After her youngest son was killed—and she's come to call him Boomer now as often as she calls him Andrew—she realized she'd missed the mark a little. "I've had to revise that and say I really hadn't met the true cream of the crop," she says, "because those people who volunteer within hospital care, as much as they give of themselves, they're not risking their lives."

Not until after Andrew's death did she and her husband, Hans, meet most of Andrew's friends and colleagues. After all, he was stationed in Edmonton, and though he kept talking about bringing his buddies out to Comox to go fishing, the plan was only firming up as the end of his tour in Afghanistan approached. "But we've now since met most of them," Maureen says, "and they've come and stayed here, and they're welcome to any time. We've just expanded our family hugely."

She's taken aback both by the sort of people her son's friends are and by the work they do. "I don't think people understand," she says. "I know they don't understand what they go through. One of Andrew's buddies told me that Andrew had to scrape one of his buddy's intestines off the wall of a G-Wagon to get him all back in a body bag. When you think about that, a twenty-three-year-old kid doing that. . . . They form such close bonds over there. I saw that, you know. It's [the military] just kind of, it's a whole other world. It's really quite amazing. And how smart they are. It's not, 'Oh yeah, these are all kids who couldn't get a job anywhere else.' Andrew could have gone wherever he wanted."

She'd often wondered if, when he came back, he wouldn't end up serving in one of the Christian missions overseas, "but the more I talked to his comrades, the more I thought he wouldn't have gotten out [of the army]. I know some of his buddies who are going back. I'm just floored: They don't have to."

David Blythe is one of those buddies. "I feel like I have unfinished business," he says. "And I would like to go over and help, again. I want to be there for all those people who are going, all my friends, my medical friends and the infanteers. I want to be there again, you know? Just because of that little bit of experience I do have, I feel like maybe I could help them save people's lives. That's how I feel."

Though Blythe spent months away on courses and exercises with Boomer, and though they hung out in Edmonton and were constantly together, "Overseas, I really got to know him. We were at Patrol Base Wilson for probably at least three and a half weeks before I left to come home. He was a great guy. We had lots of deep talks. I know everybody says how goofy he was and that—and he was, the things he did were goofy—but everything inside of him was for a purpose. I don't think I could say he had one bad bone in his body. He was all good."

Blythe's personal life suffered while he was in Kandahar. He and his girlfriend, a med tech who worked at the base hospital, had bought a house together just before he left for Afghanistan. They had a golden retriever and two cats and were in a serious relationship. But when I saw him in July, Blythe was subdued: The writing was on the wall, and he suspected they wouldn't make it as a couple. "We're changed people," he said then. Though he believed that what they had seen would make them better human beings, he didn't think they were going to be able to live their lives together.

"I was right," he says. "I basically knew it was over, but you know, you kind of try to hang on to things . . ." Within two months of coming home, he and his girlfriend decided to sell the house.

Andrew was a huge help to him, Blythe says. "He was nothing but positive, and always looked for the good in everything."

Then and now, Blythe remains haunted by a Bravo Company soldier he treated on July 8, Corporal Chris Klodt. Shot during a close-quarters battle, the young man crumpled to the ground and was dragged to safety by his mates. When Blythe got to him, all that was visible was a laceration to his neck. It was bleeding, but not badly. "And he was unconscious and then he was conscious and then he wasn't. He was all over the place, so me and another fellow jumped in the back of the Bison and took off with him." All around them, the battle raged.

Only later did they learn that a piece of shrapnel had lodged in Klodt's back, paralyzing him. "We felt terrible for that," Blythe says. "[Under] the circumstances, it wouldn't have made sense to do spinal precautions, but it's something I guess we have to live with. I've pretty much accepted it now, but I don't think [Klodt] can move his legs and stuff now, he's basically a paraplegic . . . not necessarily because of what we did. I don't know, I don't think we could have stopped it."

Blythe was back in Canada for only four or five days when he got the call about Boomer. He drove to Comox for the funeral. "I was the only one there that was overseas with him," he says, "so I would have been the last one to see him, and that was kind of hard." He met Maureen. "It was a very tough time just seeing her," he says. "It still doesn't feel real to me because I never actually saw his body."

Maureen Eykelenboom's faith in her son's fellow soldiers is such that when she began setting up Boomer's Legacy, the charity established in her son's name, she insisted it be directly linked to the Assistance to Afghanistan Trust Fund, a trust that had been established by the military when it received an unsolicited private gift of $10,000. That fund, which can be accessed quickly and with a minimum of paperwork by soldiers of the Provincial Reconstruction Team in Kandahar, will be the recipient of Boomer's Legacy monies.

"They'll be accountable to tell us what they spend it on," she says, "but they won't have to go through hoops." Though the end goal is education for Afghan children, in the short term, she says, schools and books are of little use to youngsters who don't even have enough food or fresh water. Thus, Boomer's Legacy will put money into the hands of the soldiers at the PRT, who have the most intimate contact with Afghans, and are best positioned to know what will do the most good.

Maureen had to browbeat the military brass a little to have it all approved, but with Rick Hillier's help, she got it done. It was one of those rare instances when she had to get the okay first. "I usually like to ask forgiveness," she says, "not permission. Andrew had a little bit of that in him, too. He didn't always abide by the rules."

He was no goody two-shoes, she knows. In fact, until he was about ten, "I'd pray, I'd say, 'Lord, why did you give me this boy? What am I going to do with him? I don't know what to do with him.' I wanted to hang him up by his thumbnails. Because he was into everything," pulling every fire alarm, "testing every test he could find."

But when he turned ten, she says, almost overnight, "he was a really good kid. He did a few dumb stunts, but for the most part was a really, really good kid. It was just such an amazing difference." He grew into a teenager who said, "'Yeah, I'm gonna go to this party but I'm staying overnight, because we're gonna have a few beers' or 'I'm not hanging out with them, because they're smoking dope.' He had a very strong faith," she says, "and a very strong sense of what was right and what was wrong."

However, he was mischievous, and in minor trouble all the time, particularly before the troops went to Kandahar. Garrison life, with its regulations and make-work projects, was not for him. He was late, would forget to set his alarm or sleep through it, so often that he regularly was assigned to lock up the buildings before everyone went home. His room in the barracks was messy enough that there were extra inspections. He would often sneak off to the transportation quarters, hide in their lounge, watching a movie and eating popcorn, while they covered for him if anyone came looking.

He had a battered old Toyota 4 x 4 truck. "It was kind of legendary around there," his mother says. He'd get the mechanics to help him fix it, get tips from them. After he was killed, the transport guys gave the truck a tune-up and an oil change, tied yellow ribbons all over it, and parked it on their lot.

Maureen hopes to get to Afghanistan herself in spring of 2008, when some of Andrew's medic friends will be back there with the troops of 3rd Battalion, Princess Patricia's Canadian Light Infantry. She and Jim Davis, father of Paul, who was killed instantly in the March 2, 2006, vehicle crash that also proved fatal to Tim Wilson, are planning to go together. Davis is a trustee of Boomer's Legacy, and Maureen's peer-support buddy. They want to go with a great whack of the fifteen thousand Boomer Caps—hats for Afghan babies—that knitters and crocheters across the country have made in honour of Eykelenboom.

It will be their own recce mission: "If you're going to do fundraising," Maureen says, "you have to know what the money is for, and if you don't see it with your own eyes, you can't sell it as well." She also wants to give "a whole bunch of them a big hug."

Andrew James Eykelenboom was wearing the huge stainless steel cross Maureen had sent to him when he died. He was who he was. It was the same when he had come home for Christmas two years earlier and shown her the tattoo he'd got across his back—two wings, with an enormous cross in the middle.

"Here I am, a Christian," Maureen says, "and I said, 'Why would you get that tattoo, you know where you're going [to a Muslim country]?' The mother in me came out first, to protect my son."

Boomer Eykelenboom looked at her like she was sick, she says. "Mum," he told her, "That's the whole purpose. No matter what, they're going to know what I stand for."

When Rosie DiManno wrote about her long trip in the LAV with Boomer, she described how during the night, in those cramped quarters, when she'd stretched out her legs and "rested stinky feet in his lap," he didn't complain.

Maureen read that and smiled through her tears. The Eykelenbooms have a U-shaped couch. Whenever Boomer was home, she'd sit at the short end and he'd fold his six-foot-two frame onto the long end. "Whoever could get their feet on top of the other one first would get a foot rub. So when she talks about putting her feet up on his lap, it was just very good. I could just visualize that. It would seem normal to him."

Several months after Boomer's death, Maureen got a note from Dave Ferris, her son's platoon commander for much of his tour. Berating himself for not writing sooner, Ferris told her that they'd fought to keep Boomer as their medic—even hiding him in their Big Ass Tent on the rare occasions they were back at KAF, so no one could find him or steal him away—and about how he'd saved the life of Junior, their beloved interpreter who'd had his legs blown off in an RPG attack.

"Andrew kept that man alive for three hours until the helicopter was able to get him out," Ferris wrote. "I miss Boomer every day, and I know he would not have had things turn out any other way—all the men and women that he looked after on a daily basis, including me, made it home."

Then in a postscript, Ferris returned the favour as best he could. "And in all the other photos where he may be holding a cigarette," he wrote, "he was holding it for me."

Lt.-Col. Ian Hope, Commander of Task Force Orion

30 August 2006

—

They swung aboard at once, they sat to the oars in ranks
And in rhythm turned the water white with stroke on stroke.
And from there we sailed on, glad to escape our death
Yet sick at heart for the comrades we had lost.

—ODYSSEUS, FROM HOMER's *Odyssey*,
TRANSLATED BY ROBERT FAGLES

I FIRST MET George Petrolekas in late July 2006 at a café in my airport hotel in Frankfurt. I didn't realize it at the time, but he had driven about three hours from Holland to make lunch. Our meeting was in lieu of a proper visit to the Landstuhl Regional Medical Center, the U.S. military hospital located about five klicks down the road from Ramstein Air Base, an American-run facility home to a variety of national forces and considered a NATO support installation. I'd been trying to find time, on my way either in or out of Afghanistan, to visit the hospital. It's a key stop on what the Canadian military calls the "casualty evacuation chain" and many gravely wounded soldiers are treated there. Thus far, all I'd managed was this quick meal between flights.

Then the Canadian liaison officer to the International Security Assistance Force to Afghanistan (ISAF) at NATO joint forces command in Brunssum, Petrolekas was a frequent visitor to the hospital. He'd emailed me several times, telling me of the compelling stories unfolding there and imploring me to visit. He also introduced me, via email, to Mike Capstick, then the head of the largely unheralded Strategic Advisory Team in Kabul—SAT is a Rick Hillier invention whose members, most of them high-level military planners, are embedded in the Afghan government and help map the country's road to economic recovery—whose hospitality I later enjoyed several times.

Remarkably well connected (when Petrolekas once responded to a toast by quoting Thomas Jefferson, Hillier said, "George probably knew him too"), he's a bright, thoughtful guy. He's also a good friend of Ian Hope, the Patricias' CO in Kandahar. When Petrolekas suggested that I fly to Germany, visit Landstuhl, and spend a day or so with Hope and his RSM Randy Northrup as they made their way out of Afghanistan and home to Canada, I was intrigued but dubious: Surely they wouldn't want a journalist hanging around as they went through the first stage of what the mental health folks call "decompression." But when I emailed Hope to ask what he thought, he warned me that he didn't know how much one-on-one time he'd have, but said I was welcome to tag along.

Thus, on August 25, 2006, I found myself in Petrolekas's Mercedes-Benz ragtop on a couple of German *Bundesautobahns* for the ninety-minute trip to the gorgeous Kaiserslautern district in the southwest corner of the country. Soon after, I checked in to the fortuitously named Hotel Christine in the town of Landstuhl. This part of the country borders the Palatine Forest, and in late summer was all of a lush green piece. It could not have been more starkly different than southern Afghanistan, with its deserts, dust, and astonishing heat. It rained a little on each of the three days we were there. At one point, needing to be alone, Hope just stood for a while outside the hotel, letting the rain wash over him and breathing in the fresh dampness.

He, Northrup, and Petrolekas were ensconced in the hotel bar, The Cockpit Lounge, each with a glass of German beer, when I walked in about an hour after checking in. What followed was a long and lazy dinner, with several bottles of red wine. At some point, Hope's brother Paul joined us, and I limped off to bed not having taken a single note.

The next day, a Saturday, was busy: Hope and Northrup went to Fisher House, the homey Ronald McDonald–style residence adjacent to the hospital where the families of many Canadian wounded have stayed, for a cheque presentation. The cheque was presented on behalf of the PPCLI Association by Patricia Grimshaw, the sister of Bravo Company's commander, Nick Grimshaw. It was for $20,197.61—raised in less than four weeks from the approximately 2300 troops at Kandahar—and part of a total of about $120,000 the Canadian military has raised thus far for Fisher House. The CO and

his RSM then went to the hospital itself. There they handed over to
the intensive care unit a framed print of a photograph called *Fallen
Comrades*, famous within the CF, by Canadian journalist Silvia
Pecota. And they personally thanked doctors and nurses for having
looked after their boys.

Some wounded Canadians were still there, one of them twenty-
four-year-old Jesse Melnyck, who, having been on the ground in
Afghanistan for only five or six days, was injured in a Taliban ambush
less than a week before Hope's visit. Riding as air sentry in the left
rear hatch when his convoy was ambushed, Melnyck turned around
to return fire and cover for his fellow sentry, whose weapon had
jammed. A bullet hit the rim of his helmet and tore through his fore-
head and into his right eye. He tumbled backwards into the vehicle.
"I kind of knew instantly my eye was gone," he said. "I started to
come to grips with the fact."

Melnyck was grateful to be alive and optimistic that he could
remain in the army (after a battle with bureaucrats and help from
Rick Hillier, he is staying in, and has been accepted at RMC). He
was so cheerful he noted that a one-eyed padre already had been to
see him, and he cursed the $5000 he'd spent on laser eye surgery the
year before deploying. "Trauma's not part of the lifetime guarantee,"
he said with a grin.

That night, one of Hope's dearest friends, Kathy Amponin, a fellow lieutenant-colonel in the U.S. Air Force then stationed at
Ramstein, was having an end-of-tour party for him at her home. She
and Hope had served together at ISAF headquarters in Kabul in
2004, when Rick Hillier was the boss. Amponin subsequently
briefed and staffed successive ISAF staffs, including Canada's SAT,
and now was part of the air division that provided intelligence and
air support to the Canadians in southern Afghanistan. She'd also
taken it upon herself to visit Canada's wounded in Landstuhl, and
her reports to Hope on the status of his men, in what he calls "those
dark hours," meant the world to him.

She's tiny, short, dark haired, and quick in her movements, a pistol of a woman. She and her husband organized a lovely party, with

many young American officers; Hope's brother Paul; and food and plenty to drink, including a stash of special red wine—Penfold's Bin 389, I think—for the guest of honour. As Randy Northrup said later, for a gathering of U.S. officers, notoriously conscious of rank, it was as low key and relaxed as the hostess.

Hope stayed overnight. On Sunday morning, the man who for seven months had "put the mask on," as he calls it, who had walked through fire and refused ever to run (otherwise, he said, "You can actually feel the moral courage of people slipping; it's almost tangible"), had a quiet coffee with Amponin. She asked him what he expected would be the toughest part of the reintegration back home. "'Seeing the wounded,' I said, and I broke down."

That was one of the few times I wasn't there as a fly on the wall, listening to Hope and Northrup talk, watching them begin to unwind, hardly wanting or daring to intrude. Only once, early on Saturday morning, did I corner them in the hotel's small lobby and make them sit down for an interview. It was a less than clever choice of location: My tape is full of the hotel's coffee machine grinding and roaring into action, and the noise of guests checking in and out. By this point, Hope and Northrup were finishing one another's sentences and stories, as good COs and RSMs do.

Hope's Tac was bombed three times—once, of course, when he wasn't there and Mike Loewen nearly had his right arm torn off, and then twice one day in June as they were coming down from Ghorak, northwest of Kandahar. The first bomb that day went off just behind them—a plastic mine designed to take out a vehicle's wheels, which it did to the Golf Niner LAV—and the second came as they were moving with the recovery convoy through the city. That time it was a suicide bomber, who detonated beside Hope's vehicle, shrapnel basically slitting Master Corporal Greg (the Whiteman) White's arm through to the bone.

"Blood was just literally pouring like a waterfall," Hope said, "and he got on the ICS [the internal radio system] and said, 'I'm losing blood fast, you better stop.'" Hope called for a chopper, but "it was getting dark in a bad place" and it would take too long, so he sent the rest of the convoy back to KAF and made a one-vehicle run to the Provincial Reconstruction Team office nearby, the incomparable Stitch Hayward at the wheel.

They were on the west side of Kandahar and had to drive across the whole city—now crowded with shoppers, the punishing sun having fallen—to get to the PRT. "It took twelve minutes," Hope said. "Very good, slick driving." Throughout, the Whiteman's defiant demeanour never altered.

A medic was waiting at the PRT, got an IV into White and was able to stabilize him, and the chopper arrived a bit early. "It came in a dust storm," Hope said. "It was pitch black, and I helped put him on the bird. And as the bird was lifting, dust was everywhere. The bird hovered toward the main building and was two feet away when it stopped. I think by force of will it went up, thank God for that."

Naturally, when Master Corporal Jason Froude replaced White as the crew commander of Hope's LAV, they told him, "Loewen got it in the right wing, White in the left: Yours is gonna be centre mass." The teasing never bothered Froude. "He knew the guys' intentions were pure, not to hurt. He was forever in the hatch," Northrup said. "He never once said, 'Someone want to take this?'"

"We had some fear in the last few weeks," Hope said, "but not him."

Another time, Northrup said, Froude came out of one of the back hatches to try to jump into the crew commander's hatch and got stuck when they were under RPG fire. "One just missed him," Northrup said. "The second hit in front of us. Stitch said, 'That's number two; you got eight seconds [to get in] or I'm backing outta here.'"

Hope talked about the day that the Royals' CO, Omer Lavoie, came to PBW for the first time. "I was lighting up one of those little cigars, saying, 'Welcome to Patrol Base Wilson,'" Hope said, when they were mortared. "A round landed right by him," Northrup said. "I told him to put his fucking gear on. 'Karen [Hope's wife] will kill me if I let anything happen to you.' Fear of the woman is big."

Even from their worst day, August 3, they were able to remember a light moment.

Chris Reid had been killed in the IED strike; the medics, Nic Lewis and Jason Lamont, were sweating in the heat as they vainly kept up CPR until the chopper arrived. Shortly afterwards, the platoon was about to begin their dismounted attack, so the EOD team checked the road for bombs. They found a handful, too, in various states of readiness.

EOD teams are usually made up of combat engineers and navy officers. As the soldiers were pounding back water, they were bugging the navy fellow about being from Shearwater, Nova Scotia. "'Shearwater, you pussy,' that sort of thing." Then the firing started, and the navy guy, Hope said, "who had never been near a fight, got his weapon, and he's like John Belushi in *The Blues Brothers*." Such a sight did he make that in the middle of the fight, while taking fire, Jeff Schnurr of recce platoon actually got out of his G-Wagon and banged on the window of the next vehicle "to draw attention to this, he thinks it's so funny," Northrup said.

Much later, when the troops were receiving some medals, Northrup said to Schnurr, "Perhaps you wouldn't mind showing what drew you out of the vehicle under fire to go tap on the window of another guy who was taking fire . . ."

"These are the things you dwell on," he said. "It was good."

Hope's biggest concern was that because of the intensity of the mission, few logs and war diaries were kept. He feared their seven months in Afghanistan had happened as if in a vacuum. "Men's lives changed; people were wounded; people died. None of that is reflected in history. I'm worried that the mission was not understood, that the task force won't be understood and recorded properly, and that soldiers won't have the right thing to fall back on. As I told many soldiers coming home, that medal [the South-West Asia Service Medal] you wear on your chest means a lot. Take the time to challenge anyone who attempts to diminish what you did. Don't get mad, but take the time."

Hope and Northrup were both sure that they would have little or no trouble readjusting. I remember being surprised by that; even my brief exposure to combat, and the longer period I'd spent in the company of soldiers, had me pining a little at home.

"Won't it pale just a bit?" I asked. "Aren't the colours brighter in Afghanistan?"

Hope said that he had recently told Chief of the Land Staff, Lieutenant-General Andy Leslie, in an email, "I need a friggin' break. You're talking to a man who wakes up in the morning and whose first thought is, 'Am I gonna see a sunset and if I do, am I gonna make any stupid decisions between now and then that cost us?' The horizon is twelve hours in Afghanistan, not two years, not a career path."

"We sit back," Northrup said, and think "fuck, we're gonna take a run tomorrow to Gumbad. Two ways in. Am I going to be able to call the wife tomorrow? Don't dwell on it; move on. If it takes you longer to motivate yourself in the morning than it does to shave, get out."

For Hope, Ulysses S. Grant, the leading Union general in the American Civil War, is history's greatest soldier. "The quote I like best: 'War is simple. Find the enemy. Move to him as fast as you can, hit him as hard as you can. Move on.' Do not dwell on what just happened, on the loss or the victory. Compartmentalize and balance. . . . You've got to compartmentalize to stay in this business."

Both the CO and the RSM were looking forward to that next compartment: family, children, and home. In Northrup's family was evidence of a career that has taken him across Canada and into the world: Chad was born in Lahr, Germany, where Northrup was stationed for four years at the Cold War–era Canadian base; Nicolas was born in Annapolis, Nova Scotia; Bettina Rose in Pembroke, Ontario. "My mission now is to make up for lost time," he said. "It's no different with the colonel and his youngsters."

Hope and his wife, Karen, have two spirited, stubborn kids; "my monsters," he calls them. Emma, then about to turn eight, is the oldest; Alec, then all of six, is the baby. "He's a boy," Northrup said. "All boy."

Alec has a habit of hiding a key piece of his father's equipment every time he leaves on an exercise or trip. One time, he took Hope's sword out of the scabbard, a misappropriation discovered when Karen found him chasing his sister around the house with it. Another time, when Hope was heading to Ottawa for a combat briefing, he hid one of his father's boots. "I get to the hotel room," Hope said, "and I have only one boot." He phoned home, and talked to Alec.

"Where's daddy's combat boot?" he asked.

"Under my bed," Alec said. "When you coming back to get it?"

Another time, Hope discovered he had no helmet with him. "I call home, speak to Alec. 'Where's my helmet, Alec?' 'Hee hee hee. You gotta come back now, Daddy.'"

Late on Sunday night, over drinks in a quiet corner of the hotel bar, George Petrolekas ran upstairs to get his laptop. He popped in a DVD showing the ramp ceremonies for Reid, Keller, Dallaire, and Ingram. Someone had set the scene to music—Sarah Brightman singing "Time to Say Goodbye."

On Monday, August 28, we caught the flight back to Edmonton. We flew Air Canada, Hope and Northrup sitting six or seven rows behind me, far enough away that I was able to slip a note explaining who they were to the flight attendant. I asked her to give it to the pilot. A few minutes later, the captain came on the air, announced that the commander of the Canadian battle group and his RSM were on the flight, heading home fresh from months of combat in Kandahar, and thanked them. The passengers burst into spontaneous applause and prolonged cheers.

A short time later, the flight attendant reappeared and asked me what Hope and Northrup liked to drink. Soon after, she and her colleagues presented them with a bottle each, a pair of glasses, and homemade cards of thanks, signed by the crew.

It was a long way from the army's darkest days, post-Somalia and the brutal 1993 beating death of teenager Shidane Arone by men from the Canadian Airborne Regiment (CAR). Of the handful of soldiers charged in the teenager's death, the most prominent was Private Kyle Brown, who was convicted of manslaughter and torture. The court martial of a second, Master Corporal Clayton

Matchee, was halted when a failed suicide attempt left him brain-damaged and unfit for trial. As an independent commission of inquiry later found, the problems of the CAR weren't confined to a small group of lowly soldiers, but were tied to the quality of their leadership, preparation, and training and to a poisonous culture that had been allowed to develop in the regiment.

If the explanation for what had happened was enormously complex—and it was—some of the fixes made by the federal government and the military itself were stupidly simple. The CAR, with its long, mostly unblemished, and indeed properly proud history, was abruptly disbanded in 1997. On and off throughout the decade, soldiers across the country were frequently told and sometimes ordered not to wear their uniforms in public.

Ian Hope was one of them.

Told by senior officers, mostly of the rank he now holds, "that we should not wear uniforms in civil society lest we invoke controversy," Hope continued to wear his anyway, "but sensed the question marks." This all began to change, he said, with the Manitoba floods of 1997 and the Quebec ice storm the following year. Then Canadians saw their soldiers working to save their homes and help their fellows. (I interviewed one long-time reservist, Sergeant Matt Kirkpatrick, who within a couple of months in that period had fruit thrown at him in the downtown Hamilton, Ontario, farmers' market and had a grateful Manitoban show up at the sandbag line with a roasted Thanksgiving turkey for him and his soldiers.)

Hope was a platoon commander in the CAR for two years, ending in 1990, and then the exchange officer from the regiment to the British Army's Parachute Regiment. The CAR, he told me later, had "discipline problems related to the institutional way it was manned and led, not because of its reason for being." Like many soldiers, he was disappointed that the regiment was disbanded, especially since its last commander, Lieutenant-Colonel Peter Kenward, "was forging a path of disciplinary change and setting it on the right path."

The CAR's difficulties were on the minds of Hope and Northrup as they prepared for Kandahar. "We were determined not to allow transgression of discipline or establishment of subversive sub-cultures," Hope said. "Hence, Task Force Orion was created—a new organization unbounded by any narrow norms or attitudes of a minority group. All military occupations, all ranks, all services, and both genders—and any sexual orientation—were automatically part of TF Orion. Randy would ensure iron discipline; we both would ensure that the collective identified above all with Canadian Forces values, and therefore Canadian values."

It was precisely for this reason that Hope and Northrup were for-ever alert to any sign of too-strong unit loyalties (actually removing from the field a much-valued NCO who refused to stop wearing an unofficial A Company badge). They insisted that the troops shave every other day, even at remote bases where water was scarce, and warned them not to pretend they were special forces. Once, in March at Gumbad, I'd watched Hope stand in the flickering light of a firepit and say, "We need discipline and we need to keep up our professionalism—that's what distinguishes you from every other guy with a gun in this country."

On the plane that day late in August, I could see that Hope and Northrup were touched. But, as was usual, it was my own tremulous emotions that threatened to spill over, not theirs, and I didn't ask them about it then.

In spring 2007, however, I did.

"We never felt the same as we did that day when we came home from Afghanistan," Hope wrote in an email. "It was deeply moving to be on that aircraft with that kind of response. I will never forget the Air Canada crew—and still have all their names. I was totally disarmed, and remember feeling how so distinctly different that moment was, especially compared to that era when we were asked to feel ashamed."

What the flight crew didn't know, and couldn't have known, was that for some of that trip, Hope held in his hands the six worn sheets, printed with the names and zap numbers of all his soldiers, he had so often before had to search.

—

THE NEXT DAY, the last chalk (army-speak for planeload) of Patricias arrived home. Misjudging the size of Edmonton, a city I didn't know well in those days, I took a cab from my downtown hotel out to the base and arrived almost $50 poorer and two hours early. Soon, families began arriving in little groups, and the bleachers of the cavernous Lecture Training Facility started to fill up with young wives dressed in sexy camisoles and floaty dresses, parents and grandparents—and everywhere, babies in strollers, children, and dogs.

I met Gina MacArthur, whose husband, Clayton, worked as a trucker with the National Support Element. "I thought he'd be at the airfield," she said, "but he was out [beyond the wire] a lot." The flight had been delayed a day, she told me, and "the last twenty-four hours were as tough as the first. When I went to bed last night all alone, the sadness and emotion and loneliness was the same as the day he left." A former reporter for small-town papers, and a news junkie, MacArthur knew many women who disconnected the Internet and the cable, but she wasn't able to do it. The consolation, she said, was knowing that if she was watching it on the news, Clayton wasn't involved. "It was, 'Thank God.' Then, 'Oh, that poor family.' And then you'd feel guilty for thinking that." She arrived with a quart of milk and Oreos for Clayton; their boys, Ian and Gerard, then ten and thirteen, had made signs. Gerard's read: *I'm not cutting my hair.*

I talked a little to Mary Coghlan, whose husband, Matthew Tibbetts, was one of those intimately involved, and but for his grit nearly felled by the heat, in the August 3 battle. She was there with their baby, Wesley, and the two Nolans, one his son from a former relationship and one hers, both about the same age. When I asked her what Matt did, she smiled and said cheerfully, "He's in the army. That's all I know." Mary is gorgeous, and was all dressed up in strappy heels.

At some point, I stopped trying to talk to anybody: These folks were so clearly holding their breath, eyes glued to the door where the guys would come in. I found I was holding my own breath.

As the troops got off the plane, there was fresh Tim Hortons coffee waiting for them, and buses, and an escort of military police and city police lined up to give them a salute. The buses entered the base via 97th Street, known locally as the Yellow Ribbon Highway. In the air overhead was an escort of jet fighters.

They arrived at 4:56 p.m.

People lined up closest to the door the soldiers would use to enter the drill hall. A few men clutched flowers for their returning wives. I wondered, had things worked out differently, if Jay Beam would have been there with a bouquet for Nichola, or if their hello would have been as private as their farewell.

At 5 p.m., the first of the men came through the door. I found myself scanning the faces as keenly as the wives and mothers. The first person I spotted was Bill Fletcher and I yelled out his name, which is how the poor OC for Charlie Company came to be first greeted, and embraced, not by his lovely young wife, Daria (of whom he once said, "I got lucky: I married a great girl with poor eyesight and lousy judgment"), but by the old reporter who had dogged him overseas.

Ian and Karen Hope mingled quietly in the centre of the hall, talking to the men and their folks. Randy Northrup was swallowed up in the arms of Judy and their daughter Bettina Rose. I met Patrick Tower's parents, raved like a lunatic about him, and then followed Hope and Karen outside.

Jon Hamilton was just getting out of a vehicle, hopping about on crutches. The flight that was a day late had arrived a half-hour early. Hamilton got there in time to see Mars Janek, Pat Tower, and the CO, but he'd missed Willy MacDonald.

Hope's change-of-command parade was held the morning of Wednesday, August 30. He was handing over the 1st Battalion to Lieutenant-Colonel Dave Anderson; that night, Dave Fraser, who still had months to go in Kandahar, would do the same with 1st Canadian Mechanized Brigade Group to Colonel Jon Vance. These are long-standing ceremonial occasions in the military held to mark a change of commanding officer or RSM.

Hope's was, as editor John Weingardt later wrote in the base
paper, *The Western Sentinel*, no ordinary one, but "a moment in history. It was the last time that Lt.-Col. Hope and the soldiers of
1PPCLI would wear their desert tans together." In attendance were
more, and more distinguished, guests than normal—notably, the
regiment's eighty-two-year-old colonel-in-chief, the Countess of
Mountbatten or "Lady Patricia" as soldiers call her, who had made
the trip from England and presented the soldiers with their medals
in her little gold shoes. Also present were Alberta Lieutenant-
Governor and ex–Canadian Football League star Norman Kwong;
the regiment's colonel, Major-General (Retired) Robert Stewart;
and generals and brass galore, including Chief of Defence Staff
Hillier and Chief of the Land Staff Andy Leslie.

The troops had assembled outside, in the parade squad, at the
usual ungodly early hour. They stood in the damp chill for almost an
hour. The injured and healing, some in wheelchairs and others on
crutches or canes, were at the front on one side of the room; I was
in the press section, sitting on the floor to stay out of the way of the
TV cameras, on the other. The speeches by Lady Patricia, the
lieutenant-governor, incoming CO Anderson, and Leslie were short
and graceful.

Fraser spoke at greater length, but I stopped taking notes when I
realized that he was actually going to keep his back to the fighting
troops—assembled behind him—the entire time, and indeed he
did. Every soldier I have spoken to about this day had noted it, and
taken offence: Whatever Fraser had to say was lost forever when he
gave the soldiers his back.

Hope came to the microphone then. He looked directly at his
troops, as skinny and brown from the sun as he was, the entire time.
His remarks were for them, not for the guests sitting behind him.
He thanked the soldiers. He spoke of the wounded and the dead
and the families of the dead. He told them of his Dolby-sound,
Technicolor dream, in which he hears the steady and welcome beat
of the 25 millimetre cannons on the LAVs. "Boom-boom-boom," he
said. "Boom-boom-boom." He exhorted them not to fall victim,

either to the political winds of controversy that swirl about the Afghanistan mission or to their memories, but to choose to become better citizens. He told them to speak of their experience, everywhere they go, and to talk to one another.

Afterwards, I saw some of the soldiers I knew head to a quiet room reserved for the injured; I couldn't bring myself to go inside, though I think I might have been welcome, and I didn't attend the reception, though I was invited. It made me a bad reporter, but I couldn't bear the thought of intruding on moments of such intimacy.

Later, Willy MacDonald told me that he and Jon Hamilton finally hooked up that night, went to the seediest bar they knew, and "proceeded to get so incredibly drunk that the next day was a chore for both of us." That very next morning, Hamilton flew out on the first leg of a trip that saw him begin a new job at CFB Gagetown and join Carolina and the kids in the house she'd bought them in New Brunswick. That day or the one after, Ian Hope and Karen retrieved their youngsters, packed up their car, and began driving. Like Hamilton, they had already moved out of their house.

Within the following days and weeks, many more soldiers left Edmonton for new postings, and those who remained tried to shake themselves into a new focus. Task Force Orion—whose name Hope had chosen so carefully for its hunting themes and aggressive spirit and for the stars he knew were prominent in the skies over Afghanistan—was history.

Eight months later, Hope answered my email from an airport lounge somewhere. I wrote back to tell him one of the stories—bawdy and funny, loving and sad, always brutally honest—I'd heard from the troops.

"You must miss them so fucking much," I said. "I can hardly bear to write about them sometimes, I find them so beautiful."

"You understand what I miss," he wrote back. "I am Odysseus."

Capt. Andrew Hamilton Gault, founder of the Princess Patricia's Canadian Light Infantry

11 November 2006

—

"So we did what you do in Newfoundland. We pretended everything was okay, had some laughs, drank lots of booze, then we all cried together. Then we laughed some more at what a bunch of pansies we were."

—WILLY MACDONALD, ON REMEMBRANCE DAY IN BURGEO, VAUGHAN INGRAM'S HOMETOWN

In September 2006, Dave Anderson, the new CO for 1PPCLI, was on tricky ground. He'd taken over the battalion from Ian Hope just as the last of the weary soldiers of Task Force Orion were returning from Canada's first combat mission in five-plus decades, minus nineteen of their friends who were killed and with seventy-five others wounded, thirty-five of those seriously. After a few half-days back at work, intended to ease the shock of the sudden change in tempo, the troops went on about five weeks' leave. In addition, about a third of those who were returning—including a good chunk of the officer and NCO leadership—were being posted out right after their leave, and in some cases before, to teaching positions, in an effort to pass on combat experience to the institutional army. Over the course of the next six months, almost another hundred soldiers from the battalion were released from the forces, a number that's a little higher than normal. Many were men who had extended their contracts in order to go to Kandahar; others had decided while they were over there to get out.

In sum, Anderson was the new guy in charge of soldiers he barely knew, whose remarkable experience he had not shared, and who were now off licking their wounds. What he wanted was a "signal event" that would enable the unit to properly take note of all the task force had achieved and lost, and simultaneously mark a new chapter for the battalion.

"I spoke to a whole bunch of people about my ideas," he says, "because I'd sort of thought it through in a vacuum, while the battalion was off on leave. I was trying to figure out a way that would enable us to close the book and start looking forward, but by the same token I couldn't take away, and be seen to be taking away, from the troops, from what they had done. It's a difficult situation," he says of the delicate line he had to walk, "one where I am charged with being the keeper of the reputation of Task Force Orion, but can't be seen to co-opt it."

The Canadian army is sufficiently taxed that soon enough the 1st Battalion—like its sisters, 2PPCLI in Shilo and 3PPCLI in Edmonton, which will lead and contribute to the battle group leaving for Kandahar in February 2008—will be coughing up soldiers again. The modern pace of operations, with its short training-deployment-recovery cycle, allows little time for lazy reflection, let alone resting on laurels.

In the end, Anderson came to realize that there would be several signal events, that there could be no final farewell to Orion because the task force experience is alive in the hearts and minds of its members. He also realized that the army had screwed up in posting out so soon the returning troops and officers to new jobs at new bases.

"My biggest point, my biggest lesson learned," he says, "is that you gotta wait a year before you post them. . . . There are guys out there who are struggling a bit and they're struggling because they're not with their support network, a very hackneyed phrase but very true. There are platoons that needed their platoon commanders, and by the same token there are platoon commanders who needed to be around their platoons."

This isn't to say the returned Patricias are awash in post-traumatic stress disorder (PTSD), or anything like it. Rather the opposite, Anderson says. Before Roto 1 ended and he took over, he sat down with the army's mental health team: "The number they were quoting at me, and this was sort of the widely accepted wisdom, was that somewhere between 20 and 40 percent of the unit would suffer from PTSD." This figure was based on what was seen in Canadian troops returning from Croatia. But it is also reflective of the extreme to which both psychiatry and Western militaries have swung since 1980, when PTSD made its first appearance in psychiatry's bible, the *Diagnostic and Statistical Manual of Mental Disorders.*

While diminished in other generations of veterans as "shell shock" or "combat fatigue," PTSD entered the popular lexicon after the Vietnam War and has gained such currency that there is now a widespread expectation that soldiers will suffer from it. As Charlie Company OC Bill Fletcher says, "I still remember, coming back from Bosnia, there was kind of an unspoken rule from the mental health professionals that if you didn't have a problem, you had a problem."

Lieutenant-Colonel Kelly Farley, until late 2006 the army's top psychologist and now on the strategic joint staff in Ottawa, says that the other assumption made is that "every individual, every human being, is susceptible to mental disruption because of a single traumatic event"—or that "somewhere out there, there's a toxic dose of trauma that's enough to make anybody sick. That was a bad assumption. The reason they made it was that they felt at the time they were protecting individuals from being labelled as neurotic . . . but the problem is it led us down a track, in terms of research, that we found out ten or fifteen years later, didn't go anywhere."

More and more, Farley says, armies have to focus on what makes people susceptible to PTSD, and what works, before and after a traumatic event, to help them cope. While he would never wish for a return to the old days when men who broke down were considered weak, neither should the army "set up a culture of illness as in some cases almost desirable, or expected." The view now, he says, is to deal with a combat stress reaction as soon as possible, in the field, with the expectation that "you're going to get better and rejoin your mates. You cannot set up the expectancy that every time someone gets a little jerky, we'll ship them off."

Farley has a relative, he says, who "had full-blown PTSD, and he had it for a good reason: It was cumulative, he'd done three or four tours, been shot twice, blown up. He came home and very quickly broke down." But, he says, "He did get over it. He's recovered now. He's not in the military anymore, but he's working full time and he has a home and a family." His point: "PTSD is a statistically rare event; it's 100 percent fixable in most cases; a very small minority of folks will have long-term mental health issues."

Farley is leery of the Operational Stress Injury Support (OSIS) groups, whose members get together across the country to talk. "My concern is that at a certain point, it reinforces the illness. If you look at the literature of OSIS, [it says] 20, 30, 40 percent have PTSD when they come back. It's absolute fucking hogwash. Absolute hogwash."

In fact, absolute hogwash appears to be a fair descriptor for the predictions made for the Patricias. Dave Anderson has been told that the PTSD rate among his returning troops "is very, very low, well below 5 percent." The number is so low, he says, that the mental health professionals "won't even tell me, they can't tell me expressly how many people, because then I could work it out [who the afflicted individuals are], believe it or not."

The mission to Croatia, on which the PTSD estimates were based, he points out, "was completely different. It was shitty equipment, it was a shitty mandate, and lousy ROE [rules of engagement]. And it was very much peacekeeping." The Afghan mission is "the best equipment, at the battle group level and lower, in the world; very strong ROE; and a mission that really matters—and we're on the offence."

Those differences are critical, says former U.S. Army Ranger and psychologist Lieutenant-Colonel Dave Grossman in his book *On Combat*, because it's not action but impotence that is the big player in PTSD. So, says Grossman, are fear and horror, reactions that can be moderated by what he calls stress inoculation through exposing soldiers to live-fire exercises that simulate the madness and terrors of battle. (The Patricias did many of these.)

He, like Farley, advocates a middle ground, where PTSD is recognized and understood as the rare occurrence it is, where the stricken few are encouraged to seek and accept help as readily as they would for a physical wound, and where the remaining many are assumed to be psychologically sound and resilient. No extremes, or in Grossman's inimitable shorthand, "No macho men and no pity parties."

There's another aspect that Grossman also bravely discusses in *On Combat*—something he says could be written off as romanticizing war (usually by those who have never experienced it) but for the fact that many of those who have been in harm's way on the battlefield are keen to get back to it. "It is politically correct to say that there is nothing good about war and no one who has seen it would want to do it again," Grossman writes. "This is the obligatory nod that everyone must give when talking about the possibility of going to war, and from one perspective, it is completely true." But he knows of many Vietnam War veterans who returned for multiple tours and "every one of these individuals who I have information about is a perfectly healthy, functional human being who does not appear to have paid any significant psychological cost for his years in combat."

Grossman describes in his book how he once got an email from Monte Gould, a career cop and sergeant in the U.S. Army Reserves who'd just been told he was too old to join the U.S. Special Forces. He wrote to decry the fact that, goddammit, he'd wanted "time on target," that every time he'd turned up in a theatre of operations peace broke out. Grossman wrote back to say, "There are people who say that no one wants to go to war, and that 'A soldier hates war more than anyone else.' And I'm sure they are sincere. But I know a lot of people who would beg to differ. And best I can tell, there ain't nothin' wrong with them."

I once tried to write about this, when the Patricias returned to KAF after their long, hard foray into Helmand Province. Alas, I chose to begin by challenging the opening line of "War," an old anti–Vietnam War protest song performed by the late Edwin Starr. In attempting to illustrate that war was indeed good for something, I wrongly described Starr as British (he was Nashville born and bred, though he moved to England in the early 1970s and died there), and I went on to produce a clunker of a piece.

I should have simply done what Grossman did in *On Combat*, and deferred to Sir John Keegan, the great British military historian who, three decades ago in *The Face of Battle*, wrote the following: " . . . it would be foolish to deny that there are compensations for its cruelties: the thrill of comradeship, the excitement of the chase, the exhilarations of surprise, deception and *ruse de guerre*, the exaltations of success, the sheer fun of prankish irresponsibility."

Some of the veterans of 1PPCLI were feeling the loss of these things, and the difficulty of going, as CFB Edmonton base surgeon Dr. Will Patton says, "from being a warrior one minute to standing in a line at Loblaws the next." Soldiers have been making that adjustment for thousands of years, he says—"gone from fighting Peloponnesians to roasting their goat at home"—but the time frame is starkly different. "Before," Patton says, "when people went from Peloponnesia to Sparta, it took a year to get home. So they would decompress. Now, we go from Afghanistan to Loblaws" in days.

Three or four of Anderson's NCOs, including the recently decorated Pat Tower, and thirteen troops have already volunteered to be part of the replacement pool.

Mostly, the Patricias' hearts ache—for the friends they've lost, for one another, and for the words to properly explain all of it to those who weren't in Kandahar with them. Almost no one talks about how much, and how completely, soldiers love. Of the many things Dave Anderson did in his new job, so many of them on the money, none he got more right than Remembrance Day, because he found a vehicle for the men to briefly sun themselves once more in that warmth.

When the Kandahar vets came back to work after their leave, they found that all training scheduled for the week had been cancelled. In its stead was a week of what their new CO called "an exercise in collective wisdom." He invited in two hundred of the junior leadership, from all ranks, and "then asked them what we should be doing." For a hierarchal outfit like the army, this was a daring stroke.

As Bill Fletcher, who served as Anderson's deputy for a year in an effort to lend the new guy legitimacy and to bridge the gap between returning veterans and new faces, said shortly afterwards, "I was his foot in the door but he's kicked the door open. . . . He doesn't need that anymore."

At the same time, Anderson had found his "signal event"—November 11—and realized that what the battalion needed was "both collective and individual acts of remembrance." The genesis of the idea came from the troops themselves, as the best ideas so often do, but the CO recognized its worth and made it happen on a grand scale. There was to be a ceremony for the dedication of a Wall of Honour on the PPCLI lines on November 7, and a beer call so "we can have a beer with our fallen in our stand-easy." Beyond these events, Anderson decided the soldiers would be sent across Canada to Remembrance Day services in the cities and towns where their dead were buried. He asked for volunteers. As far west as Gibsons on British Columbia's Sunshine Coast, as far east as Burgeo on the south coast of Newfoundland, as far north as Thunder Bay, Ontario, and to the provincial and national ceremonies in Edmonton and Ottawa, the Patricias moved out.

In the end, fourteen officers and thirty-three NCOs went to seven interment sites. Another thirty troops went to Ottawa, where four of the Patricias are buried at the National Military Cemetery at Beechwood. They did double duty as part of an honour guard at the main service and then moved on to the gravesites of Nichola Goddard, Kevin Dallaire, Frank Gomez, and Jason Patrick Warren.

It was just what the soldiers needed. They met the shattered families of their lost friends, described what had happened to those sons and husbands when and if they were asked, and wept unabashedly. They presented special mugs and gifts to reserve units, Legion halls, and stricken parents. They saw veterans of the Second World War and Korea—the real veterans, they would call them—and looked into those old faces, searching for signs of the emotions that tumbled just under their own firm skin. They were together again, profane and tender, for a few precious days.

—

NOT EVERY PATRICIA was on the move. Jim (Reggie) Sinclair, a reservist with the Regina Rifles who was attached to 1PPCLI's

Alpha Company, was back home in Regina, where his mother Shirley was dying of cancer.

On November 10, he continued with what he calls his Fricking Travelling Road Show (it is a constant source of amusement to me that, with the possible exceptions of Jon Hamilton and Keith Mooney, I swear more than most soldiers) and gave a speech at Sheldon High School. By then, Sinclair had already talked to students at a half-dozen schools. He'd put his name on a list kept by the Royal Canadian Legion Branch No. 1, and when local teachers came calling, the Legion would post him out.

"I more or less talked about what Canada's involvement in Afghanistan is," he says, "and more or less talked about what I did, and talked about losing three buddies over there, and how important it is. It's why I am vocal, and talk to people, because I don't want to sit idly by and not get the word out about what Canada's doing—so basically, at the end of the day, my buddies' efforts won't be in vain." Three of his friends were killed in Afghanistan: Vaughan Ingram, Frank Gomez, and Bill Turner.

At Sheldon High School, Sinclair's audience was about six hundred strong. "They all loved it," he says. "After, there were some vets there [Sinclair doesn't consider himself a veteran], and after it was all over, the kids came by and shook their hands so it was kind of cool. I actually met a kid from Afghanistan who was there; she's an exchange student, and she came up and thanked us. It was cool."

Usually, on the Remembrance Days when he was home and not overseas, Sinclair would be on parade with his unit, his mom and aunt watching. Then they'd go to the Legion for a beer with the old fellows they knew. But on this particular November 11, Sinclair had a special 7 a.m. breakfast to attend. A secretive organization called the Order of the Crock had invited him to become a member.

Dating back to the First World War, the group has a fixed membership of only a hundred. "And every year, when a veteran dies, they invite a new guy in, so I was brought into the club this year," Sinclair says. "It's quite the deal. There's generals and politicians. Like, I'm the only corporal in the outfit." Called the crock after the container that in the old days held the rum, the men had porridge and a shot, because, Sinclair says, "That's what they would have before they went into battle. They'd give 'em warm porridge and a shot of rum and then send 'em over the top."

Breakfast was over by 8:30 or so, and normally he would have reported to the Rifles and fallen in for parade. Instead, he went home to sit with his ma, and together they watched the national service from Ottawa on the tube.

"Then she more or less said for me to go to the Legion," Sinclair says, "so I went down and met up with my buddies there." Afterwards, he and some friends were out on the range. When they finished shooting, "a few of us had a shot for my ma and it was good," Sinclair says.

Shirley Sinclair, who always hid her age ("Even as kids we had to do the math on how old she was"), died about a month later, on December 9. She was sixty-nine. They think.

Out on the east coast, Kevin Schamuhn was feeling forlorn. Posted out almost as soon as he got home, in his case to CFB Gagetown where he now teaches young officers, Schamuhn says, "I was in a deep depression those days, having to deal with leaving Edmonton, trying to sort out some renovations in our house here in Gagetown, and trying to find some incentive to go back to work. Frankly, I just didn't care anymore."

Unable to spend November 11 with the men so close to him, he and his wife, Annalise, an army logistics officer, decided to avoid it by visiting a good friend who was going to school in Charlottetown, Prince Edward Island. "I wanted to avoid any ceremonies," Schamuhn says, "because I felt like anywhere I went wouldn't do my experiences justice. I didn't want to shock my system while surrounded by strangers."

But that night, the family of their friend's friend, a musician named Ian, invited them over. "The guest of honour was Ian's grandfather," Schamuhn says, "who had served in WWII as an antiaircraft gunner in England. The family had been informed that I was coming, and was excited to witness the meeting of the old vet and the new. So, for the rest of the night I was able to share with these wonderfully perfect strangers what I went through in the war. Most of my stories were told to an audience of jaw-dropped men on the porch, who hadn't heard anything remotely close to what I was telling them. They, much like the rest of the country, heard only what was in the news, and never the personal side of the stories."

The Schamuhns plan to return to Prince Edward Island next Remembrance Day. "Except," Kevin says, "I'll probably bring my uniform and go to the cenotaph with them this time."

Randy Northrup was back home in St. Albert, a city just north of Edmonton and west of the base. "I took my wife and kids and we did the parade downtown here in the city where I live, and then we went down to the Legion, and we sat and told stories and gripped and grinned and linked up with some old faces," he says.

As battle group RSM, Northrup had addressed the troops before they scattered across the country, aiming his remarks not only at those who were heading out but also at those who, like himself, were staying put. One of the regiment's old boys, veteran Jack Cathy, was there, and Northrup says, "I likened the story to him, that when he was Corporal Cathy and was over in the Second World War, he didn't ask for the responsibility to remind Canadian citizens of what he did and what he sacrificed for his country. That was thrust upon him just by virtue of wearing the uniform.

"So what I told the troops was, when you're sitting around on the eleventh and thinking about grabbing that next bag of popcorn to watch a movie, put your uniform on and go down there and represent those who can't observe this day, and you know who I'm talking about.

"It's your responsibility, though you didn't ask for it. It's your mantle, to continue to remind Canadians what the other Canadian citizens—soldiers—are doing today. Make them see it a little clearer."

When I talked to him in April 2007, Northrup was the tiniest bit verklempt.

"Do you miss the guys?" I asked.

"I do," he said.

He sounded surprised by the admission.

Remember, he asked, how he'd once told me that being the RSM of an infantry battalion was the pinnacle of an infanteer's career? "Well," he said, "I missed the mark by a bit. Being the battle group RSM on deployment, with what we did and what we accomplished, both failings and successes, is the crowning jewel. To be the battle group RSM is truly the job, and it's those people you spend those years with—you know, I spent three years in the battalion as the RSM—and to watch them grow and change, and be as successful as we were. And I'm not padding it."

His greatest frustration was that they'd had to retake the same piece of ground—the Panjwaii-Pashmul area—over and over again. "That's hard for our soldiers to swallow, the same piece of ground. 'We've been here twice now.' 'Three times now.' And each time it costs you. And that's probably the hardest thing to swallow, that cost, and it's probably the highest cost you can pay.

"But I miss the guys," he said. "The comradeship, how I'd always sit and talk with the troops and get the tailgate stories. Once they get to know you and you've got their trust, how easy the stories come. And they don't embellish them; they give it to you.

"To sit and talk with [other] people, you get that look, just of non-believers. And that's just what irks me to no end: You talk about Afghanistan and some guy rolls back to when he was in Bosnia, on Roto 10.

"You know what, my son? Kudos to you for making it through, but it's not the same thing."

Pat Tower was originally slated to go to Burgeo for the service in Vaughan Ingram's town. However, little more than two weeks before Remembrance Day, the big announcement came from Governor General Michaëlle Jean's office: He was awarded the Star of Military Valour, second in prestige only to the relatively new Canadian Victoria Cross.

Four others—Sergeant Michael Denine; Master Corporal Collin Fitzgerald of 2PPCLI; medic Jason Lamont; and Captain Derek Prohar, a Canadian liaison officer with the U.S. Special Forces—were awarded the Medal of Military Valour. The awards were announced on October 27, together with a slew of Mentions in Dispatches.

The two decorations are awarded for acts of valour, self-sacrifice, or devotion to duty "in the presence of the enemy." Neither had been awarded since 1993, when Canada created its own military honours, separate and distinct from the traditional British awards.

Months later, Bill Fletcher became only the second Canadian to be awarded the Star of Military Valour; it was via the formal announcement that I learned, to my delight, that his middle name was Hilton.

Though none of these announcements received much media attention, they were a big deal in the Canadian Forces. General Hillier invited Tower and the others, each plus a family member, to join him in Ottawa for the national ceremony, and to fly there with him in a government Challenger.

The trip had its moments: Shortly after takeoff, Fitzgerald, intending to propose to his girlfriend, realized he'd forgotten to bring along a ring and had to borrow Hillier's wedding band. It did the trick.

But as good as the experience was, especially being able to share it with his proud father, Tower suspected he was missing out on something special.

—

MATT GAULDEN WAS ONE of ten who went to Thunder Bay for the service in Tony Boneca's town. A sergeant with twelve years of service, Gaulden was Boneca's section commander, but he was also the young man's friend. "He was buddies to everybody," Gaulden says, "including me."

The same day Boneca was killed in one of the many battles of Pashmul, Gaulden threw a grenade and snapped his ankle. He made it back for Boneca's ramp ceremony at KAF, but it wasn't enough for him, or his troops. The nature of these ramp ceremonies is that they are but a brief pause; most of the dead soldier's mates are back in the field the same day or the next one. As Gaulden says, "We basically picked up his coffin and threw him on a plane and that was it."

The troops had been asking about doing this sort of thing since Rob Costall's death—craving it—so were grateful, Gaulden says, that the CO got the approval to "send out a crew to kind of pay their final respects."

The first thing they did was get in touch with Boneca's parents, Antonio and Shirley. "His dad came out and we had a couple of things to present to him," Gaulden says. They gave him a regimental coin and a Task Force Orion beer stein engraved with his son's name. To the Lake Superior Scottish Regiment, or Lake Sups, they gave Boneca's helmet, left behind in the compound in the rush to carry him out. "We had it encased in a shadow box, and then we presented that to his unit," Gaulden says, "and I think it's sitting right at the front door now, and it has his picture."

They then went to a little pub with Mr. Boneca. "He asked us a few questions—basically, 'Was it quick?', stuff he had to get off his chest. We told him straight out what happened." The family was "so happy to have us down there, we were treated like family the whole weekend. Both his mum and dad treated us like family, like they were there the whole time."

On two of their four nights in Thunder Bay, the boys sat downstairs in the Boneca home ("he's like old Portuguese, where the women aren't allowed") and drank the old man's strong homemade wine. "They were still really upset," Gaulden says, "but I think having us out there kind of helped them out a bit. I wish we could be out there more, but obviously we can't."

The soldiers were acutely aware of the brouhaha that had surrounded Boneca's death, its roots in what his fiancée had told her dad, which he had repeated to reporters, about Boneca having been unhappy and desperate to go home. When they met the young woman, they asked her directly about all that, and "she said she was right out of 'er at the time, that she spoke and didn't know what she was saying. . . . She took back what she said, which is good, because we were pretty pissed off about that to begin with, because that was totally untrue."

It wasn't what Boneca had told her or not told her that galled the troops, Gaulden says, but rather that their friend's trust had been breached. "All of us probably said it at one time," he says. "I know I probably called my wife and probably said to her, 'You know what? I could probably get home by telling them I'd commit suicide,' you know what I mean? Not seriously, just as a joke." A soldier's wife, or girlfriend, Gaulden says, "They're your rock. You gotta have them to get through it."

On Remembrance Day itself, he says, "we formed up behind the unit [the Lake Sups] as the Patricias, as a foreign unit, and marched behind their group. And then we went out to actually see his grave afterwards, and that was just his unit and us, and the bagpipes, and that was pretty emotional, like we laid down our poppies on his grave and gave him a big high-five there, a salute, and everyone's bawling. You've got a bunch of experienced guys, sergeants and down, three to ten years' experience, and everyone's bawling, and you've got all these new guys from his unit, who didn't know him and aren't even trained soldiers yet and probably going, 'What the fuck's going on here?' That was that day, and it was rough. And then we went back to the Legion and drank for him."

The boys needed to see Tony's parents, he says. "Tell them what happened, if they wanted to know. His mum didn't. His dad, he cried, but he took it like a man, you know?"

On July 5, 2006, when Charlie Company was still at Spin Boldak, Portugal played France in a World Cup semifinal. Tony Boneca ran about the base with a Portuguese flag. Portugal lost in penalty kicks. Four days later, the exuberant twenty-one-year-old was dead, and Antonio and Shirley Boneca had lost their only child.

As Boneca's section was heading to Thunder Bay, fourteen soldiers, including pretty much everyone in Rob Costall's section, flew into

Vancouver, rented vehicles, and took the ferry up to Gibsons. For the soldiers of Charlie Company's 7 Platoon, their Remembrance Day trip was more like a pilgrimage.

Costall was killed at FOB Robinson on March 29, 2006. Because the remote base remained under threat of imminent attack for four days afterwards, the platoon was unable to make it back for their friend's ramp ceremony. "We put a dent in [the Taliban] that night," says Master Corporal Chris Fernandez-Ledon, "but they were basically regrouping and coming to attack us again." The troops understood better than anyone the impracticality of returning to KAF in time, "but we were still hurt, you know, that we couldn't go for Rob."

They'd attended the small service at the FOB held by the Americans for their soldier, medic John Thomas Stone, who had been killed the same night, "and they mentioned Rob and that he was killed, which was really nice. It helped a bit." When they returned to KAF, five days later, they got a week or so off, to regroup and talk about their friend.

Early that May, when he came home on leave, Fernandez-Ledon visited with Chrissy Costall and baby Collin, which "was probably the hardest thing I've ever had to do."

Ceremony is particularly important to soldiers, schooled in and accustomed to the formal acknowledgement of significant occasions, and for 7 Platoon's remaining five months in Afghanistan anything resembling this necessarily was put on hold.

Upon arriving in Gibsons, the first thing they did after getting their rooms was to link up with Costall's parents, Bonnie and Greg, his sister Ashley, and Chrissy. "We needed to talk [with them]," Fernandez-Ledon says. "And sit down and just get shit-faced, you know, and just talk. We had our bouts of crying and stuff like that. We got a lot of stuff out, generated a lot of ties . . . it was good. The thing is, afterwards, when we got back and everything, [Costall's parents] came out to visit us, and we're actually trying to keep a pretty close tie with them. They're wonderful people."

They raised a glass to Costall. "Many," he says. "There was lots of booze floating around, and we shared a lot of memories and stories and stuff." They gave a picture of the platoon to his family, and another, of the whole company, to the Legion right beside the cenotaph where the Remembrance Day service was held. "The main thing was for his parents," Fernandez-Ledon says, "so they know we're always thinking about him."

Fernandez-Ledon was Rob Costall's fire-team partner, was within nudging distance of him on the night he was killed, and loved him for his willingness, reliability, and silly practical jokes. "He was just one of those guys you almost envied. He just enjoyed everything he did."

When the troops returned to Edmonton on November 12, "what we really needed to do was get back in the routine of working, our normal thing, and that's pretty much what we did. It helped. It helped a lot."

For Marc Thompson, the trip to Burgeo, Newfoundland, on November 11 was his second there in four months. As part of the battalion's rear party left at home in Edmonton, Thompson was a member of the honour guard team that, in August 2006, participated in a dreadful series of three funerals and one internment, in three different provinces, within seventy-two hours: Kevin Dallaire's funeral in Ottawa on a Friday, Chris Reid's in Truro, Nova Scotia, on Saturday, Vaughan Ingram's in Burgeo on Sunday, and then back to Truro for Reid's internment.

The honour guard team had travelled by bus from Ottawa. By the time they got to The Rock, they were reeling with exhaustion. Don Reid, the rear party's sergeant-major, remembers that while still two and half hours away, as the buses moved along the road that leads only to Burgeo, every flag they saw was at half-mast in honour of a Newfoundland son. Proud as he was to have been in the honour guard, they were so pressed for time, Thompson says, that they barely had time to mingle with their friends' grieving families.

Thompson is a Newfoundlander himself, from Point Leamington on the northeast coast, and his own parents came down for November 11, as indeed they had for Ingram's funeral.

"Vaughan was always the clown," Thompson says, "screwing around, drinking and partying and everything else. But when he put that fucking uniform on . . . he could switch, when he put the uniform on. His troops worshipped the ground he walked on, because he was the one who taught them something, right?"

Like many soldiers, Ingram had an in-the-event-of-my-death letter with his final instructions. Left with his brother in Edmonton, the letter set aside $2000 for Pat Tower to throw a party. "And if Tower's dead," Ingram wrote with a soldier's pragmatism, "give the money to the warrant."

Thompson went to that party, at which Tower had placed a big picture of Ingram in a chair so they could raise a glass to him. "It was the same sort of thing we did for the funeral," Thompson says.

By rank, Ingram was entitled to a gun carriage and a historical vehicle at his funeral, but what was sent to Burgeo was basically an old wooden Jeep. Within hours of arriving, the rear party OC, Major Rich Raymond, and Ingram's dad, Clayton, were on the Ingrams' deck, building a decent trailer to carry the casket behind the old Jeep.

The night before the funeral, Ingram's casket was placed on the trailer and covered with a tarp. The boys joined him under the tarp for a few drinks. After the funeral, after they folded the flag and presented it to the family, the trailer travelled to the local fire hall, where the troops were staying. This was where the hearse would pick up the casket and take Ingram for cremation.

"When we got back," Thompson says, "we had the guard all stand at ease outside the fire hall, and we closed the fire hall doors and sat inside, and everybody said a piece on Vaughan and we sat there and drank two cases of beer. Vaughan wouldn't have wanted it any other way."

So that had been the funeral, and then Thompson was back in Burgeo for Remembrance Day.

It was amazing, he says, "because we got to spend a week there, and we got to spend the time we didn't at the funeral. So we met not only Vaughan's family, but his friends also and the community. It's

Newfoundland, right? Nobody's gonna snub you off or anything. We got treated really well there."

With him, among others, were Keith Mooney, who was injured in Pashmul in July ("Oh, that savage," Thompson says with a snort of delight); Jon Hamilton, seriously wounded in the same fight in which Ingram died; and Willy MacDonald, who was with the big man when he took his last breath.

Hamilton wrote of this visit in an email sent three days later: "Burgeo is a small town in the southwest part of Newfoundland. . . . I had never been to Newfoundland before, but it was how I would have imagined—traditional Maritime houses placed on the hills of rock along the shore. As soon as I stepped off the plane in Deer Lake, I honestly felt I was somewhere special.

"On Remembrance Day, we began by attending a service at the Anglican Church. The local sea cadets played 'O Canada' and 'God Save the Queen.' The minister read prayers, hymns were sung, and readings were heard on the importance of remembrance and peace. The church itself was full of people from Burgeo.

"We then marched from the church together with the towns-people to the cenotaph. It was also an unveiling. As I understand it, at one point the name of Burgeo's servicemen and war dead were hidden away in a town building (sorry, I forget which one). Due in large part to Vaughan's family, the names were engraved on a new monument, never to be lost again.

"The monument named the veterans of WWI, WWII, and of course Afghanistan—Vaughan. The monument also contained the names of Vaughan's grandfather, great-grandfather, and an uncle. During the ceremony, the sky was grey and there was a strong, cold breeze. The sun did, however, manage to appear from behind the clouds for a little while during the ceremony at the cenotaph. To all those who are faith-minded, I would say that it was symbolic.

"Later that day, we returned to Vaughan's parents' place and recalled stories of the type of person and soldier Vaughan was. We remembered his strength, courage, professionalism, sense of humour, and his willingness to help anyone in need.

"Clayton and Lyn thanked us for coming, but there was no other place any of us who went would want to be. In actuality, it is us who should thank them. They gave us Vaughan Ingram."

MacDonald's version of the trip came months later (though within hours of my asking for it). It was, like its author, frank and funny.

"I've always held that day in very high regard, and have always been a bit of a sap myself for it. I think really the only thing going through my mind was how weird it was to be an actual vet and wondering what it was like for the other vets from past wars. I honestly tried not to overthink it, because I usually get a bit emotional when that happens.

"Meeting Vaughan's mom and dad was very hard. They are wonderful people and they still miss Vaughan very much. I try to keep in touch with them every couple of weeks.

"So we did what you do in Newfoundland. We pretended everything was okay, had some laughs, drank lots of booze, then we all cried together. Then we laughed some more at what a bunch of pansies we were."

From Mooney, himself from St. Mary's Bay, I got his usual raw mix of magnificent Anglo-Saxon expletives and explosive emotions, delivered over the phone at high speed and with an accent that got thicker by the second.

"Burgeo," he said, "is like any other place in Newfoundland, a little bigger than where I'm from. People are friendly.

"When we left to go, it was a nice night, it was gonna be a good trip, see Iggy's parents." They went to a little sports bar at the Edmonton airport for a few beers. Then it began to snow, their flight was first diverted then delayed, and they ended up sleeping at the airport. "We got to Deer Lake at midnight."

"Well, half the boys never had Newfoundland beer, and the corner stores are open till 2 a.m., so we got our cabs, filled the cars with beer."

At Cornerbrook, they stopped for something to eat, and then headed down to Burgeo on a highway "with more moose than cops. I'll never forget it, driving across this barren, rugged marsh. It was raining too, which just added to it. It's funny, it was just like home."

When he was young, growing up in St. Mary's Bay, Mooney imagined the west and east coasts of Newfoundland as being incomparably huge, two different places, with wildly different people. "When you're young," he said, "you don't know that much: Everyone's the same."

In Burgeo, they got their rooms, picked up some more beer, and headed right over to Clayton and Lyn's, bearing a two-four (Mooney thinks it was a dozen Blue Star and a dozen Black Horse or Canadian) and a pewter Task Force Orion mug with Ingram's name on it. "We walked in the door with our twenty-four beer," Mooney said. "I looked at his mother and said, 'This is our tour gift.' I broke down, I didn't know what to say. It was almost like he never died. Fucking everybody started bawling then."

They stayed upstairs for a while, with the Ingrams, "beautiful people, strong people. They knew what Vaughan was doing, that he had a risky job."

Then they went downstairs with Clayton, who brought out two 60-ouncers, a bottle of Golden Wedding rye, and another of Lamb's rum. "We started drinking," Mooney said, "and there's only one beer left, and I said, 'I can't drink that old liquor, boys. Last time I drank I ended up in hospital.'"

But he did, of course, "and that's all I fucking remember. . . . There was a full bottle, then there was an empty bottle. It would have killed a small African country."

By 10 p.m., he was back in the hotel in bed.

The days were "more fish than you can shake a stick at," the nights spent pounding beer, remembering Iggy (every night they were at KAF, Mooney played poker with Vaughan, who was a spectacularly bad player in that you could read him like a book), and talking to his folks. After the service on Remembrance Day, they went to Vaughan's parents' place again, and Mooney asked if Clayton had a guitar. He didn't, but he made a call, "and buddy comes over with a guitar," and that was that. Only then, at the end of the day, did Clayton Vaughan cry.

Mooney had been Bill Fletcher's signaller, and was at Spin Boldak on August 3. He remembers Fletcher coming to break the news about Chris Reid, killed in an IED blast. "I knew Chris, too," Mooney said, "and I knew him for a long time. I went in my room and was fucking bawling." He was working nights, and as they were forming up that evening, Fletcher had to tell them they had three more Canadian fatalities.

"Three fucking more? All I'm thinking is fucking Vaughan Ingram," Mooney said. "I dropped to my fucking knees."

On that trip to Burgeo, Mooney realized how much he missed Newfoundland. "It takes a while for an individual to figure out who they are," he said. "I also figured out how mean the world can be."

—

WHEN DR. WILL PATTON TURNED FORTY, he took a sabbatical from his job in emergency medicine at the University of Alberta, where he was an associate professor and worked as an attending emerg doc, and went with the Canadian Forces to Syria and the Golan Heights. He'd been a member of the reserves for almost seven years, but when he returned to Canada, "I realized, you know what? I've done my job in emergency medicine . . . I want to do something different. So I closed my practice down and moved from the reserves to the regular force."

He'd had a satisfying career with prestige and stability, and believed that he'd made a difference in many lives, but he came from a military background—his great-grandfather was in the flying corps, his grandfather was a Patricia, his dad a career Mountie. While he knew that emergency medicine mattered, he wanted something more.

There was, too, the state of the Canadian health care system, what he calls the "practice environment." He asked himself, "Do I want to be in a practice environment where an old lady with a rib fracture waits eight hours? Do I want to be in a type of practice where I'm caring for someone who three days later is lying in the same hallway on a stretcher?"

Arriving at CFB Edmonton as base surgeon in December 2005, he was just in time for Roto 1. "So I do my transfer and the next thing, I wake up and I'm in a war." He was alert to the mission, was himself coming out of "essentially a war environment in an emergency department," understood that the injuries he'd see would be mainly complicated blast wounds usually involving the limbs. His job was to make the care pipeline from Kandahar to Edmonton as seamless as possible, line up the specialists (mostly orthopedic surgeons) at the University of Alberta and Glenrose Rehabilitation Hospital, and arrange for community care afterwards.

But still, ready as he was, Patton was floored by his patients. "They arrive, when I take them off the plane," he says, "they're still mission-focused, it's 'When can I go back?' They want to be with their buddies. Here are these guys with very serious wounds, and they have no complaint; they're worried about the guys they left behind. I've had soldiers come back who we all agreed, myself and the attending civilian physicians, that the prognosis was very, very poor, and these individuals have surprised me to my bone marrow, and I think it's a testament to their underlying physical health. . . . We've had individuals who were critically injured, who in my almost two decades of downtown emergency work I would have harboured a guess would have a very poor outcome, and they've made me look like a fool. All I have to do is go away for a weekend and come back and the guy's at the door saying, 'Hi, Dr. Patton,' whereas a few days before he was in a coma and I'm trying to prepare the family."

The strength of his patients' families also moved him. "Here's a young boy," he says, "with pretty significant injuries, and Mom and Dad are there, next to the boy. Only a few years prior, that boy was holding his dad's hand. If that was my kid, I'd be losing it. And you know what? These are strong people, and without complaint. No one has ever questioned why they're injured, not one has questioned why, or he shouldn't have been there, or why it happened to him. No questions like that. No 'why me?' These are people of small-town Alberta, small-town Saskatchewan, small-town British Columbia. They're amazing."

Patton says he has "heard not one comment [against] Afghans, or any other individuals. I agree that most people are strong but these aren't planned-for injuries, and there are career implications, and despite all that they are accepting, resilient, and supportive of their son or daughter."

On leave in 2006, Patton went with his wife to Vimy Ridge, only to find it closed for renovations (it reopened the following April with the newly restored monument rededicated on the battle's ninetieth anniversary). They went for a walk in a graveyard there. "I could see my patients here," he says. "Eighteen, nineteen, you think they're thirty-year-old guys but they're not. In Toronto they walk around Yorkdale Mall, and here the West Edmonton Mall. I look at these young boys and what we expect of them, and what they show us back. . . . We take a nineteen-year-old boy, and you can trust him with the lives of others, you can trust him with a heavy machine gun . . . and they give back and give back."

—

JOHN CONRAD, CO of the support crew in Afghanistan, was still having dreams about Kandahar when Remembrance Day rolled around—dreams about the logistics problems he'd had to solve or the regular rocket attacks at KAF. On November 11, he and his family attended the service in Bowmanville, Ontario, where they live. They were greeted at the Bowmanville cenotaph by the town's Second World War vets, one of whom teaches one of Conrad's sons the bagpipes. At the first note of "The Last Post," Conrad was transported back to KAF, to the aluminum caskets draped with the Canadian flag, to the fallen soldiers he knew personally (Ray Arndt, Nichola Goddard, and the two men he'd seen blown up in front of him).

The sinews of his family had been strained by the war: His wife, Martha, endured reports of rocket attacks on the base and worried until she heard from him. Their daughters, Harriet and Grace, lived with the vague idea that their dad might be hurt. Their two boys, who are a little older—but particularly Aidan, the oldest—"made bold efforts to demonstrate his courage and preparedness to step in as the man of the family, plaid shirts, cowboy hat, and all" if the worst happened. This Remembrance Day, Conrad says, was not only a day to remember the sacrifices of the soldiers, but also "unique because in a small, mysterious way, I felt this day was for us: A time to begin healing as a family."

As a young sea cadet lowered the flag, Conrad was struck by the contrast between "the vitality of a fit soldier and the cold permanence of violent death," understood better the "unspoken language of our aging veterans." Though he was homesick for his men and Task Force Orion, "I drew comfort from a crowd that was supportive, grateful, and willing to have me back.

"We all come from villages, from a sense of community. If you are a soldier, and if you are lucky, at the end of the day you will return to your village one way or another.

"Two months after arriving back in Canada, I started to come home. My nightly dreams of Kandahar began to ebb. My first positive step to becoming once again a father, a neighbour, and a friend was taken." He felt tears wet on his cheeks: "I love that flag. I love it and am abundantly familiar with what it costs."

In Tampa, Florida, where he was then the Canadian liaison officer to U.S. Central Command (CENTCOM) headquarters, Ian Hope secretly longed to go to Ottawa for November 11 and stand by the statue of Hamilton Gault, the man who founded the PPCLI at the outbreak of the First World War. On Elgin Street across from the National War Museum, Hope says, the statue "reminds me so much of my grandfather, Corporal Clarence David Hope, 1st Canadian Field Ambulance, 1914–1919." He wanted to be with the honour guard there. He wanted to be at Beechwood and see his fallen. He wanted to go to Newfoundland to see his Sergeant Vaughan.

However, he'd already accepted Dave Fraser's invitation to attend the annual Vimy Dinner the following week, where Fraser was presented with the Vimy Award by the Conference of Defence Associations Institute. Another trip back to Canada, for his own purposes, would be hard to justify.

His boss at CENTCOM, Navy Captain Kenneth Stewart, wanted to organize a ceremony there as they would do in Canada. Veterans Day in the United States, also celebrated on November 11, is small compared to Canadian Remembrance Day affairs, and nothing had yet been planned. Hope organized the event, helped send out the invites, made the recordings of anthems and songs, and created the centrepiece memorial, a tablet of names and units of the thirty-six soldiers from CENTCOM who had fallen since November 11, 2005.

"All this work kept me very busy and unthinking until it was over," he said later in an email. "Then I had my own, quiet, sorrowful moment.

"At the end of the ceremony, I spent the rest of the day with my family, but after supper I took a glass of good red wine and a chair and went out back of the pool, and under that wonderfully comforting constellation—Orion—that blesses fall-winter-spring skies, I drank a glass and wept for my troops, the dead, the wounded, the untouched. I am not given to wallowing, so this did not last long, but it was long enough to reaffirm my commitment to them all."

In the full analysis, he said, Remembrance Day was probably less emotional for him than for all the others, "because I made it so, and because every day is a day of remembrance for me."

A week later, on November 18, Hope stood beside Hammy Gault and went to Beechwood Cemetery to pay his respects. As he wrote in another note, in what I think is the most profound statement about the loneliness of command, "Each soldier grieves the one, two, or three buddies he lost. I grieve all of them, and all the wounded I said goodbye to, and all the remainder—still familiar in that brotherhood I cannot, by rank, truly belong to."

Jon Hamilton has been back to Edmonton a couple of times, most recently in the spring of 2007, on the occasion of Lady Patricia's handover as Colonel-in-Chief of the PPCLI to former governor general Adrienne Clarkson, who is now the regiment's colonel-in-chief. It was the first time he, Willy MacDonald, Jeff Schnurr, and

Mars Janek had been together since Afghanistan, just the four of them, men he misses so much.

Hamilton said, "It's painful inside, honestly, Christie. There's days it brings me to tears."

I told him that everyone was feeling much the same way.

Good soldier to the end, he replied, "Oh, I'm not alone. I know that. And that's, I think, what saddens me even more. If it was just me, I think it would be easier to take."

It is being around men like this—Willy MacDonald, who Hamilton knew would get to him, somehow, when he was hit and bleeding; that sweet savage Mooney demanding that the OC check the state of his nuts; Pat Tower with his glasses sliding down his nose as he ran through fire; Vaughan Ingram looking after another soldier even as he was dying—that drives the best officers.

"The higher you go, the less and less opportunity you get to do that, to be grounded by the troops, who call bullshit when it's bullshit," Bill Fletcher once told me, as he contemplated his coming year at staff college in Toronto.

Many nights, just before he fell asleep, Fletcher would think of them. "Sometimes it's just a snatch of a memory, you know, whichever guy happens to pop up. Sometimes it's just replaying a scene through my head." He thinks of guys "like Sergeant Tower, who started August 3 as a section commander and ended up as the platoon commander, with his best friend dead. . . . Little things, like Mooney who gets his thigh torn apart, and after I checked his penis for him—and that's my worst story ever—to see him immediately buoy up and go out and grab his replacement, all the while still putting pressure on his wound. 'Here's the radio, here's the frequency, here's what you gotta do.' . . . Little things, to see the injured guys not want to leave theatre, to a man saying, 'Can-we-stay-can-we-stay-we-want-to-stay?' Where do you stop?"

Nine times out of ten, Fletcher said, "by virtue of rank, I'll never be friends with the guys I command."

I didn't say it, but what I thought was: Love, that's a different matter. Who could not love them?

Afterword

—

I WAS HOPING—planning—to go back to Kandahar again before the paperback edition of *Fifteen Days* came out. In the end, even though some of the soldiers I have come to consider my guys, from the Princess Patricia's Canadian Light Infantry, were there in the spring and summer of 2008, a few for the second time, I didn't.

I think I was still and am yet decompressing, as the modern soldier's lexicon has it—in my case, less from the stresses of combat (I have been caught in only one protracted firefight, which trust me is plenty) and more from emotional overload. In the course of four trips to Kandahar in less than eighteen months, after countless interviews with the troops and with their families back home, I am wrung out.

Even now, I haven't been able to read my own book. When it was first published in the fall of 2007 in hardcover, all I could do at first was look at it. Within a couple of weeks, I was able to stomach the pictures. But I still can't read it, which is astonishing for someone who races to read her own words in the newspaper every morning, ever on the prowl for mistakes or typos.

I bawled pretty unashamedly as I wrote *Fifteen Days,* but am a little afraid now to open it all up again. I do not compare my sorrow to that of Maureen Eykelenboom, whose son Boomer was killed in

August 2006, and who in the summer of 2008 went to Kandahar herself, only to discover that, as one soldier put it, if she was dealing
with things perfectly well in her head, her heart was still a raw
wound. But I know what it means.

Two of the soldiers mentioned in *Fifteen Days* have been killed
since publication, both on their second tour to Afghanistan. Master
Corporal Jay Boyes of the 2PPCLI, based in Shilo, Manitoba, died
in an explosion on March 16, 2008; less than two months later, on
June 7, Captain Jon Snyder, whose beautiful face I remember
clearly from my time in 2006 with the Edmonton-based 1PPCLI,
was on night patrol when he fell into a deep well called a *kariz*. As
his mates tried desperately to save him, Jon, weighed down by the
infantryman's usual seventy pounds of gear, drowned.

My other boys, I think, are doing all right, though some have
struggled a little to find their feet back home.

Some of the principals of the book have gone on to new challenges,
new jobs, new additions to their families.

Patrick Tower is now living in Calgary, where he is an operations
and training officer with the Calgary Highlanders, a reserve regiment that figures prominently in *Fifteen Days*. He has also started
his own public speaking firm as a sideline, drawing on his military
experience to talk about leadership. And Pat is engaged now to Kelli
McMillan.

Captain Jon Hamilton and his wife, Carolina, have a new baby
girl (Connie, born April 25, 2008). As Jon said in an email, "She was
8 pounds, 5 ounces . . . she actually came in a lot more coherent and
functional at 3 a.m. than I ever have."

Jon is now officer-in-charge of the urban operations cell at the
Canadian Forces' infantry school in Gagetown, New Brunswick.

Sergeant Willy MacDonald is now a warrant officer, stationed at
Wainwright, Alberta, and running basic infantry courses; I saw him
on my book tour and in the summer of 2008, at baby Connie
Hamilton's christening. Three months before, Willy learned that he
had been awarded the Star of Military Valour (the same decoration
given to Patrick Tower) for "leadership and courage under sustained

and intense combat" in the fierce battle of August 3, 2006.

For the longest time, Willy didn't even mention the award to me, and when he finally did, he seemed more pleased that Bryce Keller, who was killed that awful day, had been posthumously awarded the Medal of Military Valour for his gallantry.

The leader of Task Force Orion, the 1PPCLI–led battle group, Ian Hope, is now a full colonel, though he points out with wariness borne of wisdom that it is only a WSE (for "whilst-so-employed") promotion while he is an international fellow at the U.S. Army War College at Carlisle Barracks, Pennsylvania, not far from Gettysburg.

There, in the summer of 2008, he received not one but three of eleven prestigious student writing awards, an astonishing, and unprecedented, feat. It is ample evidence that he is as much the author, as well as the guiding spirit, of *Fifteen Days* as I am.

We are still in irregular contact by email. I miss him dearly, and Jon and Willy and the others. I still intend to go back to Kandahar again, but I know now that it will never be the same as it was in the summer of 2006. Ian and his soldiers had more freedom to plan and conduct their own operations than any Canadian contingent since, had the imagination and intellectual ferocity to do so, and suffered from less bureaucracy and B.S. than is probably possible now. They were (and are) the best of a very fine lot, and I was lucky enough to be there with them for a while. It was the experience of my life.

July 13, 2008, Toronto

Acknowledgements

—

I NEED TO THANK all those who told me the stories in this book and then endured months of my email and phone harassment as I tried to get my civilian brain around things military. If despite their help there are mistakes on these pages, they are mine alone.

Thanks also to the soldiers who told me stories which didn't make it into the book; I've never written one of these before and imagined I had endless room and space. Turns out, even with a book, I didn't. The fault was not in you the story-tellers, and certainly not with those you spoke about, but in my clumsy inability to weave it all together. I am so sorry.

In particular, I want to thank Ian Hope, Jon Hamilton, and Willy MacDonald for their unfailing good humor, patience and trust. You gave me the chance to carry the torch; I only hope I held it high enough.

To John D McHugh, the fine photographer whose pictures appear throughout the book and who went to bat to get them for me, I am very grateful. John was shot and seriously wounded while on the job in Southern Afghanistan in the spring of 2007. God speed your recovery, John—or as your friends in recce platoon would say, get your lazy arse back in gear.

Thanks also to Mike Capstick for his fine eye (and, in Kabul during 2006, his hospitality) and to Martha Kanya-Forstner, my editor, who brought to the job the clear intelligence and tender heart of Susie, one of her two splendid little daughters.

I couldn't have done this without the indulgence and support of my masters at *The Globe and Mail*, particularly Colin MacKenzie.

I wrote this thinking often of my late father, former Flight-Lieutenant Ross Blatchford, 422 Squadron, Royal Canadian Air Force, whom I loved so much.

Photo Credits

—

Page 264 AR2006-P007-0030, Kandahar, Afghanistan, Sept. 15, 2006, National Defence. Reproduced with the permission of the Minister of Public Works and Government Services, 2007

Page 284 CP PHOTO/Kevin Frayer

Page 290 courtesy of Maureen Eykelenboom

Page 310 courtesy of Lt.-Col. Ian Hope

Page 326 John Major, *Ottawa Citizen*

INSERT I

Page i courtesy of Sgt. Patrick Tower

Page ii (top and middle) courtesy of Corporal Keith Mooney; (bottom) courtesy of Darcia Arndt

Page iii courtesy of Major Nick Grimshaw

Page iv (top and bottom) courtesy of John D McHugh

Page v (top) courtesy of Sgt. Patrick Tower; (bottom) courtesy of Capt. John Croucher

Page vi (top) courtesy of Major Bill Fletcher; (bottom) courtesy of MWO Wayne Kelly, B Coy, Sergeant Major

Page vii (top) courtesy of John D McHugh; (bottom) courtesy of MWO Wayne Kelly, B Coy, Sergeant Major

Page viii courtesy of Sgt. Patrick Tower

INSERT II

Page i courtesy of Sgt. Dennis Power

Page ii (top) AR2006-M013-0019, Kandahar, Afghanistan, Nov. 29, 2006, National Defence. Reproduced with the permission of the Minister of Public Works and Government Services, 2007; (bottom) courtesy of John D McHugh

Page iii (top) AS2006-0351, Kandahar, Afghanistan, May 17, 2006, National Defence. Reproduced with the permission of the Minister of Public Works and Government Services, 2007; (bottom) courtesy of Capt. Dave Ferris

Page iv AR2006-A016-0009A, Kandahar Airfield, Afghanistan, Mar. 29, 2006, National Defence. Reproduced with the permission of the Minister of Public Works and Government Services, 2007

Page v (top) courtesy of Lt.-Col. Ian Hope; (bottom) courtesy of Maureen Eykelenboom

Page vi (top and bottom) courtesy of Elaine and Errol Cushley

Page vii (top and bottom) courtesy of John D McHugh

Page viii AR2006-A019-0002A, Kandahar Airfield, Afghanistan, Mar. 31, 2006, National Defence. Reproduced with the permission of the Minister of Public Works and Government Services, 2007

Glossary

——

1st Battalion Princess Patricia's Canadian Light Infantry (1 PPCLI) based in Edmonton. Alpha Company under the command of Major Kirk Gallinger and Charlie Company under the command of Major Bill Fletcher were part of the Canadian Battle Group, Task Force Orion

1st Battalion The Royal Canadian Regiment The senior regular force infantry unit based in Petawawa. It consists of two LAV III-equipped infantry companies, a combat support company, and a headquarters

1st Regiment Royal Canadian Horse Artillery (1RCHA) A Close Support Artillery Regiment. This battalion-size unit consists of two sub-units (batteries) of six artillery howitzers each, a target acquisition and surveillance battery and a headquarters. It is the oldest Regular Force unit in the Canadian Forces

2nd Battalion Princess Patricia's Canadian Light Infantry (2 PPCLI) based in Shilo. Bravo Company of the battalion under the command of Major Nick Grimshaw was part of the Canadian Battle Group Task Force Orion

Afghan National Army (ANA)

Afghan National Highway Police (ANHP)

Afghan National Police (ANP)

Afghan National Security Forces (ANSF)

Ambush Alley Highway 1 from the Panjwaii district to Kandahar City

American Embedded Training Teams (ETT) Charged with professionalizing Afghan security forces

Area of Operations (AO) In land operations, geographic areas are assigned to specific units as a method of control. In the south of Afghanistan, Regional Command–South has divided its AO and assigned specific provinces to individual nations. For example, Kandahar Province is the Canadian AO while Helmand Province is the British AO

Assisting Officer (AO) Officers who tend to the families of soldiers wounded or killed in action

Battery Commander (BC) Artillery sub-unit commander. Commands six guns and three or four Forward Observation parties. In addition to commanding the Battery, the BC coordinates all indirect fire support on behalf of the Battle Group Commander. This includes artillery, mortars, Close Air Support from fixed winged aircraft and firepower from Attack/Armed helicopters

Big Ass Tent (BAT) A tent large enough to house two hundred soldiers sleeping on bunk beds, cheek to jowl. These are the normal troop accommodations on Kandahar Airfield

Bison Eight-wheeled armoured vehicle considered a workhorse of the Canadian Forces, used as personnel carrier or ambulance. Differs from a

LAV III in that it does not have a turret or 25 mm canon. Instead, it usually carries a pintle-mounted machine gun that requires the gunner to expose part of his or her body to fire the weapon

Board of Inquiry (BOI) A BOI is convened to investigate deaths, serious injuries or any other matter that a Commanding Officer or Formation Commander needs to have investigated. It is usually comprised of three or four officers and can compel CF members to give evidence under oath. When its investigation is complete, the BOI will provide the convening authority with findings in respect to the investigation as well as recommendations

C6 General Purpose Machine Gun Medium Machine Gun held and employed at the section level. The combination of its high rate of fire and the punch of its 7.62 mm round makes it a very effective weapon in infantry combat

C7 Standard issue Canadian Forces assault rifle—5.56 mm

C8 Compact version of C7—5.56 mm

C9 Light machine gun with a higher rate of fire and greater range than C6—5.56 mm

Canadian Forces Base (CFB) The administrative title for CF Bases in Canada. May also be referred to as a Garrison. For example, CFB Edmonton is often called Edmonton Garrison so that area Army Reserve units can be included

Casualty evacuation point (CEP) A designated place on the ground where soldiers are directed to bring casualties in order to keep scarce medical resources together. Usually in an area that's easily defensible and protected by natural or man-made features such as hills or walls

Civil-Military Co-operation (CIMIC) Made up of reserve officers and soldiers who lead most village engagements and coordinate all aspects of the Battle Group's involvement with the local population, including "hearts and minds" development projects

Commander's Emergency Reconstruction Program (CERP) Funds provided to military commanders for the purpose of "quick impact" development projects—part of the "hearts and minds" aspect of counter-insurgency operations

Comms (Communications) The radios and other technical equipment needed to command and control a unit

Commanding Officer (CO) The officer appointed to command an independent unit. Major combat arms and service support units are usually commanded by Lieutenant-Colonels, such as Ian Hope and John Conrad. Smaller units, Military Police and medical units, may be commanded by Majors or even Captains. Appointment as a Commanding Officer brings powers of punishment and other authorities as defined in the *National Defence Act*

Deputy commanding officer (DCO) The DCO is the second-in-command of the unit. Usually a senior Major, each combat arm uses the DCO or 2i/c in a slightly different manner

Explosives Ordnance Disposal (EOD) The process of disarming or disposing of all types of unexploded ordnance, ranging from dud munitions to the most advanced improvised explosive devices. Teams are composed of specially trained combat engineers, ammunition technicians/technical officers, and naval officers

Forward Air Controller (FAC) Specially trained Air Force or Army officers capable of directing Close Air Support aircraft onto targets in close proximity to either friendly troops or civilians

Forward Observation Officer (FOO) Artillery officers at the front end of the front line. Their job is to watch the enemy in its positions so they can call in and coordinate the big artillery guns, 81 millimetre mortars, and attack helicopters

Forward Operating Base (FOB) Designed to establish presence in a specified area. They may be temporary or more permanent. Examples are: **FOB Robinson** Primitive patch of near-desert about 100 kilometres west of Kandahar in Helmand Province; **FOB Martello** Canadian-built FOB in Uruzgan Province

Gumbad Safe House Now-defunct remote compound, about 130 kilometres north of Kandahar, home base during Roto 1 for soldiers of Alpha Company's 1 Platoon and later, other platoons

Gun position officer (GPO) The senior gunnery officer on an artillery battery position. Responsible for the firing of guns and the attendant logistics support, the GPO works with about sixty soldiers, and two or three other officers

G-Wagons Lightly armoured, versatile utility vehicles.

Health Services Support Company (HSSC) During Roto 1, sixty medical technicians from 1 Field Ambulance in Edmonton, under OC Marilynn Chenette, looked after the ordinary health concerns of Canadian soldiers in two separate clinics, provided extra hands for the Canadian-led hospital at KAF in cases of mass casualties, and went outside the wire daily with combat platoons and logistics patrols

Hesco Bastions Container system more durable and stronger than sandbags. Hesco consists of large reinforced cylinders made of material and steel wire that can be filled with sand and gravel to provide a protective wall around facilities

Highway 1 The main highway between Kabul and Kandahar. West of the city, it runs through the volatile Panjwaii district

Home Leave Travel Assistance (HLTA) A program that provides soldiers with funding for one vacation during a six-month tour of duty. The soldier can either return to Canada to visit family, or his or her next of kin may meet the soldier in a third location. Europe, Australia and Asia are all popular "HLTA locations" for soldiers serving in Afghanistan. In many cases, HLTA is the only time-off that troops have during the tour

Immediate Reaction Force (IRF) Troops maintained at a high state of readiness to respond to emergencies

Improvised Explosive Devices (IED) The generic term for bombs assembled from ordnance such as mines or artillery shells. IEDs may be fired by remote control (cell phones, for example) or activated by pressure plates. They are usually buried in or beside a roadway and are often used in conjunction with an ambush. The use of IEDs is only limited by the imagination of the bombers, and may be hidden in vehicles (Vehicle Borne or **VBIEDS**), on the bodies of suicide bombers, or even on animals

International Security Assistance Force to Afghanistan (ISAF) The multinational, United Nations-approved mission. NATO officially took over the reins of ISAF in southern Afghanistan from the United States on July 31, 2006

Joint Coordination Centre (JCC) Provincial centre in Kandahar with the responsibility to coordinate the multiple security agencies active in the Province

Joint Tactical Air Controller (JTAC)

Joint Task Force 2 (JTF 2) Canada's elite special operations force

Kandahar Air Field (KAF) Main NATO and US base in the Southern Region of Afghanistan. KAF has held, at times, more than 13,000 troops from over 30 nations.

Lake Superior Scottish Regiment (Lake Sups) Reserve regiment from Thunder Bay

Leaguer A temporary defensive position of armoured vehicles usually set up for a speedy refuel or resupply

Light Armoured Vehicles (LAVs) The generic term for the family of wheeled armoured vehicles that are the mainstay of Canada's Army

Lord Strathcona's Horse (Royal Canadians) Regular force armoured regiment based in Edmonton

Loyal Edmonton Regiment (Eddies) Alberta's oldest infantry reserve regiment

Medal of Military Valour Awarded for acts of valour, self sacrifice or devotion of duty in the presence of the enemy

Medevac Medical Evacuation. May be by ground or air. The medevac system in Afghanistan, especially the American helicopters, has been responsible for saving the lives of the vast majority of Canadian and Allied wounded

Medium-Value Target (MVT) Usually a local or district level Taliban or insurgent commander or leader

Mentions in Dispatches (MID) Military honour awarded under the authority of the Chief of Defence Staff. It is presented for acts of superior leadership or bravery in the face of the enemy. Soldiers MID wear an oak leaf laurel on their campaign medal

National Support Element (NSE) Unit responsible for supplying troops in the field with everything from fuel to bullets, as well as providing all forms of vehicle and weapons maintenance and repair

Night-vision goggles (NVG) Term for the variety of night vision aids available to the modern Canadian soldier. NVGs are usually attached to the helmet

Niner Commanding officer is always called Niner on the radio as his radio call-sign is 9; pronounced niner for clarity on the air

Niner's Tac Commanding Officer's tactical headquarters. It includes his engineer and artillery commanders, as well as a close protection party and a small staff to assist him in exercising command and control away from the main Battle Group headquarters

Non-commissioned Officer (NCO) The army's junior and middle leadership group, composed of warrant officers, sergeants and master corporals, who provide a link between officers and troops and provide most of the training and much of the leadership

North Atlantic Treaty Organization (NATO) Originally formed after the Second World War for the defence of the Euro–Atlantic region in the face of the Soviet threat, NATO has become the primary Western military alliance and is now capable of operations outside of Europe, the Atlantic, and North America

Officer Commanding (OC) The commander of an infantry company, artillery battery, armour/engineer squadron or other sub-unit, usually a major

Operational Mentor Liaison Teams (OMLT) Canadian team charged with professionalizing Afghan security forces. This is the NATO term for organizations that perform similar functions as the American Embedded Training Teams (ETT)

Operational Stress Injury Support (OSIS) A unique Canadian military program that provides peer counsellors to soldiers suffering from Post-Traumatic Stress Disorder or other operational stress related injuries

Operation Zahar (Op Zahar) Canadian battle group operation, involving all three companies and recce platoon, two troops of artillery with their M777 Howitzer guns, a squadron from 1 Combat Engineer Regiment, and two companies of the Afghan National Army and their American Embedded Training Teams

Patrol Base Wilson (PBW) A grimy base named after Master Corporal Tim Wilson, located in the area of the Zhari District Centre

PKM General purpose machine gun still in production in Russia

Princess Patricia's Canadian Light Infantry (PPCLI or the Patricias) One of Canada's three Regular Force infantry regiments. It consists of three battalions and a small administrative headquarters to look after regimental affairs. The PPCLI is unique in that it was privately raised early in the First World War by J. Hamilton Gault and fought in France and Belgium alongside British troops

Priority 1 casualty (Pri 1) Immediate and advanced medical care required

Priority 4 casualty (Pri 4) Vital signs absent

Provincial Reconstruction Team (PRT) Small units deployed throughout Afghanistan to assist the reconstruction effort. The Kandahar PRT consists of Canadian soldiers, diplomats, and staff from the Department of Foreign Affairs, Canadian International Development officers, as well as RCMP officers and Corrections Canada officials

Psyops (Psychological Operations) The use of leaflets, loudspeakers, radio broadcasts etc. to influence insurgent behaviour. A fairly new capability for Canada's Army

Public Affairs Officers (PAO) The official spokesmen and link with embedded media

Quick Reaction Force Air mobile group on standby 24/7 to respond to emergencies for all of Combined Joint Task Force 76, operational headquarters for southern and eastern Afghanistan during Roto 1. Area is now under ISAF control

Reconnaissance (recce) platoon The CO's "eyes and ears" on the battlefield. Consists of highly trained infantry soldiers, including snipers, who are generally deployed "in front" of the companies to define enemy positions and activities

Regimental Sergeant Major (RSM) The senior non-commissioned member of the Regiment and the link between the soldiers and officers

Remote-Controlled IEDs (RCIEDs) See IED

RG-31 Nyala South African anti-mine carrier

Rocket-Propelled Grenade (RPG) Cheap and simple anti-armour weapon of Soviet design

Roto 1 Seven-month tour in Kandahar Province of Task Force Orion

Roto 2 Also known as Task Force 3–06, this group was the second to serve in Kandahar Province from August 2006 to February 2007. Composed of soldiers from the 1st Battalion, The Royal Canadian Regiment, 2nd Regiment, Royal Canadian Horse Artillery, 2 Combat Engineer Regiment, The Royal Canadian Dragoons, 2 Field Ambulance and 2 Canadian Mechanized Brigade Group headquarters and Signal Squadron, all based in Petawawa, and Alpha Company of the 2nd Battalion, Princess Patricia's Canadian Light Infantry based in Shilo

Royal Canadian Horse Artillery (RCHA) Although the horses are long gone, the title "Horse Artillery" is maintained by the 1st Regiment (Shilo) and the 2nd Regiment (Petawawa) as a means of perpetuating the traditions of Canada's Gunners. The francophone Regular Force regiment in Valcartier also maintains the "right of the line" distinction and its title is roughly equivalent to RCHA—5ieme Regiment d'Artillerie Leger du Canada (5ieme RALC)

The Royal Canadian Regiment (The RCR or the Royals) Canada's senior Regular Force Infantry Regiment, The RCR is structured in roughly the same manner as the PPCLI. Its 1st and 3rd Battalions are stationed in Petawawa and its 2nd Battalion is from Gagetown

Royal Military College (RMC) Located in Kingston, RMC is a degree granting institution that also trains junior CF officers for all branches of the service

Royal Regina Rifles Reserve regiment from Regina

Rules of Engagement (ROE) The legal document that provides commanders and soldiers with directions and guidelines on the use of force, including lethal force. It prescribes levels of authority for the use of certain weapons, as well as the basic conditions for using them. It is important to note that ROE never deny the soldier the right of self-defence

Seaforth Highlanders of Canada Reserve regiment from Vancouver

Spin Boldak The most important town on the Afghan–Pakistani border in Kandahar Province. It was intended to be Charlie Company's area of operation, but in practice almost never was

Shura Consultation with village leaders or elders. Also called a ***jirga*** in some areas

Star of Military Valour Awarded for acts of valour, self-sacrifice or devotion to duty in the presence of the enemy. Second in prestige only to the relatively new Canadian Victoria Cross

Task Force Orion Canadian battle group which served in Kandahar Province during Roto 1 from February 2006 to July 2006. Composed of the soldiers of the 1st Battalion, Princess Patricia's Canadian Light Infantry and engineers from 1 Combat Engineer Regiment, both based in Edmonton, and Bravo Company from the 2nd Battalion, PPCLI, and a battery of gunners from 1st Royal Canadian Horse Artillery, both based in Shilo

Trig marker A marker used to identify survey control points

Troops in contact (TIC) American term used to indicate troops in a firefight with enemy forces

Very High Frequency Radio (VHF)

Village Medical Outreach (VMO) Occasions for soldier medics and doctors to care for sick Afghan villagers

Wadi Dried up river bed

Index

___

British Parachute Regiment, 242,
243, 320
Britten, Brady, 138
Britten, Caiden, 138
Britten, Sergeant Guy, 132–38, 142
Brodeur, Warrant Officer Ray, 196
Brooks, Corporal James, 236
Brown, Major-General G.G., 8–9
Brown, Private Kyle, 319
Burgeo, Newfoundland, 14, 327,
334, 338, 343–48

Calgary Highlanders (Calgary), 36,
54, 356
Camp Mirage, 41, 148
Camp Nathan Smith, 96, 295
Camp Souter, 208
Canadian Airborne Regiment
(CAR), 233, 319–21
Canadian Expeditionary Force, 252
Canadian Forces Leadership
Institute, 271
Canadian soldiers: conduct of, 102,
320–21; and decompression on
returning home, 313, 317–18;
goals of, 62–63, 75–76, 100, 121,
128, 130, 156–57, 162, 244–45,
335; and post-traumatic stress
disorder, 329–31; psychological
condition of, 13, 75–77, 97,
296–97; rear party and assisting
officers (AOs), 50–51, 184, 205,
206, 207, 245, 277, 279, 343, 344;
and relations with Afghans, 2,
6–7, 100, 103–105, 110, 112,
114–15, 118, 122–23, 127, 147–48,
150–51, 156, 157–59, 160;
reservists, 36–37, 38–39, 42,
43, 59, 100, 104, 115, 123; and

universality of service require-
ment, 173, 183, 296; see also
individual regiments
Canadian Press, 204
Canadian Scottish Regiment
(British Columbia), 207
CanWest News, 85
Capstick, Colonel Mike, 166, 312,
360
Cathy, Corporal Jack, 337
CBC, 184; online programming,
299
Chao, Steve, 71, 98, 234, 297
Charlottetown, Prince Edward
Island, 146, 336
Chenette, Captain Marilynn, 118,
151–53, 296, 298, 299–300,
301–302
Cherry, Don, 191, 207
Churchill, Master Corporal Liz, 151
Civil-Military Co-operation
(CIMIC), 95, 104–106, 122
Clarkson, Adrienne, 352
Coalition forces, 4, 70, 72, 146, 159,
194, 196, 205, 214, 218, 229, 255;
American, 4, 26, 32, 69, 70, 84,
90, 94–95, 126, 152, 159, 193, 194,
196, 197, 199, 205, 214, 215–17,
218, 222, 244, 251, 314, 315, 342;
British, 7, 70, 158, 193, 194, 199,
200, 214, 217, 218, 222, 228–29,
230, 286; Canadian, 199, 218;
Danish, 199; Dutch, 111–12, 195,
199, 218; Estonian, 199; French,
199; Joint Coordination Centre
for, 146, 160; Romanian, 151, 199;
see also individual Canadian
and U.S. regiments
Coghlan, Mary, 322

MacArthur, Ian, 322
MacDonald, Sergeant Willy, 5, 6–7,
    9, 10–11, 22, 24, 25, 26, 27, 28, 29,
    32, 33, 215, 222, 224, 226–27, 323,
    325, 327, 346, 352, 353, 356, 359
MacKay, Warrant Officer Justin,
    84, 85, 93, 94, 106, 107, 108–110,
    129
MacKenzie, Colin, 78, 360
MacKenzie, Major-General Lewis,
    73
Madonik, Rick, 127
Mahlo, Private Daniel, 15l, 171,
    201–202
Maltais, Sergeant Pete, 198
Manitoba, floods in (1997), 320
Mansell, Bombardier Myles, death
    of, 107
Marshall, Corporal Sean, 126, 301
Matchee, Master Corporal
    Clayton, 319–20
May, Sergeant John, 107–108
Maynard district centre, 144
McCully, Captain John, 57
McFadden, Private Matt, 124
McFadzen, Master Corporal
    Lance, 57, 64
McGarry, Major Liam, 182
McGuinty, Dalton, 242
McHugh, John D, 122
McMillan, Kelli, 356
Meade, Captain Bob, 84, 85, 167, 224
Meaford, Canadian Forces Base
    (CFB), 273–74
Mellish, Kendra, 280–81
Mellish, Warrant Officer Frank,
    258, 280–81; death of, 258
Melnyck, Jesse, 314
Mianishin district, 106

Michalak, Tom, 71, 82, 297–98
Military honours: Canadian
    Victoria Cross, 338; Medal of
    Military Valour, 11, 258, 259, 339,
    357; Mention in Dispatches, 15,
    31, 109, 117, 339; South-West
    Asia Service Medal, 317; Star of
    Military Valour, 15, 242, 248,
    272, 338–39, 356
Military Wives Sisterhood, 184
Miller, Warrant Officer Mark, 75,
    280
Mooney, Corporal Keith, 79–80, 82,
    83, 87–88, 90–91, 335, 345,
    346–48, 353
Mountbatten, Countess of ("Lady
    Patricia"), 324, 352
Muir, Corporal Jeff, 303
Mushan, 152, 153, 161, 162

Nabi, Haji Mohammad, 105
Naim, Mohammad, 151
National Defence, Department of
    (DND), 4, 60, 194
National Investigation Service
    (Canadian Forces), 204
National Military Cemetary, 280,
    334, 351, 352
National Service Element(?), 209,
    286
National Support Element (NSE),
    30, 43, 54, 227, 231, 322
NATO, see North Atlantic Treaty
    Organization (NATO)
Nawa, 213, 218, 219, 220–22
Needham, Dave, 241, 242, 243, 245
Needham, Heather, 245
Needham, Private Will, 241–43,
    247, 256, 261, 262